Credible words are not eloquent;
Eloquent words are not credible.

The wise are not erudite;
The erudite are not wise.

The adept are not all-around;
The all-around are not adept.

The sages do not accumulate things.
Yet the more they have done for others,
The more they have gained themselves;
The more they have given to others,
The more they have gotten themselves.

Thus, the way of *tian* is to benefit without harming;
The way of the sages is to do without contending.

–from the *Dao de jing*

# *Daodejing*
## "Making This Life Significant"

*A Philosophical Translation*

Roger T. Ames and David L. Hall

Ballantine Books
New York

A Ballantine Book
Published by The Random House Publishing Group
Copyright © 2003 by Roger T. Ames and David L. Hall

Published in the United States by Ballantine Books, an imprint of The Random
House Publishing Group, a division of Random House, Inc., New York, and
simultaneously in Canada by Random House of Canada Limited, Toronto.

Ballantine and colophon are registered trademarks of Random House, Inc.

www.ballantinebooks.com

Library of Congress Control Number: 2003096751

ISBN 978-0-345-44419-6

Camera-ready copy for this book was prepared by Daniel Cole.

Cover art: The bamboo strips used as part of the cover design are photographs
representative of the three *Laozi* bundles recovered at Guodian. The strips are
reprinted here with the permission of Wenwu Publishing House. The photographic
representation of a sculpture of Qi Baishi by the Nanjing sculptor Wu Weishan on
the back cover is reprinted here with his kind permission.

Manufactured in the United States of America

First Edition: January 2003
First Trade Paperback Edition: January 2004

19 18 17 16 15 14 13 12

*"Venture not beyond your doors to know the world. . . ."*

*Making this life significant with the philosophers and friends at UTEP*

# Contents

# Preface and Acknowledgments

The *Daodejing* has probably been translated into the English language more often than any other piece of world literature. Why translate it again? An entirely reasonable question.

And a reasonable question requires a reasoned answer. Recent archaeological finds (Mawangdui 1973 and Guodian 1993) have provided us with textual materials that are physically more than a millennium earlier than previously available versions of the *Daodejing*. Such finds challenge the authority of existing translations to the extent that these new materials have increased our knowledge of the text and of the circumstances of its transmission. And there is broad scholarly agreement that these early redactions of the *Daodejing* do indeed cast important new light on the structure and the meaning of this defining document in Daoist philosophy.

In addition to providing new insights into an old document, these archaeological finds have also provided us with textual materials that are importantly different from what has been available up until now, enabling us to resolve some persistent linguistic problems. Undoubtedly the most substantial addition to the *Daodejing* are the fourteen strips—*The Great One Gives Birth to the Waters*—that appear as an integral element within one of the Guodian versions of the text. Beyond the seamless physical consistency of these strips with the rest of this early exemplar of the *Daodejing*, they contain a discussion of Daoist cosmology that not only uses the familiar *Daodejing* vocabulary, but further brings a clarity to this cosmology that enables us to understand other chapters of the *Daodejing* in a way that has not been possible before. In deference to a continuing and yet inconclusive debate on the relationship between this exciting new portion of the text and the *Daodejing* itself, we have followed the practice of excerpting this new document and of giving it the title *The Great One Gives Birth to the Waters*. We have translated it, and have discussed it in some detail, in an appendix. Whatever the ultimate status of these strips with respect to the *Daodejing* itself, their critical importance as a resource for illuminating the Daoist response to the cosmological question of the source and nature of creativity is nowhere in question.

However, beyond the archaeological finds there is, if possible, an even more compelling reason to take up the project of offering yet another English-language translation of the *Daodejing*. The *Daodejing* is a profoundly "philosophical" text, and yet it has not been treated as such. It has been translated and interpreted initially by missionaries, and more recently by sinologists. That is to say that, to date, the *Daodejing* has only incidentally and tangentially been engaged by philosophers. This assertion is meant neither to impugn the usually good intentions of the missionaries nor to pretend that there is any substitute for the sophisticated philological, historical, literary, and cultural sensibilities that we associate with good sinology. In fact, if there is an indictment to be made, it is to be directed against professional philosophy in our Western seats of learning that, in its own self-understanding, continues to insist that philosophy is exclusively an Anglo-European enterprise.

Given this marginalization of other philosophical traditions, philosophy as a discipline has an unfulfilled responsibility to our academy. An essential occupation of philosophers is to identify and describe the generic traits of the human experience in order to locate problems within the broadest possible context. And these defining generic characteristics are importantly different as we move from one cultural and epochal site to another. Philosophers have the responsibility to seek out and to understand the uncommon assumptions that distinguish cultures as a preventative against cultural reductionism and the misconceptions such ethnocentrism entails. Thus, the absence of philosophers in the interpretation of

Chinese philosophy has come at a cost. It has become a common-place to acknowledge that, in the process of Western humanists attempting to make sense of the classical Chinese philosophical literature, many Western assumptions have inadvertently been insinuated into the understanding of these texts, and have colored the vocabulary through which this understanding has been articulated. Chinese philosophy has been made familiar to Western readers by first "Christianizing" it, and then more recently by locating it within a poetical-mystical-occult worldview. To the extent that Chinese philosophy has become the subject of Western philosophical interest at all, it has usually been analyzed within the framework of categories and philosophical problems not its own.

The recent recovery of new versions of existing texts and the further discovery of many that have been long lost has occasioned the retranslation of many of the classics, and has provided both a pretext and an opportunity for philosophers to step up and rethink our standard readings. Most importantly, it has presented us with the challenge of trying, with imagination, to take these texts on their own terms by locating and interpreting them within their own worldview.

The happy collaboration of Hall and Ames has, over nearly a quarter of a century, been an attempt, however imperfect, to bring together both sinological and philosophical skills first in our interpretive studies of classical Chinese philosophy, and more recently, in our new translations of seminal texts. In developing a strategy for our translations, benefiting enormously from the participation of Henry Rosemont Jr. in these efforts, we have developed a structure that includes a philosophical introduction, an evolving glossary of key philosophical terms, a self-consciously interpretive translation, and the inclusion of a critical Chinese text.

In describing our translations as "self-consciously interpretive," we are not allowing that we are given to license, or that we are any less "literal" than other translations. On the contrary, we would insist that any pretense to a literal translation is not only naïve, but is itself a cultural prejudice of the first order. To begin with, we would assert that English as the target language carries with it such an overlay of interpretation that, in the absence of reference to an extensive introduction and glossary, the philosophical import of the Chinese text is seriously compromised. Further, a failure of translators to be self-conscious and to take fair account of their own Gadamarian "prejudices" with the excuse that they are relying on some "objective" lexicon that, were the truth be known, is itself heavily colored with cultural biases, is to betray their readers not once, but twice. Just as each generation selects and carries over earlier thinkers to reshape them in its own image, each generation reconfigures the classical canons of world philosophy to its own needs. We too are inescapably people of a time and place. And a most cursory understanding of the *Daodejing* itself would require that we acknowledge ourselves as such. This self-consciousness is not to distort the *Daodejing*, but to endorse its premises.

A lot has happened as we worked on this translation. Tragically, the David Hall side of the project that burned most brightly, also burned most quickly, and in the company of family and friends, he died in his desert one spring day.

The profound sadness and sense of loss is made bearable by a compounding of happiness in a collaboration that only got better over the years because it always attracted further collaboration. Along the way, many friends and colleagues have added to the enjoyment and satisfaction that we were always able to find in our work. The formidable D. C. Lau with a comment here and an allusion there has given us things to think about with respect to the *Daodejing* specifically, and over the years with respect to Chinese philosophy broadly, that have returned to our thoughts regularly for further reflection. Clifford Ames and Owen Lock, keepers of the English language, interrogated an earlier version of the manuscript with a thoroughness that left not a single sentence unconfessed. And Geir Sigurdsson spent many hours on the banks of Weiminghu rescuing our Introduction from itself. Xing Wen lent a steady hand to some technical problems with the text, and Danny Coyle searched the final manuscript for infelicities. Robin Yates, with remarkable tact and good sense, saved us from a reading of chapter 77 that was too clever by half. And dear Bonnie interrupted her own sabbatical to further discipline these pages. Over the years, Daniel Cole has, with precision and with art, made the most of the presentation of our work, and without him there would be far less beauty in this world. When the time came, Tracy Bernstein and Allison Dickens stepped up as editors for Ballantine, and gave us every opportunity to make the most of our efforts. Finally, I personally want to express my deep gratitude to my graduate students at Peking University who, in our comparative philosophy seminar in the fall of 2001, challenged me to think long and hard about Daoist cosmology, and who enabled me to see things that David had known all along.

Roger T. Ames
Peking University
April 2002

# Historical Introduction

## HISTORICAL CONTEXT

The Warring States Period (403–221 BCE) in which the *Daodejing* was born is fairly named. As time passed, internecine warfare raged with escalating ferocity among the contending states of the central Chinese plains. The killing field casualties rose exponentially as the "art" of warfare progressed from swarming militia to the efficiency of phalanx-like fixed troop formations. At every level of innovation, from the introduction of cavalry, to standard issue crossbows, to siege engines, these instruments of aggression made a folly of defense. Cities were walled and fortified only to be breached; borders were drawn up only to be redrawn; alliances were formed only to be betrayed; treaties were signed only to be reneged upon. For generation after generation, death became a way of life, so that mothers gave birth to sons with the expectation that they would never reach majority.

The eventual outcome was never in doubt. In the race to empire, the game was zero-sum. And to lose was to perish utterly. In the centuries of protracted labor that preceded the birth of this profoundly literate Chinese culture, the most widely circulated texts were not religious or philosophical treatises; they were military handbooks. In fact, most of the philosophers who traveled from court to court were purveyors of wisdom "guaranteed" to lead their patrons to certain victory. And even when their expositions focused on the social and political reforms necessary for a flourishing state, at some point, almost every one of the texts named for them turns to warfare and to the necessity of a strong military.

It was as a response to these darkest of days in which the blood of China's children irrigated the crops and their flesh fertilized the land that the *Daodejing* emerged as an alternative vision of what the human experience might be like. The world was wasting away, and the *Daodejing* was a mysterious elixir that offered to serve as its restorative.

## THE NATURE AND APPLICATIONS OF THE *DAODEJING*

The great French sinologist Marcel Granet observed that "Chinese wisdom has no need of the idea of God."[1] Analogously, in this Chinese world in which nothing was "created," including the world itself, the *Daodejing* too appeared without the benefit of efficient cause. Of course the text has long been associated with the sobriquet the "Laozi 老子," or "The Old Master," but the historicity of this rather generic old man is as likely as his name is informative.[2]

What do we know about this authorless text? On the basis of rhetorical patterns and rhymes, William Baxter dates the *Daodejing* to as early as 400 BCE, but suggests early or mid fourth century BCE as its most likely period of compilation.[3] Given that it is widely cited in the late fourth and third century BCE corpus—the *Zhuangzi*, *Zhanguoce*, *Lüshi chunqiu*, *Hanfeizi*, and so on—the text in some form is likely to have appeared earlier rather than later. The 1993 recovery of three distinct bundles of strips dating to about 300 BCE that together constitute a "partial" *Daodejing* from a tomb in Guodian, a village to the north of the ancient Chu capital of Jinancheng in modern-day Hubei province, is consistent with Baxter's estimate. It is not clear whether this Guodian version of the *Daodejing* is itself an interim phase circulating orally in the growth of the complete 81 chapter version, or whether it is someone's abridged version of an already existing complete text. But even in this partial text (however we choose to understand the term "partial"), the explicit anti-Confucian polemic suggests a date of compilation at which the Daoist and the Confucian lineages had already drawn their lines.

Before we speculate on the authorless origins of the *Daodejing*, it might be helpful to address the issue of orality. The relationship between the spoken and written languages of early China has had an important bearing on the past and the future of a text—that is, how a text would emerge over time out of the oral tradition, and how it would be transmitted to future generations. Elsewhere, together with Henry Rosemont, we have argued that:

> Classical Chinese . . . is like the good little boy: it was primarily to be seen and not heard. A person who tried to write a speech in *wenyan* today would end up with a soliloquy. This is not to imply that sounds were and are totally irrelevant to the written language, for some puns and all rhymes, alliteration, and so forth are obviously phonetic in character. Further, such linguistic devices were undoubtedly of enormous value in facilitating the memorization of large tracts of text that could be recalled to fund discussion. What this does imply is the following, which is an important premise for our overall position: spoken Chinese is and was certainly understood aloud; classical Chinese is not now and may never have been understood aloud as a primarily spoken language; therefore spoken and literary Chinese are now and may always have been two distinct linguistic media, and if so, the latter should clearly not be seen as simply a transcription of speech.[4]

The claim that the written language is not a transcription of speech is qualified in this argument by the acknowledgment that in a largely if not primarily oral tradition, much of the language that at some point and for specific reasons comes to be written down has earlier been transmitted from memory, and in this form, enriches refined speech much as the crafted apothegms of Shakespeare, Pope, Nietzsche, and Emerson abound in good intellectual conversation today.

D. C. Lau tells us a lot about the text. In preparing his own translation of the *Daodejing,* he has followed the ubiquitous division of the short text into two books, the *"dao"* classic and the *"de"* classic, and has also respected the further traditional rendering of the text into 81 "chapters." But he takes one additional step in dividing these 81 chapters into 196 sections with even more additional subsections, justifying this seeming fragmentation of the work on the basis of internal rhymes and the observation that there is only a very loose sense of textual coherence.[5] Lau also suggests that the rhymed passages that constitute more than half of the text were probably "learned by rote with the meaning explained at length in an oral commentary."[6]

Michael LaFargue offers us some further insight into the nature and function of the *Daodejing*. He argues that the text does not "teach philosophical doctrines" but rather contains "sayings" that fall into two groups: "polemic proverbs" that seek to correct some common assumption ("cheaters never prosper"), and sayings that recommend a certain regimen of self-cultivation.[7] LaFargue makes a further important point in insisting that, contrary to the standard handwringing about the impenetrability of the text, the words usually "conveyed a single definite meaning for a group of people with a shared competence."[8] That is, the sayings that constitute the text were largely meaningful to its anticipated audience within the context of their own historical period and life experience.

If we combine and expand upon the insights that we have rehearsed above, we can make a reasonable conjecture about the provenance, the coherence, and the applications of the *Daodejing*.

First, the fact that remarkably similar bamboo strip and silk manuscript versions of the *Daodejing* are being found in archaeological sites from significantly different times and places testifies to the probability that we are dealing very early on with a canonical "text" if not a widely popular classic. We have put "text" in quotation marks and have used the expression "classic" advisedly because the written form of the work seems to be derivative of an essentially oral tradition.

Indeed, while we might be accustomed to think of such traditions of wisdom literature as being passed down through the written word, beyond the pervasive use of rhyme, there are other rather clear indications that memorization and oral transmission probably played a major role in establishing a common frame of reference for the academic lineages of early China. The pervasive use of differing loan characters in the written forms of the *Daodejing* and other recovered texts suggests that they represented sounds first and then, by context and inference, ideas. This would mean that they were part of an oral tradition that was written down from memory for some specific purpose, perhaps in this case providing reading material for the now silent tomb occupant in the journey to the nebulous world beyond. The accumulation of written texts also seems to have had a role in the construction of court libraries at state academies that would try to attract the best and brightest scholars of their age, and thus bring prestige to their patrons.

Another factor that would have influenced this process of standardization is the relationship between a rich and redundant spoken language, and "texts" which operate as an oral corpus of economical aphorisms to capture the prevailing wisdom of the time. These combined sayings would be available in the oral language as familiar apothegms that could be used as "topics" to begin discussions, with the possibility of further elaboration occurring in the vernacular language. While there seems to be a certain fluidity in the transmission of these early documents, the recent archaeological finds are uncovering increasingly earlier versions of relatively standardized texts, the *Daodejing* among them, suggesting that rote memorization and "canonization" had some force in consolidating the texts and preserving their integrity.

We would agree with Michael LaFargue that much of the rhymed materials found in the *Daodejing* can be fairly described as a kind of "proverbial" wisdom literature that, rather than offering exposition, seeks to stimulate a sympathetic audience to conjure up the conditions necessary to make its point.[9] A significant quibble with LaFargue, however, would be that these rhymed sayings are not only mnemonic, but are also memorable in the sense of the clever West African proverb-tellers or the evocative epigramatic and scriptural sayings of our own tradition. That is to say, the aphorisms that came to constitute the *Daodejing* should not be confused qualitatively or functionally with the familiar adages that LaFargue uses to make his own point (for example, "nice guys finish last"). Such banal clichés are seldom confused with wit or wisdom. By contrast, the elegant sayings that constitute the

*Daodejing* are "the sound from the ground," sharing with other such conventional sources a widespread, often informal, dissemination, and the cultural function of sustaining a shared linguistic currency and a common wisdom within a competent population. By "competent" we are following LaFargue in describing an audience with a similar worldview and common sense—precisely those assets lacking in our own contemporary attempts to engage the "text."

It is interesting to reflect on how such conventional sources, encompassing among other things everyday popular songs and their distillation in the *Book of Songs*, functioned to produce meaning and promote different philosophical agendas in the early Chinese corpus. What can be said about this largely oral medium of transmission and communication of songs is perhaps even more true of the layer of selected wisdom sayings that constitute the *Daodejing*.

David Schaberg explores the way in which uncanonical songs underwent a process of historical framing during the Warring States Period and Qin dynasty,[10] when commentators approached a song, often enigmatic and sometimes even incomprehensible, as an encoded means of communication that could only be understood and appreciated by fitting it with, and within, a particular historical anecdote of some interesting individual or event.

A similar process seems to have been at work in the philosophical literature of this period in which canonical songs such as those collected in the *Book of Songs*, presumably widely remembered and sung by the population, were "decoded" when they were used to punctuate a particular philosophical point. That is, one intriguing characteristic of almost all of the classical texts—the *Analects*, *Mozi*, *Mencius*, *Zhongyong*, *Xunzi*, and so on—is that having presented some kind of a philosophical argument they then quite literally break into song. And there seems to be a dividend for both philosopher and song alike in participating and being used in this practice. From the perspective of the song, it is framed and clarified, and is thus reauthorized as a shared and respected repository of ancient meaning. And the philosophers for their trouble get to claim the prestige of a canonical source for the assertion at hand.

The song is a particularly effective addition to the philosophical argument for several reasons. It is persuasive by virtue of being widely known among the audience of the text. Again, the original source of the song is the daily life of the people, where each song is what Schaberg describes as "a manifestation of complete and uncontrollable genuineness."[11] This raw spontaneity and honesty lies in the fact that songs are most often the vehicles of either praise or blame: a public outpouring of approbation for some instance of virtuous conduct, or an irrepressible protest against some injustice. When these philosophical texts repeatedly burst into song, they are taking full advantage of the reader's assumption that such songs do not lie. Thus, when philosophers invoke a song, they not only seek to clarify their arguments, but also seek to attach the indisputable veracity of the song to their claims.

The song further dramatizes the argument and charges it emotionally, bringing the more general and abstract assertions of the text down to earth by locating them in seemingly specific historical situations. Thus, a well-placed song lends veridical force to the philosopher's claims, and at the same time, invests these claims with passion.

It would seem that a great many hands across an expanse of time set down, sorted, re-sorted, edited, and collated the *Daodejing* and the materials that constitute it. Little wonder that the text can initially give its readers the appearance of being fragmentary, disconnected, and occasionally, even of being corrupt. It should not be surprising, then, especially to the modern Western reader who might be used to a more linear and sequential mode of presentation, that the *Daodejing* seems to be something less than a coherent whole. But first impressions in this instance are belied as the architecture of the text emerges from different directions.

First, when we turn to reflect on how the selected wisdom sayings of the *Daodejing* function, we can assume that they, like the repertoire of songs, have a kind of unquestioned veracity that comes from belonging to the people and their tradition. We can further observe that this veracity is made corporate by a reading strategy that co-opts the reader. Two often remarked characteristics of the

*Daodejing* are palpable absences: it contains no historical detail of any kind, and it offers its readers no doctrines in the sense of general precepts or universalistic laws. The required "framing" of the aphorism by the reader is itself an exercise in nondogmatic philosophizing where the relationship between the text and its student is one of noncoercive collaboration. That is, instead of "the text" providing the reader with a specific historical context or philosophical system, its listeners are required to supply always unique, concrete, and often dramatic scenarios drawn from their own experience to generate the meaning for themselves. This inescapable process in which students through many readings of the text acquire their own unique understanding of its insights informed by their own life experiences is one important element in a kind of constantly evolving coherence. The changing coherence of the text is brought into a sharpening focus as its readers in different times and places continue to make it their own.

Again, there is a greater degree of coherence to the *Daodejing* than a first reading might suggest. Chapters are sometimes grouped around specific themes and subjects. For example, chapters 1 and 2 are centered on the theme of correlativity, chapters 18 and 19 contrast natural and conventional morality, 57 through 61 all begin with recommendations on proper governing of the state, 67 through 69 are about prosecuting war, chapters 74 and 75 deal with political oppression and the common people, and so on. We have appended a thematic index that reveals at least some of such editorial organization.

Another source of coherence in the *Daodejing* lies in the fact that it, like so many classical Chinese texts, is read and appropriated *paronomastically*. That is, a close reading of the text reveals repeated characters and metaphors that awaken in the reader an expanding web of semantic and phonetic associations.

An additional observation to be made is that the rhymed sayings are not themselves a grab-bag miscellany of clever yet sometimes contradictory insights. On the contrary, it would seem that these specific aphorisms have been selected and edited to support the broader purpose of the text. Michael LaFargue and other prominent voices (notably Hal Roth) have argued persuasively that what gives the *Daodejing* its indisputable focus is its overall didactic project. It would seem that the aim of the compilers of the *Daodejing* is to prescribe a regimen of self-cultivation that will enable one to optimize one's experience in the world. These same wisdom passages are an integral element in this process that, when authenticated in the conduct and character of the practitioners, result in their personal transformation. It is important to note that this goal of self-transformation has nothing to do with death, judgment, and an afterlife, nor has it anything to do with the "salvation of the soul" (the traditional concerns of Western eschatology). Instead, such personal growth and consummation is meliorative in the sense of producing the quality of character that makes this world itself a better place.

Having underscored the necessary collaboration between the reader and the text in the production of meaning, we are faced with the question as to our intentions in appending our own commentary after each chapter in this translation. The idea of writing an explanatory "commentary" seems to be as promising in its putative outcome as "explaining" a haiku. The commentary, then, is intended as no more than a suggestive footnote that is successful only to the extent that it sparks the reader's own engagement with the chapter itself. If it is treated as systematic or exhaustive or authoritative, it has ironically betrayed the reader that it is intended to serve.

## NOTES TO THE *HISTORICAL INTRODUCTION*

1. Granet (1934):478. In fact, many of the most prominent sinologists, Chinese and Western alike, use their own language, but are quite explicit in rejecting the idea that Chinese cosmology begins from a transcendent Absolute and entails the reality/appearance that arises from such a commitment. See Tang Junyi (1988):100–03, Xiong Shili (1977):180–91, Zhang Dongsun (1995):271–72, Graham (1989):22, Needham (1956): 290, Sivin (1995):3, Hansen (1992):215, Giradot (1983):64.

2. Graham (1990) rehearses the composite legend of a "Laozi" that first came to associate the *Daodejing* with Lao Dan at about 250 BCE.

3. Baxter (1998):233, 249.

4. Ames and Rosemont (1998):38–9.

5. The irony is that terms that are usually used to indicate inference—*gu* 故 and *shiyi* 是以 —are often used in the text as mere grammatical markers to link sections that otherwise have little or no connection. See D. C. Lau (1982):139.

6. D. C. Lau (1982):133.

7. LaFargue (1998):263.

8. LaFargue (1998):260.

9. LaFargue (1994):125–74.

10. Schaberg (1999).

11. Schaberg (1999):337.

# Philosophical Introduction
## Correlative Cosmology—
## An Interpretive Context

### I. OPTIMIZING EXPERIENCE: *THIS FOCUS AND ITS FIELD*

We will argue that *the* defining purpose of the *Daodejing* is bringing into focus and sustaining a productive disposition that allows for the fullest appreciation of those specific things and events that constitute one's field of experience. The project, simply put, is to get the most out of what each of us is: a quantum of unique experience. It is making this life significant. In his early work in articulating the assumptions underlying Chinese natural cosmology, Tang Junyi is saying something similar when he summarizes what he takes to be the most crucial contribution of Chinese culture broadly. It is

> . . . the spirit of the symbiosis and mutuality between particular and totality. In terms of our understanding this means an unwillingness to isolate the particular from the totality, and in terms of feeling, it means the commitment of the particular to do its best to realize the totality.[1]

If this is indeed the defining problematic of the text, it might help us understand at least one insight conveyed in its title, the "*Daodejing.*" The scores of translations that have introduced this text to the Western academy have deferred to the difficulty of making sense of the title by conventionally leaving it untranslated. Alternatively they have simply titled it after its putative author, "the Old Master," still leaving it untranslated as the "*Laozi.*"

While almost all translators have skirted the problem of rendering the title into English by simply romanizing it as *"Daodejing,"* a few earnest souls have stepped up and offered their best effort, each of them emphasizing either a different dimension of the work itself, or a more subjective understanding of what the text means to them. Herbert A. Giles (1886), for example, underscores the always laconic, often opaque, and sometimes even tentative diction of the text in calling it *The Remains of Lao Tzu*. G. G. Alexander (1895) takes a figurist approach, finding in the text echoes of his own religious sensibilities: *Lao-tsze: The Great Thinker with a Translation of His Thoughts on the Nature and Manifestation of God*. Seeming to rescue this protean piece of literature for perhaps gray but always responsible philosophy, Paul Carus and D. T. Suzuki (1913) render the title: *The Canon of Reason and Virtue: Lao Tzu's Tao Teh King*. But "reason" for these scholars turns out to be "Divine Reason" and the "Son of Heaven" is "the High Priest of the people who must bear the sins of mankind."[2] While sensitivity to the religious dimension of the text (albeit a sensitivity derived from a tradition radically different from its own) is its own virtue, the sin of mankind is certainly increased by half in their willingness to reduce the *Daodejing*'s exquisite poetry to rather unremarkable doggerel (even doggerel has its standards). Witness chapter 6:

> The valley spirit not expires,
> Mysterious woman 'tis called by the sires,
> The mysterious woman's door, to boot,
> Is called of heaven and earth the root.
> Forever and aye it seems to endure
> And its use is without effort sure.

Perhaps the most widely known and accepted English translation of the title is Arthur Waley's (1934) *The Way and Its Power: A Study of the Tao Te Ching and Its Place in Chinese Thought*. While seemingly secular and more dynamic, Waley's popular title still suggests our familiar "One-many" metaphysics. In this title, the demonstrative and possessive pronouns nominalize *"the* Way" and isolate it metaphysically as the "One" source of order for a universe that is ordered by it, locating the energy of creative transformation in this superordinated agency as its "Power." Further, the use of a capital "W" invests this "Way" semantically as a metonym for the transcendent and Divine. Waley's language might sound more liberating, but his title still promises a version of the *Daodejing* located squarely within a worldview more familiar to his readers than relevant to the text.

We want to introduce a translation of the title that attempts, however imperfectly, to capture the defining purpose of the text stated above: bringing into focus and sustaining a productive disposition that allows for the fullest appreciation of those specific things and events that constitute one's field of experience. Of course, there is no one correct translation of the title, *Daodejing*. Were we to give priority to the cosmological insights provided by the text, we might render *Daodejing* as: "The Classic of This Focus *(de* 德*)* and Its Field *(dao* 道*)*." If instead we wanted to emphasize the outcome of living according to this cosmology, we might translate it as: "Feeling at Home in the World." But with deliberation we choose to underscore the human project that has prompted the articulation of Daoist cosmology and is inspired by it. Thus we translate *Daodejing* as "Making This Life Significant." The Philosophical Introduction that follows will stand as our clarification of this translation, and as an argument that seeks to defend it.

## 2. DAOIST COSMOLOGY: AN INTERPRETIVE CONTEXT

We begin our argument for translating *Daodejing* as "Making This Life Significant" from Daoist cosmology. Taking a closer look at the interpretation of both the title and the content of the *Daodejing* as "The Classic of This Focus *(de* 德*)* and Its Field *(dao* 道*)*," we might first ask what does the expression "this focus" mean? The Daoist correlative cosmology begins from the assumption that the endless stream of always novel yet still continuous situations we encounter are real, and hence, that there is ontological parity among the things and events that constitute our lives. As a parody on

Parmenides, who claimed that "only Being is," we might say that for the Daoist, "only *beings* are," or taking one step further in underscoring the reality of the process of change itself, "only *becomings* are." That is, the Daoist does not posit the existence of some permanent reality behind appearances, some unchanging substratum, some essential defining aspect behind the accidents of change. Rather, there is just the ceaseless and usually cadenced flow of experience.

In fact, the absence of the "One behind the many" metaphysics makes our uncritical use of the philosophic term "cosmology" to characterize Daoism, at least in the familiar classical Greek sense of this word, highly problematic. In early Greek philosophy, the term "kosmos" connotes a clustered range of meanings, including *arche* (originative, material, and efficient cause/ultimate undemonstrable principle), *logos* (underlying organizational principle), *theoria* (contemplation), *nomos* (law), *theios* (divinity), *nous* (intelligibility). In combination, this cluster of terms conjures forth some notion of a single-ordered Divine[3] universe governed by natural and moral laws that are ultimately intelligible to the human mind. This "kosmos" terminology is culturally specific, and if applied uncritically to discuss the classical Daoist worldview, introduces a cultural reductionism that elides and thus conceals truly significant differences.

The Daoist understanding of "cosmos" as the "ten thousand things" means that, in effect, the Daoists have no concept of cosmos at all insofar as that notion entails a coherent, single-ordered world which is in any sense enclosed or defined. The Daoists are, therefore, primarily, "acosmotic" thinkers.[4]

One implication of this distinction between a "cosmotic" and an "acosmotic" worldview is that, in the absence of some overarching *arche* or "beginning" as an explanation of the creative process, and under conditions which are thus "an-archic" in the philosophic sense of this term, although the "nature" of something might indeed refer to "kinds," such "natural kinds" would be no more than generalizations made by analogizing among similar phenomena. That is, difference is prior to identifiable similarities.

The Chinese binomial most frequently translated as *kosmos* is *yuzhou* 宇宙, a term that overtly expresses the interdependence between time and space. The "world" as *shijie* 世界 is likewise expressed literally as the "boundaries between one's generation and the tradition." For ancient China, time pervades everything and is not to be denied. Time is not independent of things, but a fundamental aspect of them. Unlike traditions that devalue both time and change in pursuit of the timeless and eternal, in classical China things are always transforming (*wuhua* 物化). In fact, in the absence of some claim to objectivity that "objectifies" and thus makes "objects" of phenomena, the Chinese tradition does not have the separation between time and entities that would allow for either time without entities, or entities without time—there is no possibility of either an empty temporal corridor or an eternal anything (in the sense of being timeless).

What encourages us within a Western metaphysical tradition to separate time and space is our inclination, inherited from the Greeks, to see things in the world as fixed in their formal aspect, and thus as bounded and limited. If instead of giving ontological privilege to the formal aspect of phenomena, we were to regard them as having parity in their formal and changing aspects, we might be more like classical China in temporalizing them in light of their ceaseless transformation, and conceive of them more as "events" than as "things." In this processual worldview, each phenomenon is some unique current or impulse within a temporal flow. In fact, it is the pervasive and collective capacity of the events of the world to transform continuously that is the actual meaning of time.

A second assumption of Daoist "cosmology" (now using this term "cosmology" under advisement) that follows from this acknowledgment of the reality of both change and the uniqueness that follows from it is that particular "things" are in fact processual events, and are thus *intrinsically* related to the other "things" that provide them context. Said another way, these processual events are porous, flowing into each other in the ongoing transformations we call experience. Formation and function—the shape of things and what they do to whom—are interdependent and mutually determining characteristics of these events. It is for this reason that things resist "definition" in the literal sense of *finis*—a practice that delineates some ostensibly discrete boundary around them, and thus reduces all relations to external, extrinsic transactions. With fluid and shifting boundaries among things, integrity for any particular thing does not mean *being* or *staying* whole, or even actualizing its own internal potential. Rather, integrity is something *becoming whole in its co-creative relationships with other things*. Integrity is consummatory relatedness.

Integrity in this sense of becoming whole in one's relations with other things is a co-creative process in which one shapes and is shaped by one's environing circumstances. Not only is change an integral characteristic of things, but real creativity is a condition of this continuing transformative process. That is, our immediate experience is composed of fluid, porous events that entail both persistence and the spontaneous emergence of novelty, both continuity and disjunction. In this evolving order, there is at once a familiar rhythm to life, and the newness of each moment.

The irrepressible presencing of novelty within the context of what already exists guarantees the uniqueness of each emerging event, and preempts notions such as strict, linear causality, absolute predictability, and reversibility. The world is ever new. And the propensity of things—the force of circumstances—inching ahead in its seeming ineluctability, is always underdetermined, attended as it is by the contingency of real novelty.

In our introduction to *Focusing the Familiar: A Translation and Philosophical Interpretation of the* Zhongyong, we introduce a distinction between power and creativity, and follow A. N. Whitehead in questioning the appropriateness of using "creativity" in the familiar *creatio ex nihilo* model that we associate with Judeo-Christian cosmogony. Whitehead argues that any robust sense of creativity requires that creativity itself is more primordial than God.

In the received Judeo-Christian tradition, the all-*power*ful God *determines* things, *makes* things. God, as Omnipotent Other Who commands the world into being, is *Maker* of the world, not its

*Creator*. In the presence of the perfection that is God, nothing can be added or taken away. There can be no novelty or spontaneity. Thus, all subsequent acts of "creativity" are in fact secondary and derivative exercises of power. Creativity can make sense only in a processual world that admits of ontological parity among its constitutive events and of the spontaneous emergence of novelty.

Power is to be construed as the production of intended effects determined by external causation. Real creativity, on the other hand, entails the spontaneous production of novelty, irreducible through causal analysis. Power is exercised with respect to and over others. Creativity is always reflexive and is exercised over and with respect to "self." And since self in a processive world is always communal, creativity is contextual, transactional, and multidimensional. Thus creativity is both *self*-creativity and *co*-creativity. Either everything shares in creativity, or there is no creativity. Indeed, it is this transactional, co-creative character of all creative processes that precludes the project of self-cultivation and self-*creation* from being egoistic.

One further point can be made with respect to the creativity that the spontaneous emergence of novelty makes possible. The radical sense of creativity that we associate with "bringing into being" in a *creatio ex nihilo* sensibility is too isolated and extreme for this idea within the Daoist tradition. The term *dao*, like the terms "building," "learning," and "work," entails both the process and the created product. It is the locus and the time frame within which the always contextualized creativity takes place.

When the *Zhuangzi* observes that "we are one with all things 萬物與我爲一," this insight is a recognition that each and every unique phenomenon is continuous with every other phenomenon within one's field of experience. But is this an exhaustive claim: are we talking about *all* phenomena in the continuing present? Because the world is processional and because its creativity is *ab initio* rather than *ex nihilo*—a contextual creativity expressed across the careers of its constitutive phenomena—any answer to this question would have to be provisional. Phenomena are never either atomistically discrete or complete. The *Zhuangzi* recounts:

With the ancients, understanding had gotten somewhere. Where was that? Its height, its extreme, that to which no more could be added, was this: Some of these ancients thought that there had never begun to be things. The next lot thought that there are things, but that there had never begun to be boundaries among them. . . .[5]

A third assumption in the Daoist "cosmology" is that life broadly construed is entertained through and only through these same phenomena that constitute our experience. The field of experience is always construed from one perspective or another. There is no view from nowhere, no external perspective, no decontextualized vantage point. We are all in the soup. The intrinsic, constitutive relations that obtain among things make them reflexive and mutually implicating, residing together within the flux and flow.

This mutuality does not in any way negate the uniqueness of the particular perspective. Although any and all members of a family have implicated within them and thus present (rather than represent) the entire family, all members constitute and experience the family from their own particular point of view. And members in making the family their own quite appropriately have a distinctive proper name.

A corollary to this radical perspectivism is that each particular element in our experience is holographic in the sense that it has implicated within it the entire field of experience. This single flower has leaves and roots that take their nourishment from the environing soil and air. And the soil contains the distilled nutrients of past growth and decay that constitute the living ecological system in which all of its participants are organically interdependent. The sun enables the flower to process these nutrients, while the atmosphere that caresses the flower also nourishes and protects it. By the time we have "cashed out" the complex of conditions that conspire to produce and conserve this particular flower, one ripple after another in an ever-extending series of radial circles, we have implicated the entire cosmos within it without remainder. For the Daoist, there is an intoxicating bottomlessness to any particular event in our experience. The entire cosmos resides happily in the smile on the dirty face of this one little child.

If the insistent particular (*de* 德) is holographic, how does differentiation occur among particular things? In the human community, for example, what does it mean for a person to become distinguished and an object of deference?

First, this holographic sensibility is not simply Daoist, but a shared commitment of classical Chinese natural cosmology. The Confucian Mencius, for example, is also articulating this classical Chinese common sense when he interprets the field of *qi* in terms of moral energy and offers his advice on the attainment of human excellence. He speaks of his ability to nourish his "flood-like *qi* (*haoran zhi qi* 浩然之氣)," describing this *qi* as that which is "most vast (*zhida* 至大)" and "most firm (*zhigang* 至剛)."[6] Restated in the language of focus and field, Mencius is saying that his "flood-like *qi*" has the greatest "extensive" and "intensive" magnitudes. This language of extensive field and intensive focus suggests that one nourishes one's *qi* most successfully by making of oneself the most integral focus of the most extensive field of *qi*. In this manner, one gains greatest virtue (excellence, potency) in relation to the most far-reaching elements of one's environs. As we read in the *Mencius*:

> Everything is here in me. There is no joy greater than to discover creativity (*cheng* 誠) in one's person and nothing easier in striving to be authoritative in one's conduct (*ren* 仁) than committing oneself to treating others as one would oneself be treated.[7]

Our argument for translating *cheng* 誠 as "creativity" in this *Mencius* passage is that its more familiar translations as "sincerity" and "integrity" in fact reference a creative process. "Sincerity" as affective tone is the ground of growth in mutual relationships, and "integrity" is the "becoming one" that occurs as we become intimate. The deepening of these relationships that in sum constitute us as a person is a profoundly co-creative process of "doing and undergoing," of shaping and being shaped.

The Daoist variation on the efficacy of one's "flood-like *qi*" is the way in which the intensive focus of one's insistent particularity (*de* 德) provides the most extensive range of influence or potency in shaping one's world. Said simply, persons who "have their stuff together" change the world around them. In chapter 54 of the *Daodejing*, the cultivation of personal excellence is described as the starting point in world-making and in enhancing the ethos of the cosmos:

> Cultivate it in your person,
> And the character you develop will be genuine;
> Cultivate it in your family,
> And its character will be abundant;
> Cultivate it in your village,
> And its character will be enduring;
> Cultivate it in the state,
> And its character will flourish;
> Cultivate it in the world,
> And its character will be all-pervading.

This relationship between intensive resolution and extensive influence is also captured in chapter 23:

> Thus, those who are committed to way-making in what they do
> Are on their way.
> Those who are committed to character in what they do
> Achieve this character
> While those who lose it
> Are themselves lost.
> Way-making is moreover enhanced by those who express character,
> Just as it is diminished by those who themselves have lost it.

Optimizing experience by getting the most out of it requires a kind of "husbanding" of one's resources, where "husbanding" is understood as a combination of cultivation and frugality. High resolution in one's character elevates one as a focal presence and as an enduring influence on the extended community through the patterns of deference that have come to define one's person. This achieved character provides the world with a resource for resolving its problems as they arise. Such is the import of chapter 59:

> For bringing proper order to the people and in serving *tian*,
> Nothing is as good as husbandry.

It is only through husbandry that you come early to accept the way,
And coming early to accept the way is what is called redoubling
your accumulation of character.
If you redouble your accumulation of character, all obstacles can be
   overcome,
And if all obstacles can be overcome, none can discern your limit.
Where none can discern your limit,
You can preside over the realm.
In presiding over the mother of the realm
You can be long-enduring.

In this processual Daoist cosmology, continuity is prior to individuality, and the particular character or disposition of each event is thus an ongoing distinctive achievement. That is, each event distinguishes itself by developing its own uniqueness within the totality. And freedom is neither the absence of constraint nor some isolatable originality, but the full contribution of this achieved uniqueness to a shared community.

   A fourth presupposition of Daoist cosmology is that we are not passive participants in our experience. The energy of transformation lies within the world itself as an integral characteristic of the events that constitute it. There is no appeal to some external efficient cause: no Creator God or primordial determinative principle. In the absence of any preordained design associated with such an external cause, this energy of transformation is evidenced in the mutual accommodation and co-creativity that is expressed in the relations that obtain among things. When turned to proper effect, this energy can make the most of the creative possibilities of any given situation. This kind of responsive participation we have characterized elsewhere as *ars contextualis*: the art of contextualizing.[8] *Ars contextualis* is a way of living and relating to a world that quite simply seeks to get the most out of the diversity of experience.

## 3. GETTING THE MOST OUT OF ONE'S INGREDIENTS

The reality of time, novelty, and change; the persistence of particularity; the intrinsic, constitutive nature of relationships; the perspectival nature of experience—taken together, these several presuppositions that ground the Daoist worldview and provide Daoism with its interpretative context set the terms for optimizing our experience. Or said in a more metaphorical way, there is a strategy in the *Daodejing* for getting the most out of the ingredients of our lives.

The Confucian focus on the family (*jia* 家) serves as a starting point for understanding this Daoist sensibility, for the Confucian project of self-consummation, although decidedly different in its parameters, has a similar objective. We have argued elsewhere that the family serves as a pervasive metaphor for social, political, and even religious relations within the Confucian worldview.[9] The *Analects* 1.2 states explicitly that the way of conducting oneself most productively as a human being emerges out of the achievement of robust filial relations:

> Exemplary persons (*junzi* 君子) concentrate their efforts on the root, for the root having taken hold, the way (*dao* 道) will grow therefrom. As for filial and fraternal responsibility, it is, I suspect, the root of authoritative conduct (*ren* 仁).

The underlying assumption is that persons are more likely to give themselves utterly and unconditionally to their families than to any other human institution. Thus, the family as an institution provides the model for the process of making one's way by allowing the persons who constitute it both to invest in, and to get the most out of, the collective human experience. Promoting the centrality of family relations is an attempt to ensure that entire persons without remainder are invested in each of their actions.

The power of the family to function as the radial locus for human growth is much enhanced when natural family and communal relations are perceived as being exhaustive, without being construed as a distraction from, in competition with, or dependent upon any more fundamental relations, especially those characteristic of transcendental religiousness. It is from the family expanding outward that persons emerge as objects of profound communal, cultural, and ultimately religious deference, where the focus of religious reverence remains ancestral rather than supernatural or otherworldly. Human relations, far from being subordinated to one's relationship with one's God, are the concrete locus out of which religious feelings emerge.

Ambrose King makes the argument that relationships within the classical Chinese cosmology are construed broadly in familial terms.[10] We have gone further in suggesting that family is a more adequate metaphor than Joseph Needham's notion of "organism" for thinking about Chinese cosmology, and that arguably *all* relationships within this world are familial.[11] This metaphor certainly has application to the *Daodejing,* where rulership as an institution is naturalized on the model of the family, and explicit images of human procreativity—mother and infant—are projected onto the cosmos.

In fact, the sustained Grand Analogy that pervades the *Daodejing* is: *dao* is to the world as ruler ought to be to the people. *Dao*—the discernible rhythm and regularity of the world as it unfolds around and through us—is nonimpositional: "Way-making (*dao*) really does things noncoercively."[12] This attitude is carried over into the human world. In governing effectively, coercion is perceived as impoverishing and dehumanizing. So the consummate political model in Daoism, corresponding to the consummate experience itself, is described as *wuwei* ("noncoercive activity") and *ziran* ("self-so-ing," or "what is spontaneously so"). As stated in chapter 17, under the sway of nonimpositional rulership, the people are able to be spontaneous.

> With the most excellent rulers, their subjects only know that they
>     are there,
> The next best are the rulers they love and praise,
> Next are the rulers they hold in awe,
> And the worst are the rulers they disparage. . . .
> With all things accomplished and the work complete
> The common people say, "We are spontaneously like this."

Spontaneity must be clearly distinguished from randomness and impetuosity. In fact, far from being "uncaused," it is the novelty made possible by a cultivated disposition. Spontaneity is the punctuated flow and pressure of the calligrapher's brush; it is the singing dexterity of Cook Ding's cleaver.

Spontaneous action is a mirroring response. As such, it is action that accommodates the "other" to whom one is responding. It takes the other on its own terms. Such spontaneity involves recognizing the continuity between oneself and the other, and responding in such a way that one's own actions promote the interests and well-being both of oneself and of the other. This does not lead to reductive imitation but to complementarity and coordination. Handshakes and embraces are actions that presuppose a recognition of the relational stance of the other, and that complete that stance. In the dancehall of the cosmos, when the music for the next dance starts to play and partners open their arms to each other, the dance proceeds as a dyadic harmony of nonassertive actions.

## 4. APPRECIATING THE PARTICULAR

This Daoist theme of optimizing experience might be explored more concretely by borrowing a memorable passage from William James. James alludes to a classical Western nursery rhyme—yet another kind of "sound from the ground"—to reflect on precisely the issue of how to get the most out of one's life experience. He at once asks and answers the question "What Makes a Life Significant?":

> Every Jack sees in his own particular Jill charms and perfections to the enchantment of which we stolid onlookers are stone-cold. And which has the superior view of the absolute truth, he or we? Which has the more vital insight into the nature of Jill's existence, as a fact? Is he in excess, being in this matter a maniac? Or are we in defect, being victims of a pathological anesthesia as regards Jill's magical importance? Surely the latter; surely to Jack are the profounder truths revealed; surely poor Jill's palpitating little life-throbs *are* among the wonders of creation, *are* worthy of this sympathetic interest; and it is to our shame that the rest of us cannot feel like Jack. For Jack realizes Jill concretely, and we do not. He struggles toward a union with her inner life, divining her feelings, anticipating her desires,

understanding her limits as manfully as he can, and yet inadequately, too; for he is also afflicted with some blindness, even here. Whilst we, dead clods that we are, do not even seek after these things, but are contented that that portion of eternal fact named Jill should be for us as if it were not. Jill, who knows her inner life, knows that Jack's way of taking it—so importantly—is the true and serious way; and she responds to the truth in him by taking him truly and seriously, too. May the ancient blindness never wrap its clouds about either of them again! Where would any of *us* be, were there no one willing to know us as we really are or ready to repay us for *our* insight by making recognizant return? We ought, all of us, to realize each other in this intense, pathetic, and important way.

If you say that this is absurd, and that we cannot be in love with everyone at once, I merely point out to you that, as a matter of fact, certain persons do exist with all enormous capacity for friendship and for taking delight in other people's lives; and that such persons know more of truth than if their hearts were not so big.[13]

What is particularly instructive about this excerpt from James is his claim that the site of knowing the truth about Jill is Jack's heart. Both the magical importance of Jill as someone valued and the absolute truth about Jill as a matter of fact are realized concretely in these immediate feelings. Persons are constituted by their relationships, and these relations are valorized and made real in the process of persons bringing their fields of experience into focus. And it is Jack who focuses Jill with optimum resolution. The unmediated acknowledgment of Jill as one of the wonders of creation resides in the affective relationships that give her context, particularly, her Jack. This is only to say that the creative transactions—the doings and undergoings among persons—are a disclosure of their feelings for one another. Thus, affective tone and the subjective form of feeling are always entailed in the uniquely perspectival locus of the co-creative process. We feel our way forward into novel experience.

When we turn to the Chinese language in which this Daoist worldview is sedimented, James's insight into the inseparability of fact and value—the cognitive and the affective, thinking and feeling—is revealed in its own way. The character *xin* 心, often translated rather awkwardly as "heart-and-mind," is itself an argument for the assumed indivisibility of knowing and feeling within this antique tradition.

*Xin* is a stylized pictograph of the aorta, associating it quite immediately with the "heart" and the emotional connotations that attend it. The fact that the character *qing* 情 that we translate as "emotions" or "feelings" is a combination of this *xin* 心 and a phonetic element, *qing* 青, justifies this understanding.[14] Indeed, many if not most of the characters that entail some dimension of "emotions" and "feelings" have *xin* as a component element.

However, the fact that *xin* has as often been rendered as "mind" should also alert us to the possible inadequacy of simply translating it as "heart." Many if not most of the Chinese characters that refer to different modalities of "thinking" are also constructed with *xin* as a component. Indeed, there are many passages in these classical texts that would not make sense in English unless the *xin* "thinks."

The point is that in this classical Chinese worldview broadly conceived, the mind cannot be divorced from the heart. There are no altogether rational thoughts devoid of feeling, nor any raw feelings altogether lacking in cognitive content. Having said this, the prejudice to which Daoism is resolutely resistant is the dichotomy between the cognitive and the affective that would privilege knowing as some separate cognitive activity. A. N. Whitehead expresses this same concern when he observes that: ". . . mothers can ponder many things in their hearts that words cannot express."[15] Concrete feelings, the real site of knowing, become selectively abstracted and impoverished when they are resolved into the rational currency of names, concepts, and theories without adequate deference to the affective ground of this cognitive superstructure.

In this early Chinese natural cosmology in which process and change have priority over form and stasis, it is frequently observed that, with respect to the common sense understanding of the human body, physiology has priority over anatomy, and function takes precedence over site. In this resolutely nondualistic worldview, the *xin*, then, is primarily a dynamic system that is metonymically associated with but in no way exhausted by, its dense center, the anatomical heart-and-mind. This being the case, it might well be argued that *xin* means primarily "thinking and feeling," and then derivatively and metaphorically, the organs with which these experiences are allied.

In the passage cited above, James allows that every Jack is "enchanted" by the charms and perfections of his own particular Jill. The enchantment in the "thoughtful" feelings of Jack and Jill emerges in their mutual and reciprocated sensitivity and awareness. This kind of shared appreciation means several things. Certainly, they recognize better than most the quality, significance, and magnitude of each other, and in so doing, admire each other greatly. But this burgeoning capacity for mutual appreciation goes well beyond simply a personal enjoyment of each other that begins and ends in their relationship. Indeed this appreciation spills over to become "value-added"—quite literally raising the value of the cosmos in which they occur. Their shared cosmos is much appreciated, becoming a more magnificent time and place because of the profound feelings Jack and Jill have for each other. It is this capacity of the human experience to enchant the cosmos, then, that is the more important meaning of "appreciating the particular."

## 5. THE MUTUAL ENTAILING OF OPPOSITES

In the *Book of Changes*, experience itself is defined simply as a succession of *yin* and *yang* phases: 一陰一陽之謂道. This description is an abstract way of making the empirical observation that all predicates give way to their opposites: order and disorder succeed each other, and so on. This characteristic of experience is ascribed to the natural cyclical movement of *qi* rather than some supernatural force, and is captured and made explicit in the metaphorical language of *yinyang* 陰陽 and the five phases 五行 cosmology.

As chapter 40 of the *Daodejing* observes, the mutual entailing of opposites means that whatever "goes out" and becomes consummately distinct, also "returns":

"Returning" is how way-making moves,
And "weakening" is how it functions.
The events of the world arise from the determinate,
And the determinate arises from the indeterminate.

The most basic meaning of "returning" restates what has been said above. As Tang Junyi reports, cosmology is not simply a linear zero-sum victory of order over chaos driven by some external cause, but rather is the endless alternation between rising and falling, emerging and collapsing, moving and attaining equilibrium that is occasioned by its own internal energy of transformation.[16] This cosmic unfolding is not "cyclical" in the sense of reversibility and replication, but is rather a continuing spiral that is always coming back upon itself and yet is ever new.

It is the disposition of all things that their present condition entails its opposite. The *Daodejing* observes in chapter 58:

It is upon misfortune that good fortune leans,
It is within good fortune itself that misfortune crouches in ambush,
And where does it all end?

This insight into the mutuality of opposites has several implications. Perhaps most obviously, young is "young-becoming-old"; dark is "dark-becoming-light"; soft is "soft-becoming-hard." In the fullness of time, any and all of the qualities that define each event will yield themselves up to their opposites. Those who are born into the world and live to grow old will eventually die. Anything that embarks upon this journey toward fruition has in its first few steps set off on the long road home. And it is at the moment of setting out as a newborn infant that a person has maximum potency. Thus, the journey can fairly be characterized both as a returning and a gradual weakening of one's initial promise. And it is by effectively husbanding this potency over one's career that one is able to make the most of one's experience.

By anticipating the changes in your conditions, and by remaining focused despite the unavoidable vicissitudes that are visited upon you as you move along the continuum from beginning to end, you are able to optimize the possibilities at each moment and thus enjoy the ride to its fullest. Cultivating a proper disposition and being prepared for the seasons through which you pass from birth to death will enable you to consistently get the most out of your circumstances. It is your resolution—the intensity found at the center—that will keep your life experience in focus, establish you as an object of deference, and enable you to enjoy both a productive life and a healthy death.

Said another way, to lose focus and stray off course along the way while on this journey will precipitate reversion. Squandered energy while young will age you prematurely. As it says in chapter 55:

> For something to be old while in its prime
> Is called a departure from the way of things.
> And whatever departs from the way of things will come to an untimely end.

Aggression directed at others will, like Monsieur Guillotine's guillotine, come back to shorten your own life. Again, as in chapter 74:

> To stand in for the executioner in killing people
> Is to stand in for the master carpenter in cutting his lumber.
> Of those who would thus stand in for the master carpenter,
> Few get away without injuring their own hands.

The world around us is always an interface between persistent form and novelty, the familiar honeycombed by the unexpected. The new emerges within the context and the security of the ordinary, and in due course, what was new overtakes and supplants the ordinary, and what was ordinary becomes an increasingly fragile memory for those who can still remember. In time, the new becomes the newly ordinary, and the ordinary returns whence it came.

## 6. AESTHETIC HARMONY

At this point we would like to introduce a few technical terms of aesthetic analysis that might be applied in explaining the particularly Daoist mode of attaining and sustaining harmony. This vocabulary is drawn from the work of A. N. Whitehead's *Process and*

*Reality*, a philosophical work that is grounded in an aesthetic sense of order.[17]

According to Whitehead, there are four fundamental variables that contribute to the achievement of that harmony deriving from a balance of simplicity and complexity. These variables are *triviality, vagueness, narrowness,* and *width.*

*Triviality* involves an excess of differentiation. It is complexity without contrast. An order is trivial when it is characterized by an excess of differentiation among its elements, all of which are entertained equally and are given equal importance. Systems theory would call triviality an excess of information leading to the production of dissonance: it is mere "noise." It is chaos. There is no organizing strategy, no hierarchy, no differential importance. This is sheer multiplicity without focus or discretion.

*Vagueness,* as Whitehead uses the term, is an excess of identification. In a vague order, the differences among items are irrelevant factors in constituting the order. It is simplicity without contrast. The vague order displays an undifferentiated commonality of character. Vagueness is a bland field without particular focus; it is the facile and unconsidered use of generalizations.

*Narrowness* is an emphasis upon certain components in an order at the expense of others. It is simplicity in search of intense contrast. An order dominated by narrowness has an intensity of focus that backgrounds all other strongly differentiated factors. Matter-of-fact gives way to importance.

Finally, *width* involves the coordination of differentiated elements, each with its own unique contribution to the order. It is complexity that sacrifices some contrast for depth and scope. The kind of discussion one would hope to have in an interdisciplinary university seminar would likely contribute to an order characterized by width. Width involves the balancing of narrowness and vagueness.

A productive order has all four characteristics in various forms of background/foreground combinations. Vagueness, and the mild identification it entails, when focused by the narrow, produces the contrasts appropriate to the production of harmony. Contrast involves the interweaving of triviality and vagueness through a shifting foreground/background gestalt, while the depth of contrast in an order is a function of its degree of complexity.

The *Daodejing* centers its discussion on cultivating the most productive relationship between the vagueness of the continuous field of experience and the narrowness of the insistent particulars. One pervasive theme of the text is that coercive, contentious activity diminishes the balance between focus and field. On the other hand, noncoercive relatedness encourages width, and the alternation between vagueness and triviality provides contrast.

The abstractness of the *Daodejing* and the absence of any concrete, illustrative examples trades potential complexity and intensity that would be provided by these specific cases for an accommodating width, thus allowing it to be broad in its relevance and application. The role of the reader, then, is to supply the narrowness needed to create the intensity and deepen the degree of contrast.

This language of aesthetic analysis can be regarded as germane to the dispute between the naturalistic Daoists and the more narrowly human-centered Confucians that we find both in the *Daodejing* and the *Analects of Confucius,* and in the tradition more broadly conceived. From a Confucian point of view, the vagueness of human relatedness is brought into focus through the performance of hierarchical roles and formal practices (*li* 禮). Through these ritualizing institutions all human beings are able to take a stand, and to find their place by establishing a value that is relative to the value of other members of their community. Ritualized living is an instrument for personalizing institutions and registering the narrowness and intensity of each human perspective, while allowing for enough width to promote effective tolerance. The Confucian argument would insist that the narrowness of human concerns provides the necessary intensity, while the Daoist's exaggerated inclusiveness would move humanity beyond productive "width" in the direction of a nonproductive vagueness.

Thus, the central complaint of the Confucian about the Daoist vision of things is in the vagueness of the latter. In fact, the Confucian accuses the Daoist explicitly of sacrificing the intensity that comes with a narrow focus for an inclusiveness that is too thin and diffuse.[18]

In response, the Daoist, as a student of the arts of the Chaos clan, would insist that the Confucian claim to narrowness is bogus. Indeed, the insistent particularity *(de)* of human beings and the possible intensity of their natural feelings is trivialized by recourse to contrived rules and artificial relationships that are dehumanizing, and by strategies for social regulation that privilege an ordered uniformity over spontaneity. Further, the absence of concern about the natural environment transforms Confucian narrowness into a kind of intolerance and exclusiveness that jeopardizes the depth of contrast and the intensity of one's experience provided by appropriate width. Confucian narrowness, the Daoist might well argue, leads socially to nepotism, parochialism, and jingoism, and within the natural environment, to anthropocentrism, speciesism, and the pathetic fallacy.[19] For the Daoist, the only guarantee of a viable narrowness would be to allow for the nontrivialized expression of each perspective in the environment to be registered and accounted for, human and otherwise. Indeed, *li* and its perceived intolerance of the world beyond the human community leads to a thinness of experience, and with it, a diminution of imagination and creativity.

The Daoist's guarantee against vagueness lies in an achieved disposition that is made manifest in the appropriate exercise of the *wu*-forms: *wuwei* 無為, or noncoercive actions in deference to the *de* ("particular focus") of things; *wuzhi* 無知, or knowing that does not have recourse to rules or principles; and *wuyu* 無欲, or desiring that does not seek to possess or control its object. The deference implicit in these *wu*-forms facilitates width as an appropriate combination of triviality and vagueness, while maintaining the narrowness and the focus of insistent particularity.

The point of this technical aside is a simple enough one: The interfusion of the variables leading to a balanced complexity of experience involves recourse to distinctly nonlogical criteria. There is no means of establishing the superiority of triviality, or vagueness, or narrowness, or width, one over the other because these are all presuppositions of a realized order. Nor is there any final science that could advise one as to the correct intermixing of these aspects of order.

Similarly, consistent with the Daoist resistance to asserting any certitude or final vocabulary, there is no way of saying that Confucianism or Daoism is ultimately superior to the other by virtue of an appeal to univocal criteria. Nor is there any means of separating the two movements into distinctive schools on the basis of orthodoxies of belief or practice. There is no final truth either about the nature of things, or about the means whereby that nature is sought. The achievement of order and harmony in nature and society— that is to say, the achievement of effective way-making or *dao*—is a multifaceted effort that is dependent less upon uncovering true principles or right forms of conduct than on the exercise of imagination and creativity within the most deferential of contexts. In fact, the broadest context—the one leading to the richest resources for Chinese "way-makers"—has been built from the contributions of both the Confucian and the Daoist sensibilities.

## 7. AWARENESS

The *Daodejing* encourages a comprehensive, processual view of experience that requires a full understanding of the larger picture and the ability to locate and appreciate the particular event within it. This broad view of the field of experience allows one to contextualize particular events, and it provides the peripheral vision needed to stay focused at the center while at the same time anticipating future turns.

What does it mean to achieve resolution in one's disposition by "keeping to the center" and "remaining focused"? By appealing to what Tang Junyi has captured in the expression *yiduo bufenguan* 一多不分觀—translatable as "the inseparability of one and many, of continuity and multiplicity, of *dao* and the myriad of insistent particulars (*de*)"—we can identify two mutually reinforcing levels of awareness advocated in the *Daodejing*: what we might call focal awareness and field awareness.

In order to influence and anticipate the general flow of circumstances, we must have a focused awareness of each of the particular events that constitute our experience. We must be aware of the one as it is implicated in and influences the many. This kind of awareness is to see the world focally in terms of the insistent particulars (*de*) that constitute it. And in order to best understand any one of these events and bring it fully into focus, we must be aware of the field of conditions that conspire to sponsor and sustain it. We must be aware of the many conditions as they are implicated in and are continuous with the one event. This kind of awareness is to see the insistent particular more broadly in terms of the continuous flow of experience (*dao*). The field can only be entered through the particular focus, and the complexity of the focus can only be appreciated by extending the field. Thus, a focal awareness and a field awareness presuppose each other.

One insight governing field awareness is that it requires a full cognizance of the mutual entailment of opposites, allowing one to track one's collaboration in any particular situation through its inevitable process of reversion. It foregrounds the relational character of the elements within the matrix of events, and the symbiotic continuities that obtain among them. This kind of insight—the capacity to see where a situation has come from and to anticipate where it is going—discourages any proclivity one might have to isolate things, and to make exclusive judgments about them on the basis of any particular phase in their continuing narrative.

A student of the martial arts may become discouraged because his or her initial attempts at reproducing the proper form of a roundhouse kick are slow and embarrassingly unsuccessful, while at the same time other more supple students may gain immediate proficiency. A field awareness would anticipate that this student's initial lack of suppleness will, in the course of training, be transformed into the tension that, like a taut spring, produces the power of the properly executed technique. A weakness becomes a strength when what is inflexible becomes more supple.

Focal awareness, on the other hand, is the full appreciation of the particular foci that constitute any particular field as the concrete medium through which field awareness is sustained. A subtle understanding of the uniqueness of each event and the attention to the minutia that affect it enables one to anticipate the evolving order, and to encourage or discourage fluctuations at an incipient phase before they have evolved into the full-blown weight of circumstances. All major events are modest in their beginnings, and minor alterations introduced at an early stage of an ongoing event can have cascading consequences for the outcome.

Several defining aspects of focal order condition our awareness of it. The first of these conditions is the temporal immediacy of the continuing present: order is always located in the "very now." The second condition is spatial immediacy: order starts here and goes there. Third, focal order is always collaborative: all relations, while they are intrinsic and thus constitutive, are also projective and recursive. And finally, equilibrium in one's disposition allows one to contextualize events on their own terms and to achieve an optimally productive harmony.

The "art" in any martial art lies in tailoring it to the strengths and weaknesses, both psychological and physical, of the particular student. The fullest degree of competence comes as a function of optimizing this uniqueness. A great deal of care must be taken at the most elementary stages of training to establish "habits of mind and body," again both psychological and physical, that lead to a maximizing of the developing skill and allow for the emergence of one's particularity. Training is a combination of awareness and feeling. And one must remain resolutely focused in one's entire person through the changing seasons of one's practice. Success in the martial arts, as in all experience, lies ultimately in the satisfaction students gain in knowing that they have made the most of their experience in all of its changing phases.

A full appreciation of particularity requires that we understand and be responsive to the complex patterns of relatedness implicated in any event. These patterns are endlessly manifold and diverse, and their ever-changing novelty makes them constantly unique and distinctive. But again this novelty is always *ab initio* and *in situ*, occurring within an already familiar context. Indeterminacy and the possibility for spontaneity are real, and there are gaps in the sequence of events that preclude absolute predictability and precise causal analysis. But there is also a fluid continuity that is captured in expressions such as "passing" and "returning." It is in appreciating both this continuity and the emergent novelty of experience that we are able to deal with events in terms of the mutual implication of opposites.

The *Daodejing* enjoins us to cultivate those habits of awareness that allow us to plumb and appreciate the magic of the ordinary and the everyday. Indeed, it is by enchanting the routine that we are on the way to making this life truly significant.

## 8. THE *WU* 無 -FORMS

The compilers of the *Daodejing* seek rather explicitly to develop a contrast between the glimpses of insight this text strives to impart, and the substance of other philosophical doctrines. Many if not most doctrines evolve with their antecedents in an elaborate genealogy of values and ideas. These philosophical doctrines are often hierarchically structured by precepts and governing principles, and they may well require an extended course of study for their mastery and transmission. The precepts that inform these "doctrines" are professionalized by their learned "doctors," and within their marble academies these erudites—for appropriate status and recompense—are only too glad to amaze the *hoi poloi* with the flashing dexterity of their philosophic thrusts and parries.

What the *Daodejing* has to offer, on the other hand, is much simpler. It encourages the cultivation of a disposition that is captured in what we have chosen to call its *wu*-forms. The *wu*-forms free up the energy required to sustain the abstract cognitive and moral sensibilities of technical philosophy, allowing this energy, now unmediated by concepts, theories, and contrived moral precepts, to be expressed as those concrete feelings that inspire the ordinary business of the day. It is through these concrete feelings that one is able to know the world and to optimize the human experience.

The abstraction of the concrete ethical dimension of such felt knowing into a formal moralist vocabulary is rehearsed in chapter 38 of the *Daodejing*:

> Thus, only when we have lost sight of way-making is there excellence,
> Only when we have lost sight of excellence is there authoritative conduct,
> Only when we have lost sight of authoritative conduct is there appropriateness,
> And only when we have lost sight of appropriateness is there ritual propriety.
>
> As for ritual propriety, it is the thinnest veneer of doing one's best and making good on one's word,
> And it is the first sign of trouble.
> "Foreknowledge" is tinsel decorating the way,
> And is the first sign of ignorance.
>
> It is for this reason that persons of consequence:
> Set store by the substance rather than the veneer
> And by the fruit rather than the flower.
> Hence, eschewing one they take the other.

The moral precepts described in the first two stanzas emerge as objects of reverence, but as hallowed as they might become, they are anemic when compared to the love and life of concrete, spontaneous feelings. It is the "substance" and the "fruit"—the passionate experience of life itself—rather than a catechism of bloodless ethical principles, that is the real site of knowing. Such felt knowing is an ongoing process of focal and field awareness—of way-making—that can only be sustained with indefatigable resolution.

Indeed, it is not an easy business to stay focused. Even though the *Daodejing*'s teachings on how to cultivate the most effective disposition for making one's way in the world could not be put in more straightforward terms, still "when the very best scholars learn of way-making they are just barely able to keep to its center" (chapter 41).

Were we to search for something like a central insight that defines the Daoist sensibility, we might discover that a "single thread" pervades the text. The central focus of the Daoist way of thinking is the decisive role of deference in the establishment and preservation of relationships. As we have said above, integrity in a processual worldview is not *being one*, but *becoming one* in the consummatory relationships that one is able to achieve within a context of environing particulars. Deference involves a yielding (and being yielded to) grounded in an acknowledgment of the shared excellence of particular foci (*de*) in the process of one's own self-cultivation. Deferential acts require that one put oneself literally in the place of the other, and in so doing, incorporate what was the object of deference into what is one's own developing disposition. And one's own disposition thus fortified becomes available as a locus of deference for others.

In Confucianism, self is determined by sustained effort (*zhong* 忠) in deferential transactions (*shu* 恕) guided by ritually structured roles and relations (*li* 禮 ) that project one's person outward into society and into culture. Such a person becomes a focus of the community's deference (*junzi* 君子) and a source of its spirituality (*shen* 神).

Daoism, on the other hand, expresses its deferential activity through what we are calling the *wu*-forms. The three most familiar articulations of this pervasive sensibility are: *wuwei* 無爲, *wuzhi* 無知, and *wuyu* 無欲. These are, respectively, noncoercive actions in accordance with the *de* ("particular focus") of things; a sort of knowing without resort to rules or principles; and desiring which does not seek to possess or control its "object." In each of these instances, as in the case of Confucian *shu*, it is necessary to put oneself in the place of what is to be acted in accordance with, what is to be known, or what is to be desired, and thus incorporate this perspective into one's own disposition. Our chief aim here is to demonstrate how this explicitly Daoist understanding of deferential activity presupposes a focus-field model of self.

Given our discussion of the inseparability of feeling and thinking—the affective and the cognitive—in the Daoist heart-and-mind (*xin*), the conflict associated with the self that the Daoist sage must overcome cannot be a struggle among some compartmentalized rational, appetitive, and emotional faculties. Indeed, given the relational and unpartitioned model of the self characterized by *xin*, it is difficult to imagine how there could be anything like an internal dynamics that would be a source of agitation. It is unlikely that we would find Hamlets or St. Pauls prominent among the Daoists.

If the problematic of unrealized selfhood does not entail a self divided against itself, what is the source and the nature of the disturbance that the cultivation of the Daoist disposition is meant to overcome? If it is not referenced primarily within an individuating soul, it can only be a disturbance in the relationships that constitute the context of self-consummation. Said another way, if a person is not in fact constituted by some essential, partitioned "soul," but is rather seen as dynamic pattern of personal, social, and natural relationships, agitation must arise as a consequence of poor management of these constitutive roles and relationships. Hence, agitation in the heart-and-mind is not narrowly "psychological," but is more accurately conceived of as of broad ethical concern: How should we act and what should we do?

To summarize the three most prominent examples of the *wu*-forms that we have discussed in more detail elsewhere,[20] *wuwei* 無 為, often translated (unfortunately) as "no action" or "non-action," really involves the absence of any course of action that interferes with the particular focus (*de* 德) of those things contained within one's field of influence. Actions uncompromised by stored knowledge or ingrained habits are relatively unmediated: they are accommodating and spontaneous. As such, these actions are the result of deferential responses to the item or the event in accordance with which, or in relation to which, one is acting. These actions are *ziran* 自然, "spontaneous" and "self-so-ing," and as such, are nonassertive actions.

It is not through an internal struggle of reason against the passions but through "acuity (*ming* 明)"—a mirroring of the things of the world as they are in their interdependent relations with us—that we reach a state in which nothing among all of the myriad of "the goings on" in the world will be able to agitate our hearts-and-minds, and we are able to promote the flourishing of our world. In other words, we defer in attaining integrity with those things that contextualize us, establishing a frictionless equilibrium with them. And it is this state of achieved equilibrium that is precisely the relationship most conducive to symbiotic growth and productivity. The Daoist sages in *Zhuangzi* are described in such terms:

> The stillness of the sages is not simply a matter of their saying: "Stillness is good!" and hence they are still. Rather, they are still because none of the myriad things are able to agitate their hearts-and-mind. When water is still, it illuminates one's whiskers and eyebrows, and in its placidity, it provides a standard so that skilled artisans can take their measure from it. If the stillness of water provides illumination, how much more so one's spirit. The stillness of the heart-and-mind of the sage makes it mirror to the whole world and the looking glass for all of the myriad things. [21]

The notion of *jing* 靜—stillness, tranquillity—that is often used to characterize this posture, far from being simple passivity, is an ongoing, dynamic achievement of equilibrium that requires constant monitoring and adjustment. It is important to remember that all correlative pairs entail their opposites in the sense that *jing* is "tranquillity-becoming-agitated." Thus, tranquillity (*jing*) stands in a dominant relationship in its partnership with agitation (*dong* 動); it does not negate or exclude its opposite. The same qualification has to be brought to bear on other familiar pairs that might otherwise mislead us: for example, emptiness (*xu* 虛) and fullness (*shi* 實), and clarity (*qing* 清) and turbidity (*zhuo* 濁).

*Wuzhi* 無知, often translated as "no-knowledge," actually means the absence of a certain kind of knowledge—the kind of knowledge that is dependent upon ontological presence: that is, the assumption that there is some unchanging reality behind appearance. Knowledge grounded in a denial of ontological presence involves "acosmotic" thinking: the type of thinking that does not presuppose a single-ordered ("One behind the many") world, and its intellectual accoutrements. It is, therefore, *unprincipled* knowing. Such knowing does not appeal to rules or principles determining the existence, the meaning, or the activity of a phenomenon. *Wuzhi* provides one with a sense of the *de* of a thing—its particular uniqueness and focus—rather than yielding an understanding of that thing in relation to some concept or natural kind or universal. Ultimately, *wuzhi* is a grasp of the *daode* 道德 relationship of each encountered item that permits an understanding of *this* particular focus (*de*) and the field that it construes.

Knowledge, as unprincipled knowing, is the acceptance of the world on its own terms without recourse to rules of discrimination that separate one sort of thing from another. Rules of thumb, habits of mind and action, established customs, fixed standards, received methods, stipulated concepts and categories, commandments, principles, laws of nature, conventions—all of these prejudices require us to intervene and "welcome things as they come and escort them as they go," resulting in what Steve Goldberg has described as "a hardening of the categories." Having stored past experience and organized it in terms of fixed standards or principles, we then recall, anticipate, and participate in a world patterned by these discriminations.

Sages, however, mirror the world, and "neither see things off nor go out to meet them." As such, they "respond to everything without storing anything up." They mirror the world *at each moment* in a way that is undetermined by the shape of a world that has passed away, or by anticipations of a world yet to come. As the *Daodejing* asks in chapter 10:

> In scrubbing and cleansing your profound mirror
> Are you able to rid it of all imperfections?
> In loving the common people and breathing life into the state,
> Are you able to do it without recourse to wisdom?
> With nature's gates swinging open and closed
> Are you able to remain the female?
> With your insight penetrating the four quarters
> Are you able to do it without recourse to wisdom?

The Daoist project is neither passive nor quietistic. Water is the source of nourishment; the mirror is a source of light; the heart-and-mind is a source of transformative energy. To "know" as the mirror "knows" is not reduplicative, but is to cast the world in a certain light. Such performative "knowing" is for one to actively interpret and realize a world with healthy, productive effect. These metaphors for *xin* entail a presentation rather than a representation, a coordination rather than a correspondence. "Mirroring" then is best seen as synergistic and responsive, where all of the elements are in the stream and constitute a fluid interdependent continuity.

Perhaps the best rendering of the term *wuyu* 無欲 is "objectless desire." Since neither noncoercive action nor unprincipled knowing can in the strict sense *objectify* a world or any element in it—that is, make discrete and independent objects out of one's environing experience—the desiring associated with the Daoist sensibility is in the strictest sense "objectless." The "enjoyments" associated with *wuyu* are possible without the need to define, possess, or control the occasion of one's enjoyment.

Thus, *wuyu*, rather than involving the cessation and absence of desire, represents the achievement of *deferential desire*. Desire, based upon a noncoercive relationship (*wuwei*) with the world and a "mirroring" understanding (*wuzhi*) of it, is shaped not by the desire to own, to control, or to consume, but by the desire simply to celebrate and to enjoy. It is deference. Desire is directed at those things desirable because they *stand to be desired*. But those things which stand to be desired must themselves be deferential, which means that they cannot *demand* to be desired. For to demand to be desired is to exercise a kind of mesmerizing control over the desirer. In a world of events and processes in which discriminations are recognized as conventional and transient, desire is predicated upon one's ability at any given moment to "let go." It is in this sense that *wuyu* is a nonconstruing, objectless, desire.

The Daoist problem with desire does not concern what is desired, but rather the manner of the desiring. Enjoyment for the Daoist is realized not in spite of the fact that one might lose what is desired, but because of this fact. The world is a complex set of transformative processes, never at rest. *Wuhua* 物化, the metamorphosis of things (and not to be confused with the *wu*-forms), means that we can never pretend that what we seek to hold on to has any permanent status. In Daoism, transient desire is the only desire that lets things be, that does not construe the world in a certain manner, that does not seek to apply the brakes on a world of changing things.

The key to an understanding of *wuyu*—indeed of all these *wu*-forms that comprise the Daoist disposition—lies in the contrast between "objects" and "objectivity." Using Western epistemological terms, the thoughts about the world expressed in both the *Zhuangzi* and the *Daodejing* represent what we might call a realist perspective.[22] Beyond the mediating confusions introduced by language, and by layers of our own distorted perceptions and tendentious categorizations, there is nevertheless, with properly Daoist qualifications, an "objectively" real world. Our task is to experience that world as "objectively" as possible.

From the Daoist perspective, the problem begins when we insist that the "objective world" is a world made up of objects—namely, concrete, unchangeable things that we encounter as over against and independent of us; things which announce themselves to us by asserting "I object!" For the Daoist, the objective world cannot be objective in this sense because it is a constantly transforming flow of events or processes that belie the sorts of discriminations that would permit a final inventory of the furniture of the world.

Paradoxically, for the Daoist the objective world is objectless. Sages envision a world of changing events that they can, for whatever reason, choose to freeze momentarily into a distinct pattern of discrimination, but that they recognize, when they see clearly, as being beyond such distinctions.

For the Daoist, the consequence of this transformed vision is that knowing, acting, and desiring in the world are no longer based upon construal. Feeling ourselves in tension with objectified others can lead us to act in an aggressive or defensive manner in order to effect our will. Principles and fixed standards can lead us to construe the object of our knowledge by recourse to such principles. In this way, an item becomes one of a *kind* (rather than *one-of-a-kind*) or an instrument for the achievement of an end (as opposed to an end in itself). Desire motivated by an object of desire leads us to seek possession of that which is desired, allowing it significance only insofar as it meets our needs. A self that is consumed by objects of desire narrows, truncates, and obfuscates the world as it is.

On the other hand, noncoercive action, unprincipled knowing, and objectless desire have the following in common: To the extent that a disposition defined in these terms is efficacious, it enriches the world by allowing the process to unfold spontaneously on its own terms, while at the same time participating fully in it. We may say that the implementation of the *wu*-forms allows us to leave the world as it is. But we may make this claim only if we recognize that "world" in this context means a myriad of spontaneous transactions that are characterized by emerging patterns of deference to acknowledged excellences. In Daoism the self is forgotten to the extent that discriminated objects no longer constitute the environs of the self.

These three *wu*-forms—*wuwei, wuzhi, wuyu*—all provide a way of entertaining, of deferring to, and of investing oneself in an objectless world. Thus, in their governing of the people the sages are concerned with embodying and promoting the sort of acting, knowing, and desiring that does not depend upon objects. In fact, when these *wu*-forms are understood as the optimum dispositions of the Daoist self, whether in the person of the sage or the people, they provide us with a way of interpreting passages in the *Daodejing* that are frequently construed unsympathetically as recommending imposition and control. Chapter 3 is an example:

Not promoting those of superior character
Will save the common people from becoming contentious.
Not prizing property that is hard to come by
Will save them from becoming thieves.
Not making a show of what might be desired
Will save them from becoming disgruntled.

It is for this reason that in the proper governing by the sages:
They empty the hearts-and-minds of the people and fill their
    stomachs,
They weaken their aspirations and strengthen their bones,

Ever teaching the common people to be unprincipled in their
    knowing
And objectless in their desires.
They keep the hawkers of knowledge at bay.
It is simply in doing things noncoercively
That everything is governed properly.

But the *wu*-forms are not just *wuwei, wuzhi,* and *wuyu*. In fact,
*wu*-forms are pervasive in the *Daodejing*. One additional *wu*-form,
for example, is *wuming* 無名: translated as "the nameless," but
actually suggesting a kind of naming that does not assign fixed
reference to things.

    In order to function effectively in negotiating our environment,
we need to rely upon our ability to make distinctions. These distinctions in themselves are certainly functional and enabling, but
can distort the way in which we understand our world. We can
easily fall into the fallacy of what Whitehead describes as "mis-
placed concreteness," reifying what is abstract and treating these
hypostatized "things" as more real than the changing events of our
experience. We can easily and at real expense overdetermine the
continuity within the life process as some underlying and unchanging foundation. Such linguistic habits can institutionalize and enforce an overly static vision of the world, and in so doing, deprive
both language and life of their creative possibilities. The referential
use of language as someone's technical morality—expressing the
way the world *ought* to be—can too easily lay claim to the power
and control that would make it so.

    Naming as power undermines the importantly creative aspect
in the effective use of names. In a processual world—a world ever
under construction—to be able to name something is to be able to
trace out its concrete relation to you and the world, and on that
basis, respond to it productively. While naming can be understood
as an abstractive and isolating gesture, Daoist naming personalizes
a relationship and, abjuring any temptation to fix what is referenced,
instead understands the name as a shared ground of growing
intimacy. Such naming is presentational rather than just representa-
tional, normative rather than just descriptive, perlocutionary rather

than just locutionary, a doing and a knowing rather than just a saying.

Naming as knowing must have the provisionality to accommodate engaged relationships as in their "doing and undergoing" they deepen and become increasingly robust. Such knowing is dependent upon an awareness of the indeterminate aspects of things. The ongoing shaping of experience requires a degree of imagination and creative projection that does not reference the world as it is, but anticipates what it might become.

In the *Classic of Mountain and Seas*, an ancient "gazetteer" that takes its reader on a field seminar through unfamiliar lands, the calls of the curious animals and birds that are encountered are in fact their own names. They (like most things) cry out what they would be. And having access to the "name" of something is not only a claim to knowing it in a cognitive sense, but more importantly, to knowing how to deal with it. Naming is most importantly the responsiveness that attends familiarity. Hence such knowing is a feeling and a doing: it is value-added. It is naming without the kind of fixed reference that allows one to "master" something, a naming that does not arrest or control. It is a discriminating naming that in fact appreciates rather than depreciates a situation.

Another important *wu*-form is *wuxin* 無心, literally "no heart-and-mind," that might best be interpreted as "unmediated thinking and feeling." As the *Daodejing* observes in chapter 49:

Sages really think and feel immediately (*wuxin*).
They take the thoughts and feelings of the common people as their own.

The sages do not compose the score for social and political order. The music is the natural expression of the common people. The role of the sages is to listen carefully to the songs of the common people and to orchestrate their thoughts and feelings into consummate harmony. Since the people themselves are the immediate source of communal order, they are in this respect the emerging content of the hearts-and-minds of the sages. The heart-and-mind is the product rather than the source of the flourishing community. The people do not speak to one another because they have hearts-and-minds; rather, they have *become* whole-hearted members of the community through full participation in the communicating community.

An obscure passage in the *Zhuangzi* becomes less so when we read it and its key notion *wuqing* 無情 as a *wu*-form—not "no-feeling," but rather "unmediated feeling." This understanding of *wuqing* can provide us with a useful gloss on this chapter 49 of the *Daodejing*.

> Hui Shi said to Zhuangzi, "Can someone be a person without feelings?"
>
> "Not a problem," replied Zhuangzi.
>
> "But how can someone be called a person," asked Hui Shi, "if they don't have feelings?"
>
> Zhuangzi said, "Their context provides them with the appearance and the shape of a person—why wouldn't we call them such?"
>
> "Since we are already calling them persons," asked Hui Shi, "how could it be that they are lacking feelings?"
>
> "This is not what I mean by feelings," replied Zhuangzi. "What I mean when I say that they are '*wuqing*' (lit. 'without feelings') is that they do not injure their own persons with likes and dislikes, and are always responsive to what is natural without trying to increase life."[23]

Persons such William James's "Jack and Jill" reside in their immediate affective relationships. For such persons to lose sight of these important relations by buying into a regimen of contrived values distances them from their concrete circumstances and makes them less human than they were.

Another *wu*-form that we find repeated in the *Daodejing* is *wushi* 無事, interpreted as "no-business." As a *wu*-form it means "to be non-interfering in going about your business." In chapter 57, it has a specifically political application that explains itself:

> The more prohibitions and taboos there are in the world,
> The poorer the people will be.
> The more sharp instruments in the hands of the common people,
> The darker the days for the state,
> The more wisdom hawked among the people,

The more that perverse things will proliferate.
The more prominently the laws and statutes are displayed,
The more widespread will be the brigands and thieves.

Hence in the words of the sages:
    We do things noncoercively
    And the common people develop along their own lines;
    We cherish equilibrium
    And the common people order themselves;
    We are non-interfering in our governance
    And the common people prosper themselves;
    We are objectless in our desires
    And the common people are of themselves like unworked wood.

One of the most pervasive ideas in the *Daodejing* that is captured in the *wu*-form *wuzheng* 無爭 is "striving without contentiousness." Chapter 66 concludes with a consideration of the conduct of the sages: "Is it not because they strive without contentiousness that no one in the world is able to contend with them?"

The *wu*-forms that we find throughout the text all advocate a personal disposition that seeks to optimize relationships through collaborative actions that, in the absence of coercion, enable one to make the most of any situation. It is the uniqueness of each situation that requires any generalization about this optimal disposition to be stated in negative terms. A voice coach can describe the constraints that students in general might have to overcome in achieving the fullness of their talent, but all of the students must sing their own unique songs.

## 9. THE *WU*-FORMS AS "HABIT-FORMING"

If we look for a more concrete way to express the cultivation of the *wu*-form disposition advocated by the *Daodejing*, we might think of "life as art." The developed customs and habits of mind of the Daoist are a resource that conditions, influences, and attempts to optimize the range of creative possibilities without in fact causally determining the crafting of novel experiences. Such aggregated habits are irreducibly social, and are the unannounced social propensity out of which individual hearts-and-minds express themselves as overt actions.

For example, the insistent particularity associated with the uniqueness of a particular person must be understood both relationally and as a dynamic process within the context of a given natural, social, and cultural world. Particular character is an interpenetration of habits that has organized and made meaningful the more primary but not more important natural impulses. Considered synchronically, persons are irreducibly relational, entailing what they do for this specific community as well as the personal enrichment they derive from participating in its communal life-forms and culture. Viewed diachronically, each particular personality must also be understood as an ongoing and unrelenting awareness that attends every gesture and thought, and that is expressed as a refined disposition in all of its activities.

For the classical Confucian, this ritualized awareness (*li* 禮)—the living of one's life within the roles and relationships of family and community—focuses one's aggregated habits as they are expressed in the events of the day. We have reflected on this Confucian notion of disposition at some length in our *Focusing the Familiar: A Translation and Philosophical Interpretation of the Zhongyong*, and attempt to locate the Daoist sensibility within this discussion here.

To begin with, for the Daoist, this focused awareness is extended beyond the immediate human community to encompass the other environments as well. The habit-informed interactions between person and environments occur within custom and culture broadly construed. This ecological sensibility is what gives Daoist philosophy its profoundly cosmic dimension.

To use the word "habits" to characterize either the Confucian *li* or the Daoist ecological sensibility might seem, initially, somewhat disenchanting, reducing the intense and elegantly productive human experience, whether human-centered or more broadly construed, to the ordinary and routine. But the claim at issue is that it is precisely in the elevation of the routine and ordinary business of the day, rather than in some ephemeral and transitory "momentous" events, that the profound meanings of a life are to be realized. And, properly understood, "habit" is essential to this process of enchanting the everyday.

We are accustomed to think of habit in a negative manner as mere routine, or as compulsively repetitive behavior that we would alter if only we had the willpower. That is, we are inclined to place habit squarely within the sphere of determined behavior. Indeed, habit as acquired disposition is of no great significance if one understands the order of the world to be the result of a transcendent Creator, or as the mechanical instancing of transcendent Laws of Nature. For in such cases, habitual actions merely replicate the necessities of things; they are the involuntary expression of our given instincts and needs.

It is only if the world is truly processive and changing in character that acquired dispositions may become a constitutive ground of the way things are. Understanding the Daoist-refined ecological consciousness as habitual behavior will be of benefit only if we rethink our own accepted senses of habit.

*Hexis* was used initially by Aristotle as a neologism. The Greek *hexus* means "having" or "being in possession of." Early on, *hexis* also had the suggestion of both "condition" and the "state" of something. It was thus used dispositionally to mean the natural or conditioned "tendencies" of things—as the "habit" of a vine. Aristotle himself sometimes uses *hexis* to refer to the natural or innate behavior of creatures. If we combine the senses of "habit" as that which is *had*—as a *state* or *condition* that something takes on, and as its consequent *tendency*—we arrive at the sense of the term that is found most prominently in the American pragmatic tradition.

John Dewey contrasts habit with essentialized notions of human nature and reason that are the backdrop of deterministic instinct theory, insisting that "the *meaning* of native activities is not native; it is acquired."[24] We are our habits, and they possess us rather than we them. So for Dewey, "the real opposition is not between reason and habit but between routine, unintelligent habit, and intelligent habit or art."[25] Habit is an acquired and cultivated *disposition* to act in one way as opposed to another. It is the significant form that bursts of energy take as they are channeled through existing patterns of associated living, dependent upon anticipated response as much as novel impulse.

It is certainly not counterintuitive to understand habit in this creative sense. Most individuals would recognize the peculiar contribution of technique to artistic endeavor. Without the ability to mentally parse and physically play musical notes and chords in a stylized fashion, neither composition nor performance would be possible. Technique, as pre-reflective and dispositional, frees the artist to perform and to create. This same relationship to spontaneity is realized throughout one's experience.

The immediacy of the aesthetic experience—that is, its *unmediated* character—does not permit of the development of rules or procedures defining how to either create or experience novelties. What is permitted is the construal of the conditions under which an unmediated experience may be provoked, varied, nuanced, and continually transformed. Habits are the acquired structures that make possible the experience of the *immediate*. Informed by good habits, what *feels* good *is* good. Although habits are the background of spontaneous, creative actions, the disposition that these habits constitute is underdetermined in the sense that it is constantly being reshaped and redirected by these novel interactions.

In the Chinese world, things do not *have* habits, they *are* habits. Habit is a mode of being. Thus habitual behavior establishes a relationship between "having" and "being" that encapsulates the manner in which the aesthetic sensibility dominates classical Chinese society. Scholars of Chinese thought, for example, have persistently noted that the Chinese lack a copulative sense of "to be" as "to exist." Rather, *you* 有 in doing the work of the copula means "to have," "to be present." The distinction between the copulative sense of being as *existing* and the Chinese sense of being (*you*) as *having* amounts to a difference between two modes of being present—the mediated and the relatively immediate.

Mediated experience entails the fact that Being, in the mode of this or that *essence,* is made manifest through the particular beings of the world. Persons are actualizations of some prior endowment or potential. Such experience is characteristic of substantialist ontologies and cosmologies that regard substance and form as fundamental, and that understand experience as being governed by a strong teleological design. Substances are known through forms or concepts that either exist prior to the substances themselves, or are abstractable from them. These forms are the evidence of a given design.

Immediate experience requires that the concrete particulars themselves are the objects of knowledge. Such particulars are not mediated but are grasped immediately in the sense that the experience of them is simply *had*. The structures that permit the having of experience and that determine its significance are the cultivated habits that dispose one toward that experience. The language of taste and of appreciation is relevant.

The notion of Being that implies a contrast between essence and existence privileges mediation and, therefore, conceptual, generic, and *essential* knowledge. An aesthetic perspective, as opposed to a rational or logical one, involves experiencing the world in a relatively *unmediated* fashion. Mediated experience requires one to grasp or comprehend the *essence* of a thing, while the unmediated aesthetic experience is simply *had* as lived experience.

A comparison with the analytical epistemic language of "getting," "grasping," "comprehending" is important here. Rather than a language of mediation in which the *essences* of things are abstracted through concepts, the Chinese language tends to be dispositional in that it promotes the "having" of the unmediated experience through a correlating and focusing of the affairs of the day. The important contrast here is between a cognitive and discursive knowing that abstracts from experience and felt experience as the concrete content of knowledge.

While the Confucian focus is on the cultivated disposition that allows for unmediated ritualized expression, we have registered the Daoist concern that too much emphasis on such cultivation will produce precisely the opposite undesired effect of overwhelming the spontaneous natural disposition with artificial human constructs.

That is, the Daoist would look to the cadence of nature as a resource for educating and refining our natural sensibilities. In the Daoist critique of Confucianism, it is assumed that *li* has ossified into a technical morality that, far from facilitating unmediated expression, dislocates the human community from its natural rhythms. As such, generic, institutionalized *li* now *mediates* behavior, and in so doing, suppresses spontaneous natural habits. Both the Confucian and the Daoist recognize the need for a cultivated disposition as the ground of felt experience; they simply disagree on how such a disposition is to be achieved and sustained.

## NOTES TO THE *PHILOSOPHICAL INTRODUCTION*

1. Tang Junyi (1988):8.

2. Carus and Suzuki (1913):18–9.

3. For both Plato and early Aristotle, *kosmos* was the "visible God" (*horatos theos*).

4. See Hall and Ames (1995):chapter 2 *passim* for the development of this terminology.

5. See *Zhuangzi* 5.2.40 and commentary on it in 63.23.58; compare Graham (1981):54 and 104, and Watson (1968):41 and 257.

6. *Mencius* 2A2.

7. *Mencius* 7A4.

8. See Hall (1987) and (1994), and Hall and Ames (1998):39–43, 111–12.

9. See Ames and Hall (2001):38–53.

10. See King (1985).

11. Hall and Ames (1998):35–7.

12. See the WB and GD versions of chapter 37.

13. James (2000): 286–87.

14. While *qing* 青 is certainly a phonetic element, the semantic reference is not irrelevant. *Qing* means "green-blue" as a color associated with luxuriant foliage, an indeterminate field of vegetation and undergrowth.

15. Whitehead (1926):67.

16. Tang Junyi (1988):13.

17. See Whitehead (1978):110–15. See also Neville (1974):10 ff. and Grange (1997):51–60 for useful applications of this vocabulary.

18. See *Analects* 18:5-7, and Hall and Ames (1998):171-80.

19. See Ames (forthcoming) for a contrast between Daoism and Confucianism on the issue of human exceptionalism.

20. See Hall and Ames (1998):45-58.

21. See *Zhuangzi* 33.13.2. Compare Graham (1981):259 and Watson (1968):142.

22. Thus, with some qualifications, we agree with Angus Graham (1989):194 in his claim that Zhuangzi "accepts without question that we have to take the world as it is. . . ."

23. *Zhuangzi* 14.5.54. Compare Graham (1981):82 and Watson (1968):75-6.

24. Dewey *MW* 14:65.

25. Dewey *MW* 14.55.

# Glossary of Key Terms

Below, to make the text more accessible philosophically, we provide an explanation of key terms and some justification for our translations. This glossary is informed by the earlier work of Hall and Ames, and of Ames and Rosemont, cited in the Bibliography.

Here as in our previous work, in seeking to challenge the existing formula of translations, we want to be at once deconstructive and programmatic. That is, we begin from the concern that the popular translations of these philosophical terms often do not adequately respect the degree of difference between our worldview and the worldview in which these early Chinese texts were compiled and transmitted. What is the most comfortable choice of language and what at first blush makes the best sense to the translator might well be taken as a signal that what is originally *not* familiar in the source language is, at a stroke, being made so. For example, the conventional translation of *dao* 道 as "the Way" or *tian* 天 as "Heaven" or *de* 德 as "virtue" will, we hope, become rather clear examples of the unfamiliar being made familiar. Such translations have been "legitimized" by their gradual insinuation into the standard Chinese-English dictionaries and glosses. And by encouraging the uncritical assumption in those who consult these reference works that this formula of translations provides the student with a "literal" and thus "conservative" rendering of the terms, these lexicons have become complicit in an entrenched cultural equivocation that we strive to avoid.

Our argument is that it is in fact these formulaic usages that are radical interpretations. To our mind, to consciously or unconsciously transplant a text from its own historical and intellectual soil and replant it in one that has a decidedly different philosophical landscape is to take liberties with the text and is radical in the sense that it tampers with its very roots. It is our concerted effort, however imperfectly accomplished, to understand the text within its own cultural terrain that is properly conservative.

But our goal is not to replace one inadequate formula with another. Our translations are intended as no more than suggestive "placeholders" that refer readers back to this glossary to negotiate their own meaning, and, we hope, to appropriate the Chinese terms for themselves. If Wittgenstein is insightful in observing that the limits of our language are the limits of our world, then perhaps in order to understand the Chinese philosophical tradition, we are going to need more language. It will only be when students of Chinese philosophy are able to bring a sophisticated understanding of *dao* 道 and *tian* 天 and *de* 德 to a reading of a Chinese text in the philosophically astute way that they understand terms such as *kosmos*, *logos*, and *nous* in their reading of the classical Greek corpus that they can really begin to take the Chinese world on its own terms.

In our introduction to *Focusing the Familiar: A Translation and Philosophical Interpretation of the* Zhongyong, we invoked Whitehead's Fallacy of the Perfect Dictionary to challenge the wisdom and accuracy of proposing "one-for-one" equivalencies in translating terms from one language to another. We introduce the notion of "linguistic clustering" as an alternative strategy to "literal translation" that allows us to put the semantic value of a term first by parsing its range of meaning according to context, with the assumption that a range of meaning with a different configuration of emphasis is present on each appearance of the term. The semantic value of a term and its subtle nuances of meaning are a product of its specific linguistic context. In the translation, we have included a romanization of the key terms, and we have provided a thematic index at the end of the book to facilitate the cross-referencing of repeated philosophical terms that always mean differently in different contexts. We hope in so doing to highlight their interdependent resonances, and to encourage an understanding of this vocabulary that is dynamic, allusive, and relational rather than simply referential.

There is one general point that we would make in our interpretation of this classical Chinese language. Above we have argued for a processual understanding of classical Daoist cosmology. If this account is persuasive, it means that the vocabulary that expresses the worldview and the common sense in which the *Daodejing* is to be located is first and foremost gerundive. Because "things" in the *Daodejing* are in fact active "processes" and ongoing "events," nouns that would "objectify" this world are derived from and revert to a verbal sensibility. The ontological language of substance and essence that is sedimented into the English language tends to defy this linguistic priority, insisting upon the primacy of "the world" rather than the process of the world "worlding" and the myriad things "happening." It is a fair observation that a careful reading of the introduction and this glossary are made necessary by the fact that our European languages can only most imperfectly "speak" the world being referenced in the *Daodejing*.

道 *dao.* Etymologically, the character *dao* 道 is constructed out of two elements: *shu* 辵 "foot," and hence, "to pass over," "to go over," "to lead through" (on foot), and *shou* 首 meaning "head"—hair and eye together—and therefore "foremost." The *shou* "head" component carries the suggestion of "to lead" in the sense of "to give a heading." *Dao* 道 is used frequently as a loan character for its verbal cognate *dao* 導, "to lead forth." Thus the character is primarily gerundive, processional, and dynamic: "a leading forth." The earliest appearance of *dao* is in the *Book of Documents* in the context of cutting a channel and "leading" a river to prevent the overflowing of its banks.

Taking the verbal *dao* as primary, its several derived meanings emerge rather naturally: "to lead through," and hence: "road, path, way, method, to put into words, to explain, teachings, doctrines, art." At its most fundamental level, *dao* seems to denote the active project of "moving ahead in the world," of "forging a way forward," of "road building." Hence, our neologism: "way-making." By extension, *dao* comes to connote a pathway that has been made, and hence can be traveled. It is because of this connotation that *dao* is often, somewhat problematically, nominalized by translating it "the Way."

In surveying the range of meaning invested in *dao* as it unfolds in the *Daodejing*, we can identify at least three overlapping and mutually entailing semantic dimensions that might have relevance in any particular passage.

First, there is the primary "momentum" sense of *dao* as unfolding disposition or propensity.[1] It is in this sense that *dao* (like Dewey's use of the term "experience") is to be understood as a generic idea such as "life" or "climate" or "culture" or "history" that resists resolution into familiar dualisms such as "subject/object," "form/function," "agency/action," and so on. It is simply the sea of our lived experience as human beings, with its cadence, continuities, and disjunctions. There is an ineluctable force of circumstances at play in this lived experience that at once accounts for the persistence and regularity of our daily lives, and also for the context that makes the sometimes delicious and sometimes poignant novelty possible. In fact, it is the richness and depth of the existing disposition of experience in our lives that allows for the most productive shaping of what is novel as it emerges.

Secondly, we as human beings have a proactive role in making our way in the world. *Dao* certainly entails the continuing disposition of experience that gives us context, and there is a palpable, glacial weight to this configuration of experience as it inches ahead. But this unfolding process is also underdetermined. Making our way includes making productive adjustments in the direction of the lived experience by manipulating the more fluid and indeterminate opportunities that come with the unfolding of experience. In the still "inchoate (*ji* 幾)" circumstances we can find the "trigger (*ji* 機)" that allows us to nudge the unfolding world in one direction as opposed to another. As such, *dao* is not only "way" but also "way-making," a forging of an always new way forward.

As way-making, *dao* is decidedly verbal. It is *dao* 導: the leading-forth, guiding and manipulating of experience through which we participate in educing a future. Importantly, "gateway (*men* 門)" is a recurring locative expression; it is the "where" and the "when."

The swinging gateway—opening and then closing—is *where* and *when dao* spontaneously "opens out" to provide creativity a space through which to make its "entrance," qualifying the processive nature of *dao* with the immediacy and specificity of the creative act. Given the pervasive "birthing" sense of an emerging world, this gateway is often construed vaginally as a dilating opening that produces the as yet unshaped potency of the newly born infant.

However, the most familiar yet derivative "pathway" sense of *dao* is a post hoc combination of its more primary meanings. The dynamic disposing of experience and our creative way-making that goes on within it is conceived of not as a process, but as a product. As a "way" that has already been laid, *dao* is stipulated and defined. This, then, is the objectified use of *dao* that would allow for the familiar demonstrative translation of the term *dao* as "the *dao*." But to thus nominalize and conceptualize *dao* betrays its fluidity and reflexivity, and to give priority to that use is to take the first step in overwriting a process sensibility with substance ontology. We can neither step outside *dao* nor can we arrest its always changing configuration. Even when we reflect on a temporally prior "way"—the way of Confucius, for example—we must allow that our present vantage point involves us reflexively in our interpretation of it, making Confucius both dynamic and corporate, rather than simply referential. As William Faulkner was wont to insist in his presentation of experience through time, there is no such thing as a "was"; there is only an "is." And as the oft-cited opening passage of the *Daodejing* itself cautions, we certainly cannot do justice to the throbbing complexity of experience by anything we have to say about it.

德 *de*. In the early philosophical literature, *de* retains a strong cosmological sense, connoting the "insistent particularity" of things generally, and usually of human beings specifically. It is for this reason that *de* is conventionally translated as "virtue," or "power," defining the particular as a focus of potency or efficacy within its own field of experience. Given the intrinsic relatedness of particulars in this conception of existence as process, *de* is both process and product—both the potency and the achieved character of any particular disposition within the unsummed totality of experience. *Dao* and *de* are related as field and focus respectively. *De* is "holographic," meaning that each element in the totality of things contains the totality in some adumbrated form. The particular focus of an item establishes its immediate world, and the totality as a noncoherent sum of all possible orders is disclosed however faintly by each item.

The central issue of the *Daodejing*—literally "the classic of this *de* and its *dao*"—is how this partipating item can most effectively excel in bringing its perspectival field into focus. It is this process of focusing *de* that, for the human being, generates cognitive, moral, aesthetic, and spiritual meaning.

The earliest Confucian literature tended to limit its concerns to the human experience, where this qualitative dimension of *de* more nearly suggests both "excellence" and "efficacy" in terms of what we can truly *be* and *do* if we "realize (*zhi* 知)" the most from our personal careers as members of a flourishing community. Like "authoritative conduct/person (*ren* 仁)," *de* can certainly be generalized, but it is an inductive generalization that must always begin from a particular instance within a particular context. The cultivation of *de* is pursued through one's full participation in the ritualized community, where achieved excellence in the roles and relationships that constitute one's person makes one an object of deference for others.

The *Daodejing* brings both a political and a cosmic dimension to this idea of effective potency. When located within the political realm, *de* describes the most appropriate relationship between a ruler and the people. In this context, *de* has a range of meaning that reflects the priority of the situation over agency, thus characterizing both the giving and the getting. That is, *de* is both the "beneficence" extended to the people in response to their worth, and the "gratitude" expressed by the people in response to the largesse of a worthy ruler. *De* encompasses both participating agency and its effects. It is the character or the ethos of the polity. On this basis, we might suggest "virtuality" in the archaic sense of the word as "having inherent virtue or power to produce effects" as another possible translation of *de*.

Recognizing the meaning-creating and meaning-disclosing power of the cultivated human being, the *Daodejing* emphasizes the way in which this personal articulation extends beyond the human community into appreciating the cosmos itself. Those of "highest efficacy" (*shangde* 上德) as paragons of achieved excellence have cosmological significance in maximizing the symbiotic relationship between the human experience and the context within which that drama unfolds.

和 *he*. *He* is conventionally translated "harmony," and we follow that rendering. The etymology of the character is culinary, harmony being the art of combining and blending two or more ingredients so that they enhance one another without losing their distinctive flavors. Throughout the early corpus, the preparation of food is appealed to as a gloss on this sense of elegant harmony. Harmony so considered entails both the "integrity" of the particular ingredient and its "integration" into some larger whole. Signatory of this harmony is the persistence of the individual ingredients, their full self-disclosure in their collborative relationship with the other ingredients, and the aesthetic nature of the resulting harmony—an elegant order that emerges out of the artful contextualization of intrinsically related details as they maximize the unique contribution of each one.

In the Confucian tradition, this sense of harmony is celebrated as the highest cultural achievement. Here, harmony is distinguished from mere agreement by defining it in terms of eliciting the optimum contribution of persons to their communal contexts through ritualized living. Within this tradition, the family metaphor is pervasive, encouraged by the intuition that this is the institution presumably within which the members give themselves most fully and unreservedly to the group in interactions that are governed by acts of deference (*li*) most appropriate (*yi*) to the occasion. Such a commitment to family harmony requires the full expression of personal integrity, and thus the family becomes the context in which one can most effectively pursue personal realization. In the *Zhongyong*, this Confucian sense of harmony (*he*) is given further clarification through the introduction of "focus" or "equilibrium" (*zhong* 中), where "focusing (*zhong*)" is directed at "the familiar affairs of the day (*yong* 庸)."

In the *Daodejing*, harmony certainly applies to the human world in characterizing appropriate familial relationships, as in chapter 18. But in chapter 42, the *Daodejing* extends this sensibility to the cosmos itself as being inclined toward harmony in the production of all of the things and events that constitute its evolving order:

> Everything carries *yin* on its shoulders and *yang* in its arms
> And blends these vital energies together to make them harmonious.

In fact, the relationship between harmony in the human context and its cosmic dimension is drawn explicitly in chapters 16 and 55. Common sense and acuity are defined in terms of an awareness of this cosmic propensity toward harmony and the ability to apply it to the affairs of the day:

> Things proliferate,
> And each again returns to its root.
> Returning to the root is called equilibrium.
> Now as for equilibrium—this is called returning to the propensity
>     of things,
> And returning to the propensity of things is common sense.
> Using common sense is acuity,
> While failing to use it is to lose control. (16)

靜 *jing*. "Equilibrium": see page 40.

明 *ming*. "Acuity": see pages 39–40.

氣 *qi*. This character *qi* might be translated variously as "hylozoistic vapors," "psychophysical stuff," and "vital energizing field." It first appears on the Shang oracle bones and on the Zhou bronze inscriptions as three horizontal lines, similar to the modern character for "three (*san* 三)," except the three parallel lines are usually shorter and somewhat more fluid. The *Shuowen* lexicon explains this graph as a pictographic character representing rising mists, and defines it as "cloud vapors (*yunqi* 雲氣)."

Although the systematized and elaborate "five phases" *yinyang wuxing* cosmology does not appear until Han dynasty sources, the idea that the world and its phenomena are perturbations that emerge out of and fold back into a vital energizing field called *qi* was already widely held in the late fourth and early third centuries BCE, attested to in the *Zhuangzi*, the *Daodejing*, and the *Mencius* as well as other early texts.

*Qi* has to be distinguished from either "animating vapors" or "basic matter" because it cannot be resolved into any kind of spiritual-material dichotomy. *Qi* is both the animating energy and that which is animated. There are no "things" to be animated; there is only the vital energizing field and its focal manifestations. The energy of transformation resides within the world itself, and it is expressed in what *Zhuangzi* calls the perpetual "transforming of things and events (*wuhua* 物化)." It is this understanding of a focus-field process of cosmic change that is implicitly assumed in the *Daodejing* and other texts of this period as a kind of common sense.

天 *tian*. *Tian* is a term that we choose not to translate, largely because we believe its conventional English rendering as "Heaven" cannot but conjure up misleading associations drawn from our Abrahamic traditions. These theological associations are largely irrelevant to the Chinese experience but they have, nonetheless, often overwritten Chinese cultural practices with presuppositions that are alien to them. In any case, we must extricate the term from these misleading associations if we are to approach a more accurate understanding of *tian*.

One reason why our understanding of *tian* is painfully vague is that the term is vague within the Chinese tradition itself. The question posed by the tradition has not so much been "What is *tian*?" as it has been "What is the most productive relationship between human beings and their environments?"

In the earliest canonical literature, such as the *Book of Documents* and the *Book of Songs*, *tian* is often anthropomorphized, suggesting its intimate relationship with the process of euhemerism—the ascent of historical heroes to the status of gods—that grounds Chinese ancestor reverence. A qualification has to be made with respect to the use of the Greek term "euhemerism" to describe this process as it unfolded in early China. That is, while in Greece "a" became "B," in China, "a" became "A." That is, there are good reasons to assume that *tian* is not an exception to the claim that Chinese gods are, by and large, dead people. Although this claim is not uncontested, at least we can say that, in the absence of some transcendent creator Deity, *tian*, in this early conceptualization, would seem to stand for a cumulative and continuing cultural legacy that is focused by the spirits and spirituality of those who have come before.

It was probably a common foundation in ancestor reverence that allowed for the conflation of the culturally sophisticated Shang dynasty's *di* 帝 (a melding of ancestral and animist spirits of nature and the land) with the notion of *tian* associated with the Zhou federation of tribes, militant and Romanesque, which conquered the Yellow river valley at the turn of the first millennium BCE. The Zhou appealed to *tianming* 天命 —"the mandate of *tian*"—as a strategy for political legitimization, claiming that *tian* commands a lineage to rule only if the descendents of that lineage, through their conduct, command *tian*'s respect. And *tian*'s judgment was to be known through the response of the people to those who would govern.[2]

There is also a strong association between *tian* and the natural environment, as well as with its ongoing operations. *Tian* does not speak directly, but communicates effectively (although not always clearly) through human-generated oracles, through perturbations in the climate, and through alterations in the natural conditions that contextualize the human world. *Tian* participates in a nonverbal discourse with the most worthy persons in the human community. Given the interrelatedness and interdependency of the various orders defining the early Chinese cosmology, what affects one, affects all. This interdependence assumes that a failure of order in the human world will be reflected by a sympathetic disintegration of order in the natural environment.

But with this assumed mutuality, there was a growing sense that proper conduct in the human world can guarantee stability in the natural world. In some of the early texts, the more spiritual dimension of *tian* continues to be emphasized. But as human beings develop a sense of control over their own natural environment, the emphasis in many texts, including the *Daodejing*, tends to shift to an increasingly impersonal *tian* that denotes the regular operations of nature. Although impersonal, this evolving notion of *tian* retains its sense of spirituality as the object of a kind of natural piety.

Carrying this connotation of the natural environment, *tian* is often used as an abbreviation for *tiandi* 天地 —"the heavens and the earth"—suggesting that *tian*, far from being independent, *is* this world. Denoting the unbounded world as it turns around us and is entertained from each particular perspective, *tian* is bottomless, ever advancing, and always novel.

The God of the Bible, sometimes referred to metonymically as "Heaven," *created* the world, but *tian* in classical Chinese *is* the world. That is, *tian* is both *what* our world is and *how* it is. *Tian* is *natura naturans*: "nature naturing." The "ten thousand processes and events (*wanwu* 萬物)"—an expression for "all things that are happening"—are not the creatures of a *tian* that stands independent of what is ordered; rather, they are constitutive of it. On this basis, *tian* can be described as the emergent orders negotiated out of the dispositions of the many particulars that are constitutive of it, human beings being no exception.

The question arises: How is *tian* and *tiandi* so described in chapters 16 and 25 to be distinguished from *dao*—a generic name for the field of experience as construed from each and every perspective? First, it should be noted that these terms are all simply explanatory categories that are organic and reflexive, where one overlaps with and leads into the next. This being said, one distinction between *dao* and *tian* lies in the intimate *yinyang* relationship between *tian* and *ren*: between *tian* and the human world. That is, while *daode* is a generic category that stipulates a correlative relationship between any particular thing or event and its field of experience, and is thus inclusive of the totality of orders, the correlative *tianren* is a dimension within *daode* that tends to highlight more specifically the relationship between human beings and their natural, social, and cultural context.

On occasion, the *Daodejing* contrasts the "ways" of *tian* and *ren* (for example, in chapters 59, 77, 81), where human beings would do well to take the operations of *tian* as a model for their own conduct. The expression *tiandao* 天道—"the way of *tian*" (chapters 9, 47, 73)—generalizes this mode of natural activity. Even so, "nature" would be an inadequate translation here because *tian* as a correlative will not accommodate any kind of severe "nature/nurture" dualism. *Tian*, far from being a grid of mechanistic laws or an impersonal force, still retains a sense of the human as well as a natural spirituality. In chapter 59, the ruler brings order to the people and "serves" *tian*.

This inseparability of *tian* and the human world is often expressed in the characterization of Chinese cosmology as "the continuity between *tian* and human beings (*tianren heyi* 天人合一)." What this means is that *tianren* is a correlative category that entails a symbiotic yet hierarchical relationship: *Tian* is shaped by the human experience, and what it means to be human is constantly being reshaped by *tian*. That is to say, *tian* is not just the natural world, independent of human artifice. Rather, *tian* is a living, cumulative regularity, inclusive of nature and nurture that is not only inseparable from the human experience, but is in an important degree expressive of it.

The contemporary scholar Pang Pu underscores the human dimension of *tian* in associating it with the "social conditions (*shehui tiaojian* 社會條件)" and the "social forces (*shehuili* 社會力)."[3] The project, then, is not to integrate two aspects of our experience that are originally independent of each other, but rather to optimize the correlative and interdependent possibilities of what is shared experience.[4]

萬物 *wanwu*. This expression is conventionally translated as "the ten thousand things" or "the myriad things." In the *Daodejing* cosmology, process is privileged over substance, and continuity over discreteness. Thus, *wu* is more appropriately understood not as static "things," but as processes, and the always transitory punctuation of these processes as consummatory events. Thus we must understand "things (*wu* 物)" as both processes (happenings) and events (happenings that have achieved some relative consummation).

We have often translated *wanwu* as "everything that is happening." This more fluid use of "thing" as "event" is not unknown in English, where we say "I have a million things to do" and "things got out of hand." *Wu* suggests the notion of things as particular processes with a career of growth, maturation, and consummation. It is the articulation of the ongoing fluid process into particular events that makes the world determinate and intelligible.

The expression *wanwu* 萬物 or "ten thousand processes or events" refers to the unsummed totality of all particular processes and events as they constitute this world: *Wanwu* is everything that is happening. The *Zhuangzi*'s expression *wuhua* 物化—"the perpetual transforming of processes and events"—suggests the mutuality and interpenetration of all forms of process, as one "thing" transforms to become another.

無名 *wuming*. "Naming without fixed reference": see pages 45–6.

無事 *wushi*. "To be non-interfering in going about your business": see pages 47–8.

無爲 *wuwei*. "Noncoercive action that is in accordance with the *de* of things": see page 39, 44–5.

無心 *wuxin*. "Unmediated thinking and feeling": see pages 46–7.

無欲 *wuyu*. "Objectless desire": see pages 42–5.

無爭 *wuzheng*. "Striving without contentiousness": see page 48.

無知 *wuzhi*. "Unprincipled knowing": see pages 40–2, 44–5.

心 *xin*. "Heart-and-mind": see pages 25–6, 38–9.

自然 *ziran*. "Spontaneously so" means literally "self-so-ing" or "self-deriving." We might play with this rather literal meaning in a Chinese "paronomastic" fashion by substituting "sow" and "sew" for "so," thereby evoking the protean images of "husbanding and cultivating" a world, and the "tailoring" of it to suit both one's own proclivities and those of one's context.

The "self- (*zi* 自)" element in *ziran* needs clarification. It is a non-reified and reflexive notion of "self-in-context," where "self-" refers to those roles and transactional relationships that locate one in a world, and that constitute one's cultivated disposition to act. In the processual Daoist worldview, creativity is recursive, and is always exercised over and with respect to "self." Spontaneity thus conceived entails both *self*-creativity and *co*-creativity.

*Ziran* is used in chapter 17 to characterize the spontaneous social and political order of the people as it emerges under the non-coercive government of effective rulers. It is used in chapter 23 to recommend against being doctrinaire by invoking the natural order as a model for human conduct:

> And if the heavens and the earth cannot sustain things for long,
> How much less the human being.

More profoundly, however, it is used cosmologically as a kind of categorical yet always contextualized dispositional spontaneity that is more fundamental than any specific expression of order. This then is its import in chapter 25:

> Human beings emulate the earth,
> The earth emulates the heavens,
> The heavens emulate way-making,
> And way-making emulates what is spontaneously so.

In this cosmological usage, *ziran* functions in a way similar to the cognate expression, "self-transforming (*zihua* 自化)," found in chapters 37 and 57 that describes the spontaneous unfolding of all of the natural processes, including the human world, when left free of interference.

The importance of *ziran* lies in the fact that it is an alternative to the notion of initial beginnings. *Ziran* is the spontaneous emergence of novelty that is manifest in the propensity of things as the "swinging gateway" of the continuing present. And "beginnings" are fetal (*shi* 始) rather than primordial.

Chapters such as 25, 42, 51, and 52 are most often read cosmogonically, wherein *dao* is interpreted as some initial "source" or "origin." While the sense of "resourcing" *dao* is certainly appropriate, such an understanding can become misleading if it is conflated with the sense of "origins" that we find in a "One-many" metaphysical tradition that appeals to some notion of originative and determinative first principles, and some initial creative act. Spontaneity in the Daoist tradition entails a contingency that attends the ever-continuing process of experience. And *dao* and the myriad things are simply two different ways of looking at the same process of experience, the same reality. They are the clearest statement of "the inseparability of one and many, of continuity and multiplicity, of *dao* and *de* (*yiduo bufenguan* 一多不分觀)."

In order to be consistent, we would have to allow that the continuing emergence of novelty in this Daoist cosmogony in the fullness of time would overwhelm any existing cognitive categories or explanatory vocabulary. We can only rely on our present vocabulary to reflect upon the most recent phases in this continuing process.

Thus, what might be read as a classical cosmogony in the sense of an initial beginning might be better understood as a kind of "epistemogony" in which the terms of art and explanation are being born. It is not only the world as such that emerges in the continuing present, but our way of understanding it as being discriminated into the heavens and the earth, the *yin* and *yang qi*, the spiritual and the numinous, the four seasons, and so on. All of these conditions are collateral and mutually entailing, collaborating with each other recursively to produce the world of experience.

It is the need to reach beyond our current language that requires the use of *dao* as a style name that suggests its bottomless possibilities rather than as a proper name that captures its present character. *Dao* is a name that evokes the power of the imagination and its capacity to inspire activity that goes beyond the horizons of our present world.

A careful look at classical Chinese cosmology reveals a world in which there is a contingency and fluidity among the animal, human, and divine worlds. While this resonating interdependence among worlds is a much advertised feature of the early Chinese cosmology, it is the actual interpenetrating of these realms that makes the *wuhua* cosmology far more radical than simply synergy or symbiosis. Much of the mythological literature of China is populated with creatures in which human and animal identities are unstable, with one form assimilating elements from the other. There is an entrenched ambiguity that attends any attempt to separate out the animal and human worlds, and there is anticipation in the *wuhua* cosmology that one order of existence gives way to another in the ongoing flux and flow of transformation.

The classical Daoist text *Zhuangzi*, for example, is explicit in challenging human exceptionalism, describing the possibility of assuming a human form as an arbitrary and not especially welcome perturbation within the larger process of transformation. Zhuangzi's response to the misgivings one might have about "death" is that there is real comfort and indeed even a religious awe in the recognition that assuming the form of one kind of thing gives way to becoming another in a ceaseless adventure. It can be argued, for example, that the *Zhuangzi*'s famous butterfly story, informed as it is by the perceived liberation from rapacious, wormlike caterpillar to the happy dance of the strikingly colored butterfly, really has as its subtext Zhuang Zhou himself dying out of one kind of life only to be transformed into another.[5]

The earliest and clearest statement of this early Daoist cosmology that distinguishes it from more familiar cosmogonies is *The*

*Great One Gives Birth to the Waters,* a document recovered as part of the *Daodejing* in the Guodian find dating to about 300 BCE. We have included this text and a discussion of it at the end of this book as an Appendix.

## NOTES TO THE *GLOSSARY OF KEY TERMS*

1. The language that François Jullien (1995) uses to define the important although less prominent notion of *shi* 勢 applies in large measure to this key notion of *dao* 道.

2. See Wang Hui (2000) for a detailed study of the history of *tian* and *di* that makes a strong argument for the ancestral content in both ideas.

3. Pang Pu (1998):91–2.

4. We make this argument in Hall and Ames (1998):174–76.

5. *Zhuangzi* 7.2.94. Compare Graham (1981):61 and Watson (1968):49.

# Introduction to the Translation

The *Daodejing* comes down to us today in several different versions. How do we decide which text to take as a master for our translation?[1]

D. C. Lau (1982:184) expresses some appropriate skepticism that there is such a thing as an "original" *Daodejing*. The recent 1993 Guodian 郭店 find (hereafter, GD) and the three bundles of *Daodejing* text it contained might well persuade us that there were likely several if not many different versions in circulation belonging to independent textual traditions at least as early as late fourth century BCE. One interesting feature of the c. 300 BCE GD text is that, apart from the appended document, *The Great One Gives Birth to the Waters* (*Taiyi shengshui* 太一生水), this version does not contain any substantial materials that are *not* included in the two Mawangdui 馬王堆 texts (hereafter referred to as MWD A and MWD B) and the Wang Bi (hereafter, WB) redactions.[2] This might suggest that, although the GD texts themselves provide only a partial version of the *Daodejing*, at least one "complete" version was in circulation at that early date.

On the other hand, the textual differences that obtain among the early versions suggest that the received text is likely an edited accretion that emerged over several centuries. In its earliest phases, the *Daodejing* was probably a work in progress. Thus, we cannot embrace the notion that the discovery of earlier texts provides us with versions of the *Daodejing* necessarily "superior" to the received text because they are closer to some "original." This way of thinking is what John Dewey calls "*the* philosophical fallacy" in which the outcome of a process is presumed to be the antecedent of that process. In fact, the received text often provides us with a fuller and more considered version of these earlier redactions.

While the earlier version of the text does not necessarily get us closer to an "original," D. C. Lau (1982:184) suggests that it does provide a vantage point prior to "the scribal errors and editorial tamperings of a subsequent age." In their introductions and notes to their MWD translations, both D. C. Lau and Robert Henricks (1989) demonstrate rather clearly that access to these new versions provides us with an opportunity to resolve what have been persistent textual problems. Also, both Lau and Henricks note that the MWD versions contain a wealth of grammatical particles that are not present in later versions, and that provide us with a somewhat greater precision in our reading of the text. It is for these reasons that we have settled upon a conflation of the two versions of the *Daodejing* buried in a tomb in 168 BCE and recovered in the 1973 Mawangdui find as our basic text.

MWD A observes no Han dynasty taboo characters, while MWD B observes only the given name of the first emperor of the Han. On the basis of the observance of posthumous taboo characters, D. C. Lau (1982:156) concludes that it is unlikely that the earlier MWD A was copied after the death of the first emperor in 195 BCE, and was possibly transcribed before the founding of the Han in 206 BCE. The MWD B text was unlikely to have been copied after the death of Emperor Hui in 180 BCE. This judgment is reinforced by the fact that the MWD A is written in an earlier small seal (*xiaozhuan*) script standardized in the Qin dynasty, while MWD B is written in a later clerical (*li*) form.

In reviewing the two MWD versions, D. C. Lau (1982:160) argues and Robert Henricks (2000:22) concurs that, in spite of their obvious yet largely superficial differences, they represent two lines of transmission from a common exemplar. Hence, we are justified in treating them as a single source.

Although we take the conflated MWD manuscripts as our basic text, we have also consulted and taken advantage of the earlier GD strips dating from as early as the fourth century BCE, as well as the received text associated with the commentary of Wang Bi (226–

249). We have noted emendations from these and other sources where they occur, but would refer the reader to the work of particularly D. C. Lau, Robert Henricks, and William Boltz among other leading scholars for the detailed textual analysis.

We have departed from the MWD master in one significant way. It is generally accepted that the *Daodejing* was parsed into the present 81 chapter text by the Han dynasty court bibliographer Liu Xiang (劉向, c. 79–6 BCE), although the two-part division into a *dao* section (chapters 1–37) and a *de* section (chapters 38–81) is much earlier. According to the account of his son, Liu Xin (劉歆), Liu Xiang attempted to work from all available resources, and thus began with a rather disparate collection of material, including multiple copies with many redundancies. Liu Xiang edited out of this collage a standardized text in two parts consisting of 81 chapters.[3] The choice of the number 81 seems to have at least as much to do with Han dynasty numerology as with any natural fault lines in the textual materials. We say "at least" because, given the punctuation marks found in the MWD and GD texts, it is clear that Liu Xiang may not have begun entirely from scratch in making his chapter divisions. Many (but not all) of these marks set off the chapters as we presently know them.

Peculiar to both the MWD texts is the reversal of the two-part division, making the text, as it were, a "*Dedaojing*" by beginning with chapter 38 of the *de* section, and concluding with chapter 37 of the *dao* section. Also, several chapters (chapters 24, 40, 80, and 81, for example) do not follow the sequence of the received text. While noting this fact, we have chosen to retain the familiar order of the WB version for the convenience of the reader.

Over the long day of Chinese history, innumerable commentaries have accrued around the *Daodejing*, with only a fraction of them surviving from generation to generation. Even so, within China today thousands of these commentaries continue to be passed on. In recent centuries the *Daodejing* has assumed the stature of a masterpiece of world literature, and the translations now available in so many of the world's languages offer often unique perspectives on this protean text. The emergence of the *Daodejing* as world literature is itself a profoundly creative process. The art of translation often challenges hardened and sometimes constricted readings of the text by infusing new insights and perspectives that unblock the flow of interpretation. At the same time, any new translation into the English language today is hugely indebted to the giants in this world tradition of scholarship, and ours is certainly no exception. Those interpretations that we have relied upon most heavily are frequently referenced in our notes, and are cited in our bibliography.

In providing a Chinese text, we have adapted the critical edition of D. C. Lau (1982). See his text and notes for a more complete account of textual issues.

### NOTES TO THE *INTRODUCTION TO THE TRANSLATION*

1. In this discussion of the text, we have relied heavily upon the research and sometimes speculative insights and conclusions of D. C. Lau (1982) and Robert Henricks (1989, 2000), and would refer the reader to their fuller accounts.

2. Although we follow convention in referring to the text that was transmitted with the Wang Bi (226–49) commentary as the Wang Bi text, taking this as our exemplar of the "received" text, it is clear from internal evidence in the commentary that Wang Bi himself was working from a textual source that sometimes differed markedly from this redaction. In fact, there is every indication that Wang Bi was consulting a text much closer to the conflated MWD version.

3. See Henricks (2000):8–9.

# Translation and Commentary

## CHAPTER I

道，可道也，非恆道也。名，可名也，非恆名也。無名，萬物之始
也; 有名，萬物之母也。故恆無欲也，以觀其妙；恆有欲也，以觀
其所徼。兩者同出異名，同謂之玄。玄之又玄，衆妙之門。

> Way-making (*dao*) that can be put into words is not really way-
> making,
> And naming (*ming*) that can assign fixed reference to things is not
> really naming.[1]

> The nameless (*wuming*) is the fetal beginnings of everything that is
> happening (*wanwu*),
> While that which is named is their mother.[2]

> Thus, to be really objectless in one's desires (*wuyu*) is how one ob-
> serves the mysteries of all things,
> While really having desires is how one observes their boundaries.[3]

> These two—the nameless and what is named—emerge from the same
> source yet are referred to differently.

> Together they are called obscure.[4]
> The obscurest of the obscure,
> They are the swinging gateway of the manifold mysteries.

## Commentary

Experience is processual, and is thus always provisional. Process
requires that the formational and functional aspects of our experience are correlative and mutually entailing. Our new thoughts shape

how we think and act. And how we are presently disposed to think and act disciplines our novel thoughts. While the fluid immediacy of experience precludes the possibility of exhaustive conceptualization and explanation, enduring formal structures lend the flow of experience a degree of determinacy that can be expressed productively in conceptual language. The relative persistence of formal structures permits us to parse and punctuate the ceaseless flow of experience into consummate yet never really discrete things and events.

Given that the things and events are invariably entertained from some perspective or other, they are always unique. And the radical temporality of experience that will neither be arrested nor denied guarantees that all attempts to theorize about these events, while often of contingent value, will ultimately be outrun by the processive character of experience.

Experience is most replete when we entertain it in both its determinate and its indeterminate aspects, appreciating both the contingent boundaries that mediate it and make it meaningful for us, and the spontaneous emergence of novelty that can only be immediately felt. The gateway is constantly swinging open and swinging shut. Swinging open, it gives rise to some degree of uncaused and thus inexplicable novelty in the world. It then swings shut as the event is born, allowing for its persistence. The inchoate, novel aspect of experience at first resists rationalization. Born into a contextualizing world and persisting within it, the event gradually and in degree allows for conceptualization, and can be understood in such terms. In the course of time, the event begins to disperse and return, at first disappointing and then ultimately compromising those same rational structures that earlier promised meaning.

The human being is not passive in this continuing process. On the contrary, the human imagination is itself the clearest example of naming without assigning fixed reference. Our thoughts and language are not tied to a world, but function actively to articulate and realize one. In Daoism there is no appeal to a static vision of a reality or a mind that passively mirrors it. It offers rather a wholly transactional relationship between a world-making heart-and-mind and a heart-and-mind-shaping world. In this process, we tap the indeterminate aspect of our experience to think and speak a novel world into being.

However we try to be precise in denoting the events that make up our experience, new associations are constantly arising that challenge our terms of reference. Process insists that these events and their meanings for us be ever fluid and changing.

To underscore the penumbral advance of the continuing present, the text allows that while *dao*-ing (translated here as "way-making") can be evoked as a "style" name (*zi* 字), it cannot be used as a proper name (*ming* 名). The style name is an attempt to illuminate the character of something and its directions; the proper name includes this present disposition as well as its inexhaustible possibilities. There is illumination, but there is shadow too.

But "way-making" is not simply about rational structures. *Zi* 字 or "styling" is also a name of affection. It means to breed, to nurture, and to caress fondly. Beyond the cognitive understanding of experience, there is the epistemology of caring. We know things most immediately and profoundly through empathic feeling. This affective form of knowing is the content of our meaningful *relationships, and the concreteness of these relations* defines what we really are. As such, our desires are specific. But just as the processive character of experience ultimately defeats all rational structures, process also renders all concrete knowledge of specific things contingent. We can only know specifically, yet process requires that we constantly surrender the specificity of what we know. Optimally, then, we must have desires while at the same time be resolutely "objectless" in these desires.

## CHAPTER 2

天下皆知美之爲美，斯惡已；皆知善之爲善，斯不善矣。有無之相生也，難易之相成也，長短之相形也，高下之相盈也，音聲之相和也，先后之相隨，恆也。是以聖人居無爲之事，行不言之敎，萬物作而弗始也，爲而弗恃也，成功而弗居也。夫唯弗居，是以弗去。

As soon as everyone in the world knows that the beautiful are
 beautiful,
There is already ugliness.
As soon as everyone knows the able,[5]
There is ineptness.[6]

Determinacy (*you*) and indeterminacy (*wu*) give rise to each other,
Difficult and easy complement each other,
Long and short set each other off,
High and low complete each other,
Refined notes and raw sounds harmonize (*he*) with each other,
And before and after lend sequence to each other—
This is really how it all works.[7]

It is for this reason that sages keep to service that does not entail
 coercion (*wuwei*)
And disseminate teachings that go beyond what can be said.

In all that happens (*wanwu*),
The sages develop things but do not initiate them,
They act on behalf of things but do not lay any claim to them,
They see things through to fruition but do not take credit for them.
It is only because they do not take credit for them that things do not
 take their leave.

## Commentary

Distinctions produce their opposites. For the Daoist, dividing up
the world descriptively and prescriptively generates correlative categories that invariably entail themselves and their antinomies. Way-
making as the field of experience does not resolve itself into ontological distinctions. In fact, on the contrary, there is an ontological
parity among the many events that constitute this process, with
none of them being more real than any other.

This correlative sensibility in the Daoist process cosmology is
the functional equivalent of the dualisms—good and evil, true and
false, objective and subjective, theory and practice, reason and
emotion, spirit and flesh, and so on—that constitute the familiar
vocabulary of a reality/appearance metaphysics. In the process

cosmology, with the absence of a putative ontological disparity between reality and appearance, the interdependent binaries, far from the "real" negating what is less so, require each other for explanation. Unlike "Being" and "Non-being," the "determinate (*you*) and indeterminate (*wu*)" (or "something" and "nothing") are not ontological categories at all, but are rather conventional distinctions that have explanatory force in giving an account of how things hang together.

Insight into this process cosmology and the interdependent character of the correlative distinctions used to interpret it provides a kind of sagacity in dealing with the world. The sages do not take sides, but are catalytic in facilitating the flourishing of the process as a whole. To favor one distinction over another—for example, the beautiful over the ugly—would make it exclusive and thus impoverishing. Given the continuity assumed within process cosmology, these categories are correlative and mutually entailing. Not only do you not get one without the other but, simply put, every constituent is necessary for every other constituent to be what it is. The job of the sage, then, is to enable each participant in the drama to contribute itself fully to the performance.

## CHAPTER 3

不上賢，使民不爭；不貴難得之貨，使民不爲盜；不見可欲，使民不亂。是以聖人之治也，虛其心，實其腹；弱其志，强其骨。恆使民無知無欲也。使夫知不敢弗爲而已。爲無爲則無不治矣。

Not promoting those of superior character
Will save the common people from becoming contentious.
Not prizing property that is hard to come by
Will save them from becoming thieves.
Not making a show of what might be desired
Will save them from becoming disgruntled.

It is for this reason that in the proper governing by the sages:
They empty the hearts-and-minds of the people and fill their stomachs,

They weaken their aspirations and strengthen their bones,
Ever teaching the common people to be unprincipled in their know-
ing (*wuzhi*)
And objectless in their desires (*wuyu*),
They keep the hawkers of knowledge at bay.
It is simply in doing things noncoercively (*wuwei*)[8]
That everything is governed properly.

## Commentary

In attempting to govern the people, acting assertively to promote
particular value judgments over others can be divisive and self-
defeating. Such conduct in favoring one thing over another encourages a contentiousness among the people that undermines rather
than fosters community. Better to be broadly inclusive of different
talents and contributions, and to strive to appreciate each thing on
its own terms, with the single proviso that coercion in any form is
impoverishing.

Under the tutelage of sagacious rule, there is a tacit celebration
of the bravery, patience, and kindliness of the ordinary person.
There is a tolerance of difference and diversity that precludes any
heavy-handed exercise of political constraints. In abjuring any appeal to political idealisms that are so often invoked by their advocates to justify the worst kinds of exclusion and coercion, those
responsible for the flourishing of community simply allow it in all
of its complexity to establish and sustain its own equilibrium. Rather
than foisting an agenda on the community, effective administra-
tors make sure that basic needs such as food and health are provided for, and then sit back to allow the character of the community to emerge synergistically out of the associated living of the
people.

The people, encouraged to be free from assumptions and inclusive of alternatives, develop a tolerance and accommodation that
immunizes them from purveyors of malignant prejudices. It is only
empathy and openness that can inspire the community to go beyond the mediocrity of unilaterally legislated values.

CHAPTER 4

道沖，而用之有弗盈也。淵呵，似萬物之宗。挫其銳，解其紛，和
其光，同其塵。湛呵，似或存。吾不知其誰之子也，象帝之先。

Way-making being empty,[9]
You make use of it
But do not fill it up.[10]

So abysmally deep—
It seems the predecessor of everything that is happening (*wanwu*).

It blunts the sharp edges
And untangles the knots;
It softens (*he*) the glare
And brings things together on the same track.

So cavernously deep—
It only seems to persist.

I do not know whose progeny it is;
It prefigures the ancestral gods.

## Commentary

It is the underdetermined nature of way-making that makes it, like
a bottomless goblet, inexhaustibly capacious. The processive and
fluid character of experience precludes the possibility of either initial beginning or final closure by providing within it an ongoing
space for self-renewal. Within the rhythms of life, the swinging
gateway opens and novelty emerges spontaneously to revitalize the
world, tempering whatever has moved to an extreme, and reclaim-
ing whatever has strayed from the path. Whatever is most enduring
is ultimately overtaken in the ceaseless transformation of things.

The depth and profundity of experience lies in the inexhaust-
ibility of its possibilities. And what makes these possibilities inexhaustible is real novelty: uncaused and inexplicable. As the creative
origin of everything that happens and the locus of all relationships,
experience itself is an appropriate object of awe and religious
deference.

In *Zhuangzi* 27, this same idea of inexhaustible novelty is applied linguistically with the notion of "goblet words (*zhiyan* 卮言 )." "Goblet" words are words that are renewed with each use because when they are filled up with meaning, they tip themselves out, only to be filled again. Such language is appropriate to the fluidity and irreversibility of experience.[11]

## CHAPTER 5

天地不仁，以萬物而爲芻狗；聖人不仁，以百姓爲芻狗。天地之間，其猶橐籥與？虛而不屈，動而愈出。多聞數窮，不若守於中。

The heavens and the earth are not partial to institutionalized
    morality.[12]
They take things (*wanwu*) and treat them all as straw dogs.[13]
Sages too are not partial to institutionalized morality.
They treat the common people as straw dogs.

The space between the heavens and the earth—
Isn't it just like a bellows!
Even though empty it is not vacuous.
Pump it and more and more comes out.

It is better to safeguard what you have within[14]
Than to learn a great deal that so often goes nowhere.

## *Commentary*

Nature and the sages too are on the side of genuine moral feeling. This chapter needs to be read together with chapters 18 and 19, in which spontaneous and immediate caring is regarded as an expression of communal morality superior to the artificially constructed catechism associated with an increasingly institutionalized Confucianism. The image of "straw dogs" can be read in at least three different yet complementary ways.

First, nature does not participate in a kind of human exceptionalism in which the human being is singled out for special treatment. Nature treats all things, human and otherwise, with the same degree of care.

Second, both nature itself and the sages who model themselves on it treat all things and all people with parity, even the seemingly least among them. They do not, on the basis of a decadent and unnatural morality, give favor to some over others.

Third, "straw dogs" as sacrificial artifacts are celebrated according to the proper season, then abandoned when that season has passed. Even a clutch of straw is entitled to reverence at the proper time and place. In the natural cycle, all things have their moment, and when that moment passes, they must pass with it. There is nothing in nature, high or low, that is revered in perpetuity.

Repeatedly the *Daodejing* expresses a fascination for the way in which an indeterminate source spontaneously and inexhaustibly gives rise to the provisionally determinate phenomena that we experience around us. This cosmic creativity is always expressed through the particular foci that constitute it. As a microcosm of this cosmic macrocosm, then, we too have a spring of indeterminate energy within us. It is by tapping this internal font of spontaneity that we are best able to engage the world aesthetically at the level of immediate feeling. Rather than relying upon externally acquired and often ineffectual learning, we should look to this inner source.

## CHAPTER 6

谷神不死，是謂玄牝。玄牝之門，是謂天地之根。縣縣呵若存，用之不勤。

> The life-force of the valley never dies—
> This is called the dark female.
> The gateway of the dark female—
> This is called the root of the world.
> Wispy and delicate, it only seems to be there,
> Yet its productivity is bottomless.

## Commentary

In chapters 4 and 5, we have the Daoist celebration of the fecundity of emptiness. The underdetermined nature of experience, like a self-emptying flask or a pair of bellows, makes it inexhaustibly productive. In this chapter and pervasively in the text, the image of the dark, moist, and accommodatingly vacant interior of the vagina is used as an analogy for this fertility.

## CHAPTER 7

天長地久。天地之所以能長且久者，以其不自生也，故能長生。是以聖人退其身而身先，外其身而身存。不以其無私與？故能成其私。

> The heavens are lasting and the earth enduring.
> The reason the world is able to be lasting and enduring
> Is because it does not live for itself.[15]
> Thus it is able to be long-lived.

> It is on this model that the sages withdraw their persons from contention yet find themselves out in front,
> Put their own persons out of mind yet find themselves taken care of.
> Isn't it simply because they are unselfish that they can satisfy their own needs?

## Commentary

The world as a process is constituted by the myriad things that find their consummation within it. Creativity is expressed through and only through each of these particular events that construes the process as its own unique field of experience. While each focus pursues its own consummation, there is no superordinate, generic agenda beyond the unsummed total of the foci themselves. There is no world qua world.

The sages in emulation of the natural processes are impartial and inclusive. Their concerns, on the model of nature itself, emerge out of the manifold of foci that are implicated within them. It is because the sages take nature as their mentor that their persons are preserved and all of their needs are satisfied.

## CHAPTER 8

上善似水。水善利萬物而又爭居眾人之所惡，故幾於道矣。居善地，心善淵，予善天，言善信，政善治，事善能，動善時。夫唯不爭，故無尤。

> The highest efficacy is like water.
> It is because water benefits everything (*wanwu*)
> Yet vies to dwell in places loathed by the crowd
> That it comes nearest to proper way-making.
>
> In dwelling, the question is where is the right place.
> In thinking and feeling, it is how deeply.
> In giving, it is how much like nature's bounty.[16]
> In speaking, it is how credibly.
> In governing, it is how effectively.
> In serving, it is how capably.
> In acting, it is how timely.
>
> It is only because there is no contentiousness in proper way-making
> That it incurs no blame.

### Commentary

The highest efficacy is a combination of the degree of benefit something bestows and the inclusiveness of such beneficence. The intensity and expansiveness of water is an appropriate analogy for such efficacy since it gives the gift of life without discrimination, and flows everywhere disdaining nothing.

In the human experience we are radically contextualized, constituted by those roles and relationships that locate us within our social, natural, and cultural environments. "Proper way-making" is getting the most out of these relationships as we make our way in the world: It is making this life significant. And getting the most out of our experience depends upon achieving and sustaining optimally productive harmony. Such efficacy depends upon always knowing where to be, committing ourselves utterly in our relationships, being generous in our transactions, making good on what we say, being successful both in service and in governance, and seizing the moment.

The greatest obstacle to optimizing relationships is coercion. If a healthy relationship is mutually accommodating, then the introduction of coercion, in which one party overwrites the importance of the other, entails a diminution in the creative possibilities of both. As Richard Rorty has observed, forced redefinition is humiliation.

In a cosmology that begins from the uniqueness of the particular, strict identity and its corollary, strict equality, are not an option. Relationships are invariably hierarchical. But hierarchy is only pernicious when it is compromised by coercion. The family as an institution is hierarchical, but appropriate patterns of deference can allow members of the family to have both dignity and parity in their relationships.

## CHAPTER 9

持而盈之，不若其已。揣而銳之，不可長葆也。金玉盈室，莫之能守也。貴富而驕，自遺咎也。功遂身退，天之道也。

It is better to desist
Than to try to hold it upright and fill it to the brim.
Pounded out to a point
Its sharpness cannot be long maintained.

When treasure fills the hall,
No one is able to keep it safe.
Those who are arrogant because of station and wealth
Bring calamity upon themselves.

To retire when the deed is done
Is the way (*dao*) that *tian* works.

## Commentary

The human experience can be maximized only by coordinating its activities with the workings of the natural environment and the propensity of circumstances. These human activities should be modeled upon the cyclical patterns of nature in which one season gives way to the next, orchestrating the full range of natural forces—sun, soil, air, moisture—to collaborate in producing a thriving environment and an abundant harvest. In these interdependent processes of nature, any diversion in the direction of excess or extreme is short lived, and is ultimately defeated by a synergistic return to moderation and balance.

But experience is directed as well as cyclical. That is, the propensity of circumstances in which we live our lives has a bearing, and is irreversible. This direction is driven by a seamless combination of natural and human forces.

Within the human world as in nature, taking any endeavor to its extreme will result in a reversal of this direction and a self-induced subversion of the enterprise. What goes up must come down.

The importance of the indeterminate aspect in preempting the reversion that comes with fullness is celebrated in what is probably a spurious chapter of the *Xunzi*. When Confucius is asked by his disciple Zilu, "Is there a way of managing fullness, Sir?" he replies, "You need a measure of ignorance to cope with an intelligence that vies with the wisdom of the sages; you need a measure of humility to cope with accomplishments that blanket the world; you need a measure of timidity to cope with courage that pervades an entire age; you need a measure of frugality to cope with wealth that fills the four seas. This is what is called the way of draining some off and reducing the amount."[17]

## CHAPTER 10

戴營魄抱一，能毋離乎？搏氣至柔，能嬰兒乎？滌除玄鑑，能毋有疵乎？愛民活國，能毋以知乎？天門啓闔，能為雌乎？明白四達，能毋以知乎？生之、畜之，生而弗有，長而弗宰也。是謂玄德。

In carrying about your more spiritual and more physical aspects
    and embracing their oneness,[18]
Are you able to keep them from separating?
In concentrating your *qi* and making it pliant,
Are you able to become the newborn babe?
In scrubbing and cleansing your profound mirror,
Are you able to rid it of all imperfections?
In loving the common people and breathing life into the state,
Are you able to do it without recourse to wisdom?
With nature's gates swinging open and closed,
Are you able to remain the female?
With your insight penetrating the four quarters,
Are you able to do it without recourse to wisdom?

It gives life to things and nurtures them.
Giving life without managing them
And raising them without lording it over them—
This is called the profoundest efficacy (*de*).[19]

## Commentary

Early Daoist cultivation certainly involved a meditative regimen
that seems to be the central issue here. In fact, much of the *Daodejing*
can be read as metaphor for breathing exercises. It is the thorough
integration of the physical and spiritual aspects of our experience
in the concentration of our *qi* that enables us to maximize our potency and invigorate our minds. Penetrating insight is not inspired
by some instrumental, enabling, "tried and true" wisdom, but is
rather an immediate and fundamentally creative activity out of which
fresh and efficacious intelligence arises to guide the way. The pol-
ished mirror that produces this insight is itself a source of energy,
with the glow of its illumination recasting the world about it. Real
wisdom, then, can only be this shaping insight into the present
moment, and engagement with the unique circumstances at play.

    The dynamic field of experience is the locus in which the stream
of phenomena is animated and achieves consummation, but all of this
pageantry occurs without the presence of some controlling hand. The

energy of transformation lies within the process itself rather than in some external agency. It is the very nature of the world to transform.

## CHAPTER 11

卅輻同一轂，當其無，有車之用也。埏埴而爲器，當其無，有埴器之用也。鑿戶牖而爲室，當其無，有室之用也。故有之以爲利，無之以爲用。

> The thirty spokes converge at one hub,
> But the utility of the cart is a function of the nothingness (*wu*) inside the hub.
> We throw clay to shape a pot,
> But the utility of the clay pot is a function of the nothingness inside it.
> We bore out doors and windows to make a dwelling,[20]
> But the utility of the dwelling is a function of the nothingness inside it.
> Thus, it might be something (*you*) that provides the value,
> But it is nothing that provides the utility.

## *Commentary*

The classical Western notion of "Being" used in a metaphysical sense is generally associated with ontological ground—the reality behind appearance—while "Non-being" is its strict negation. The Chinese existential verb *you* 有 overlaps with the sense of "having" rather than the copula, and therefore means "to be present" or "to be around." *Wu* 無 then—here translated as "nothing"—means "to not be present" or "to not be around." *Wu* does not indicate strict opposition or contradiction, but absence. Thus, the *you-wu* distinction suggests mere contrast in the sense of the presence or absence of x rather than an assertion about the existence or non-existence of x. *You* and *wu* are not ontological categories with all of the philosophical implications that would entail, but are rather the interdependent explanatory categories of "something" and "nothing," of presence and absence.

In chapters 2, 4, and 5 we witness the Daoist fascination with the correlative relationship between the indeterminate and the determinate aspects of experience—between a productive emptiness and the phenomenal world that emerges from it. Here that relationship between the indeterminate and the determinate is parsed in terms of formation and function, what later in the tradition comes to be known as the complementary distinction between *ti* 體 and *yong* 用.

## CHAPTER 12

五色使人目盲；馳騁田獵，使人心發狂；難得之貨，使人之行妨。
五味使人之口爽，五音使人之耳聾，是以聖人之治也，爲腹而不爲
目，故去彼而取此。

> The five colors[21] blind the eye,
> The hard riding of the hunt addles both heart and mind,
> Property hard to come by[22] subverts proper conduct,
> The five flavors destroy the palate,
> And the five notes impair the ear.[23]
>
> It is for this reason that in the proper governing by the sages:[24]
>> They exert their efforts on behalf of the abdomen rather than
>> the eye.[25]
> Thus, eschewing one they take the other.

## *Commentary*

The main thrust of this chapter, like so many others in the *Daodejing*, is to prevent the inner focus of vital energy from being overwhelmed by outer distractions. In a world in which things are constituted by their relationships, these relations must be properly managed. A real source of agitation is the propensity of the senses to be tempted by external diversions. The difference between the abdomen and the eye is that the stomach can be easily satiated, but when the wandering eye finally lands on something, it just wants more.

This chapter can be read as a not-so-oblique reference to a meditative regimen. The abdomen is the center for nourishing and concentrating one's vital energies. Both figuratively and literally, it is the center of the body and one's source of equilibrium. The eye, on the other hand, is a major orifice through which the *qi* can leak away.

The concern about insatiability is echoed in chapter 46, which says:

There is no crime more onerous than greed,
No misfortune more devastating than avarice.
And no calamity that brings with it more grief than insatiability.

Thus, knowing when enough is enough
Is really satisfying.

# CHAPTER 13

寵辱若驚，貴大患若身。何謂寵辱若驚？寵之為下也，得之若驚，
失之若驚，是謂寵辱若驚。何謂貴大患若身？吾所以有大患者，為
吾有身也，及吾無身，有何患？故貴為身於為天下，若可以託天下
矣；愛以身為天下，如可以寄天下矣。

"Favor and disgrace are cause for alarm."
"Value your gravest anxieties as you do your own person."

What does it mean in saying "Favor and disgrace are both cause for alarm?"[26]
It means that whenever favor is bestowed, both gaining it and losing it should be cause for alarm.

What does it mean in saying "Value your gravest anxieties as you do your own person?" The reason we have grave anxieties is because we are embodied persons. If we were not such persons, what anxieties would we have? Thus those who value the care of their own persons more than running the world can be entrusted with the world. And those who begrudge their persons as though they were the world can be put in charge of the world.

## Commentary

Most people are glad to receive favor, and are alarmed by disgrace. The Wang Bi commentary, however, warns that wherever there is favor, disgrace is certain to follow in its wake. Favor is not a legitimate response to merit, but rather a kind of patronage that is extended solely at the pleasure of someone else who holds power over you. The winds of such baseless favor are fickle, and can easily change direction. When favor is withdrawn, the absence of any prior justification for it becomes apparent, and circumstances are reinterpreted in such a manner that only humiliation and embarrassment remain.

The first apothegm here, in warning against favoritism, is making this recommendation on behalf of protecting our persons. The second saying is not unrelated. At a common sense level, anyone who is irreverent about his or her own well-being cannot be charged with any other responsibility, and certainly not with important matters of state. On the other hand, if we attend to each and every one of our responsibilities with the same care that we invest in our own persons, we can be entrusted with anything, including ruling the world.

The question then is what is appropriate attention to our own persons? While this maxim might seem to suggest that we are rightfully preoccupied with ourselves and should give priority to our own needs, such an interpretation has to be reconciled with chapter 7 in which quite the opposite is recommended:

> . . . the sages withdraw their persons from contention yet find
>    themselves out in front,
> Put their own persons out of mind yet find themselves taken care of.
> Isn't it simply because they are unselfish that they can satisfy their
>    own needs?

The message here seems to be: Treat all things with equal seriousness and respect, and our own persons will be taken care of as a matter of course. The way to be rid of personal concerns is to be rid of the distinction between one's person and the world in which we live. After all, "If we were not such persons, what anxieties would we have?"

The *Zhuangzi* offers what appears to be a gloss on this passage:

> Therefore if exemplary persons have no choice but to oversee the world, no policy is better than governing noncoercively. It is only once they govern noncoercively that they are able to be secure in the way they feel about their lives and circumstances. Thus those who value the care of their own persons more than running the world can be put in charge of the world. And those who begrudge their persons as though they were the world can be entrusted with the world.[27]

In this *Zhuangzi* commentary, ruling the world, far from being something to aspire to, is a burden best avoided. If such unwelcome responsibility cannot be sidestepped, however, the best way to govern effectively is again the best way to live one's life: *wuwei*. One is able to maximize the productivity of one's relationships and dissolve any tension between self and context through noncoercive, deferential activity. One both values one's person and loses one's person in this thoroughgoing integration with one's field of experience. After all, "those who begrudge their persons as though they were the world can be put in charge of the world."

## CHAPTER 14

視之而弗見，名之曰微；聽之而弗聞，名之曰希；搏之而弗得，名之曰夷。三者，不可致詰，故混而爲一。一者，其上不皦，其下不忽，繩繩呵不可名也，復歸於無物。是謂無狀之狀，無物之象，是謂忽恍。隨而不見其後，迎而不見其首。執今之道，以御今之有。以知古始，是謂道紀。

> Looking and yet not seeing it
> We thus call it "elusive."
> Listening and yet not hearing it
> We thus call it "inaudible."
> Groping and yet not getting it

We thus call it "intangible."
Because in sight, sound, and touch it is beyond determination
We construe it as inseparably one.

As for this "one"—
Its surface is not dazzling
Nor is its underside dark.
Ever so tangled, it defies discrimination
And reverts again to indeterminacy.
This is what is called the form of the formless
And the image of indeterminacy.
This is what is called the vague and the indefinite.

Following behind you will not see its rear;
Encountering it you will not see its head.

Hold tightly onto way-making in the present
To manage what is happening right now
And to understand where it began in the distant past.
This is what is called the drawstring of way-making.

## Commentary

Ironically perhaps, one of the more suggestive glosses on this chapter is passage 9.11 in the *Analects of Confucius,* in which Confucius's best and brightest student describes his education under the Master. For Yan Hui too, making one's way is a continuing encounter with the indeterminate.

> Yan Hui, with a deep sigh, said, "The more I look up at it, the higher it soars; the more I penetrate into it, the harder it becomes. I am looking at it in front of me, and suddenly it is behind me. The Master is good at drawing me forward a step at a time; he broadens me with culture and disciplines my behavior through the observance of ritual propriety. Even if I wanted to quit, I could not. And when I have exhausted my abilities, it is as though something rises up right in front of me, and even though I want to follow it, there is no road to take."

Yan Hui is leading us in the right direction. The difference between the Daoist conception of *dao*-ing or "way-making" recounted in this chapter of the *Daodejing* and its Confucian counterpart lies in the relative proportions of its referent. While Yan Hui is reflecting on way-making as the ritualized education that enchants life within the human community, the *Daodejing* is more overtly cosmological in its scope. An understanding of the way in which the ongoing underdetermined process of experience unfolds and the porous character of the flow of phenomena that constitutes it not only enables one to locate the human life within this process, but also is instructive as to how to optimize this opportunity. For the Daoist, it is an understanding of the profundity of cosmic way-making and full participation in charting it that can potentially enchant the ordinary business of the day. As William James observed, "We *add* both to the subject and to the predicate part of reality" to "enhance the universe's total value."[28]

The continuous flow of experience within which a life is lived teases our sensual and cultural sensoria by seeming to allow for discrimination only to defy any predication we might propose to assign it. Unlike the things we think we know, cosmic way-making will not yield itself up to our most basic categories of location and determination: bright and dark, inside and outside, subject and object, one and many. And when we know this cosmic way-making better, we come to understand that we don't really know "things" at all.

## CHAPTER 15

古之善爲道者，微妙玄達，深不可識。夫唯不可識，故強爲之容：
曰與呵，其若多涉水；猶呵，其若畏四鄰；嚴呵，其若客；渙呵，
其若凌釋；沌呵，其若樸；湷呵，其若濁；湆呵，其若谷；濁而靜
之徐清。安以動之徐生。葆此道者，不欲盈。夫唯不欲盈，是以能
敝而不成。

> Those of old who were good at forging their way (*dao*) in the world:[29]
>     Subtle and mysterious, dark and penetrating,[30]
>     Their profundity was beyond comprehension.

It is because they were beyond comprehension[31]
That were I forced to describe them, I would say:[32]
So reluctant, as though crossing a winter stream;
So vigilant, as though in fear of the surrounding neighbors;
So dignified, like an invited guest;
So yielding, like ice about to thaw;
So solid, like unworked wood;
So murky, like muddy water;
So vast and vacant, like a mountain gorge.[33]

Muddy water, when stilled, slowly becomes clear;
Something settled, when agitated, slowly comes to life.[34]

Those who prize way-making do not seek fullness;[35]
It is only because they do not want to be full
That they are able to remain hidden and unfinished.[36]

## Commentary

Persons who have been most successful at making their way in the world have been fully immersed in the process itself, assuming for themselves the profound and complex character of the experience that they have forged. Their conduct, like way-making, is meliorative in the sense that it is productive of a desirable way forward on the middle ground between extremes. In their advancing on the path, the expansiveness and intensity of their creative sensibilities require not only an appeal to the full breadth of shared experience, but also a plumbing of the vague and indeterminate elements that lie beyond the boundaries of what is known, and that give experience its novelty and inexhaustible depth. Because this appeal to the full range of possibilities defies the adequacy of general description, we must rely upon the imagistic force of concrete metaphors drawn from the familiar events of our lives to attempt to give the significance of this experience ample expression. Communication through such metaphors reveals the Daoist epistemology of feeling in which the quality of understanding is a function of the immediacy and intensity of what is felt.

The processive and synergistic forces at work in way-making render the language of discreteness and closure inappropriate. The road is always under construction, and the hands at work are many. While there is the punctuation of consummatory events that separates the paragraphs of one's lived experience, still the narrative is coherent and continuous: a never-ending story.

## CHAPTER 16

致虛極也，守靜篤也。萬物並作，吾以觀其復也。夫物芸芸，各復歸於其根。歸根曰靜，靜是謂復命。復命常也，知常明也。不知常妄，妄作，凶。知常容，容乃公，公乃王，王乃天，天乃道，道乃久，沒身不殆。

Extend your utmost emptiness as far as you can
And do your best to preserve your equilibrium (*jing*).[37]

In the process of all things emerging together (*wanwu*)
We[38] can witness their reversion.
Things[39] proliferate,
And each again returns to its root.
Returning to the root is called equilibrium.
Now as for equilibrium—this is called returning to the propensity
    of things,
And returning to the propensity of things is common sense.
Using common sense is acuity,
While failing to use it is to lose control.
And to try to do anything while out of control is to court disaster.

Using common sense is to be accommodating,
Being accommodating is tolerance,
Being tolerant is kingliness,
Being kingly is *tian*-like,
Being *tian*-like is to be way-making,
And the way-made is enduring.
To the end of one's days one will be free of danger.

## Commentary

The optimum posture of the heart-and-mind (*xin* 心) is to achieve and sustain an emptiness and equilibrium that will enable it to take in the world as it is without imposing its own presuppositions upon it, and without allowing the world to cause it agitation. It is significant that *xin*—a stylized drawing of the aorta—precludes the assumption of distinctions between thinking and feeling, or idea and affect. *Xin* is frequently translated simply as "heart," but since it is the seat of thinking and judgment, the notion of mind must be included in its characterization if the term is to be properly understood. Indeed, the functional equivalent of what we often think of as "purpose" or "intention" is also implicit in the notion of *xin*.

Going back to Plato, the Western tradition has been accustomed to construe efforts aimed at moral perfection as involving an internal struggle between reason and passion, or, with Augustine, between what we know we ought to do, and an obstreperous will that frustrates our acting upon that knowledge.

The interpenetration of idea, intention, and affect expressed in the notion of *xin* suggests that in the classical Chinese world the conflict associated with self-consummation is not turned inward as a struggle between the heart and the mind—that is, between the passions and reason, or between the will and judgment. If the dynamic of self-consummation does not entail the self divided against itself, what is the source and nature of the disturbance that the cultivation of an appropriate personal disposition is meant to overcome?

If agitation is not referenced primarily within one's soul, it can only be a disturbance in the relationships that constitute the self in its interactions with external things. It is through a mirroring of the things of the world as they are in their relations with us that we reach a disposition in which none among the myriad things is able to agitate our hearts-and-minds, and we are best able to promote their flourishing.

Throughout the *Huainanzi* we find reference to this "mirror-like knowing." For example, in *Huainanzi* 6:

Sages are like a mirror—
They neither see things off nor go out to meet them,
They respond to everything without storing anything up.
They are thus never injured through the myriad transformations they
     undergo.

This Daoist disposition is neither passive nor quietistic. "Mirroring" is best seen as synergistic and responsive, like virtuoso dancing or charioting or "push hands (*tuishou* 推手)" in *taijiquan,* where all of the elements are in step, and constitute a fluid interdependent whole. Such emptiness and equilibrium achieved at the root in the ordinary business of the day allows for mutual accommodation. And the common sense that facilitates such accommodation, far from being trite or trivial, is the distilled wisdom of the ages—a tried-and-true insight into the cadence of life—and as such, is deserving of enormous respect. It is what William James called "a stage of equilibrium in the human mind's development."[40]

   Accommodation, far from being passive or weak, is the source of the fullness of strength and influence, timeliness and efficacy. Indeed, accommodation is inclusionary, enabling one to extend oneself through patterns of deference. It is ordering the external effected through inner tranquillity; it is governing the trunk and branches by taking care of the root; it is bringing order to the myriad things by managing the gate through which they emerge. Accommodation, inclusivity, and tolerance are the most effective means of achieving a stable and enduring social, political, and cosmic order. This then is how the kingly and the numinous way is extended and maintained.

## CHAPTER 17

太上，下知有之；其次，親譽之；其次，畏之；其下，侮之。信不足案，有不信。猷呵，其貴言也。成功遂事，而百姓皆謂：「我自然」。

With the most excellent rulers, their subjects only know that they
    are there,
The next best are the rulers they love and praise,
Next are the rulers they hold in awe,
And the worst are the rulers they disparage.

Where there is a lack of credibility,
There is a lack of trust.
Vigilant, they are careful in what they say.

With all things accomplished and the work complete[41]
The common people say, "We are spontaneously like this."

## Commentary

While certainly advocating a kind of political anarchism, the
*Daodejing* still assumes the need for a hierarchical political structure,
with rulers above and the common people below. What is distinc-
tively anarchistic about the Daoist political order is the absence of
coercion. The most efficacious regime is one in which those who
rule carry out their administrative responsibilities so lightly and
unobtrusively that the people are able to go about their business
confidently without detecting any kind of manipulation. The people
are never given reason to question the credibility of this unadver-
tised and always distant source of political orchestration, and it
would not even occur to them that this good life is of anyone's
making save their own. The expectation that social order emerges
from the bottom up is a strong theme in this traditionally agrarian
culture in which most adjustments are the informal business of the
extended family.

    The grand analogy that is at work here is that in its activities
the human world does well to model its cosmic context. Just as the
boundless field of experience in which the human life is lived unfolds according to its own internal equilibrium without being se-
cured by anything beyond it, so the human social and political order should proceed according to its own internal rhythms without
relying upon some top-down source to discipline it. The ruler's oc-

cupation is *wuwei*: that is, to bring together the concerted efforts of the people and to be the coordinate around which these contributions are synchronized to maximum benefit.

## CHAPTER 18

故大道廢案，有仁義；知慧出案，有大偽；六親不和案，有孝慈；
邦家昏亂案，有貞臣。

> It is when grand way-making is abandoned
> That authoritative conduct (*ren*) and appropriateness (*yi*) appear.[42]
> It is when wisdom (*zhi*) and erudition arise
> That great duplicity appears.[43]
> It is when the six family relationships[44] are disharmonious
> That filiality (*xiao*) and parental affection (*ci*) appear.
> It is when the state has fallen into troubled times
> That upright ministers appear.[45]

## Commentary

It is philosophically significant that the Guodian find (c. 300 BCE) and the Mawangdui cache (168 BCE) contain both Confucian and Daoist documents. There are materials that are associated with the Confucian lineage extending from Confucius's grandson, Zisizi, down to Mencius, and in the same tombs, versions of the *Daodejing*. The appearance of Confucian and Daoist texts in the same tombs indicates that the occupant had an intellectual compass that would accommodate both ways of thinking. While such tolerance might suggest that the intellectual tension between these two competing traditions had not as yet become as explicit as it is in later philosophical literature, it is difficult to read this present chapter, also contained in the early GD materials, as anything other than an anti-Confucian polemic.

When the authentic way of being human is thriving in the world, the family-based natural morality of the community takes care of itself, enabling its members to flourish and prosper. It is only in a period of decadence and decline that philosophers arise to proclaim the obvious, and in so doing, ironically exacerbate the problem by institutionalizing an artificial alternative that suffocates natural unmediated sentiment. What was spontaneous natural feeling becomes external rules of conduct, where the invocation of moral rules as an alternative to the spontaneous expression of feeling is dehumanizing.

Morality in a healthy community is nothing more than the uncaused emergence of patterns of deference and respect as one generation gives way to the next. Such a morality is alive and vibrant, with new experience occasioning an ongoing revision of old ways of doing things. The unfortunate breakdown of a world that allows the unadorned expression of honest feeling to become an alternative world in which educated morality and its vocabulary of right and wrong, good and evil, lead to the stifling of true affection.

## CHAPTER 19

絕聖棄知，民利百倍；絕仁棄義，民復孝慈；絕巧棄利，盜賊無有。此三言也以爲文，未足。故令之有所屬：見素抱樸，少私而寡欲。

Cut off sagacity (*sheng*) and get rid of wisdom (*zhi*)[46]
And the benefit to the common people will be a hundredfold.
Cut off authoritative conduct (*ren*) and get rid of appropriateness
   (*yi*)[47]
And the common people will return to filiality (*xiao*) and parental
   affection (*ci*).
Cut off cleverness and get rid of personal profit
And there will be no more brigands and thieves.

But these three sayings as they stand are still lacking
And need to be supplemented by the following:
   Display a genuineness like raw silk and embrace a simplicity
      like unworked wood,
   Lessen your concern for yourself and reduce your desires.

## Commentary

A contrast is carried over from the previous chapter between a bottom-up, unmediated morality that expresses the natural sentiments of human beings in community, and an ethic imposed upon the people from outside that serves only to distort their authentic feelings and to divide them against themselves. The former is particularistic and alive, while the latter is generic, and at best an ossified remnant of what was once real morality. Given the terms used, the target of the critique is clearly an increasingly institutionalized Confucianism.

Philosophically, there is good reason for chapter 18 and 19 to be read together. While chapter 18 describes the consequences of forsaking natural morality, chapter 19 promises that by getting rid of a reliance upon an unnatural moral catechism, we can restore our pristine ethical sensibilities.

## CHAPTER 20

絕學無憂，唯與訶，其相去幾何？美與惡，其相去何若？人之所畏，亦不可以不畏。人恍呵，其未央哉！衆人熙熙，若饗於大牢，而春登臺。我泊焉，未兆若嬰兒未咳；纍呵，如無所歸。衆人皆有餘，我獨遺。我愚人之心也，惷惷呵！俗人昭昭，我獨若昏呵。俗人察察，我獨悶悶呵。忽呵，其若海，恍呵，其若無所止。衆人皆有以，我獨頑以鄙。吾欲獨異於人，而貴食母。

Cut off learning and there will be nothing more to worry about.

How much difference is there really between a polite "yes" and an emphatic "no!"?[48]

How much difference is there between what is deemed beautiful and ugly?[49]

Those whom people fear
Cannot but also fear others.

So indefinite! Does this humbuggery ever come to an end!

Most people are happy, happy,
As though feasting at the Tailao banquet[50]
Or climbing some sightseeing tower in the springtime.
I alone am so impassive, revealing nothing at all,
Like a babe that has yet to smile;
So listless, as though nowhere to go.

Most people have more than enough,
While I alone have lost out.
I have the heart-and-mind of a fool—so vacant and dull!

The common lot see things so clearly,
While I alone seem to be in the dark.
The common lot are so discriminating,
While I alone am so obtuse.
So vague and hazy, like the rolling seas;
So indeterminate, as though virtually endless.

The common lot all have their purposes
While I alone am a dull-witted yokel.

My needs alone[51] are different from other people,
Cherishing my mother's milk.

## Commentary

Learning is all about being on the right side of conventional distinctions. Yet these distinctions—assenting and rejecting, deeming beautiful and otherwise, fearing and being feared, and so on—are at best porous and perspectival.

A contrast is established in the text between the ordinary run of people on the one hand—people who know what they enjoy, who understand that more is better, who value precision and discernment, and who are sure of what they want—and Daoist adepts on the other. The Daoists, unpersuaded as to the value of this kind of discriminating education, retain an inclusive, pristine state of mind, welcoming the full sea of experience like that of an infant, a blockhead, a fool, a country bumpkin. Rather than finding their nourishment at the marble temple of learning, the Daoists remain contented at the mother's breast, suckled on the rich milk of immediate experience and unmediated feeling.

## CHAPTER 21

孔德之容，唯道是從。道之物，唯恍唯忽。忽呵恍呵，中有象呵；恍呵忽呵，中有物呵；窈呵冥呵，其中有精呵；其精甚眞，其中有信。自今及古，其名不去，以順衆父。吾何以知衆父之然也？以此。

Those of magnificent character (*de*)
Are committed to way-making (*dao*) alone.
As for the process of way-making,
It is ever so indefinite and vague.
Though vague and indefinite,
There are images within it.
Though indefinite and vague,
There are events within it.
Though nebulous and dark,
There are seminal concentrations of *qi* within it.
These concentrations of *qi* are authentic,
And have within them true credibility.

From the present moment back into antiquity,
Praise for way-making has never ceased,
And it is through way-making that we can act in accordance with
   the sire of the many.
How do I know that the sire of the many is so?
By this.

## *Commentary*

Way-making is participatory, and is thus influenced by the character of those who would act to extend it. While fluid and processual, it contains within it the eventful phenomena we identify as those "things" and "images" that make up our lives, including of course ourselves. This emerging field of experience is autogenerative, with the energy of transformation residing within it. The seminal concentrations of *qi* are fecund, giving birth to the myriad things around us, transforming as one thing becomes another. The underdeterminacy of these unique constituents makes their boundaries ever porous, but even more so at the beginning of their ascendancy and in their decline.

Way-making as the unfolding field of experience is the unsummed totality of things and events. It is unsummed because it is unbounded, and can only be known from one perspective or another. There is no single-ordered whole, no perspective outside of it. Each of the foci that in total constitute experience is holographic in construing its own field of dynamic, transforming relationships.

There is a recurrent kind of expression in the *Daodejing* that ends several chapters, including this one: "By this (*yici* 以此)." The answer to the question, "How do we know that this is so?" is "By this." This question, rephrased, is "What is your perspective on this?" Hence, the question "How?" also means "Whence?" The emphasis in this Daoist epistemology of feeling, then, is neither the external environs as an object of knowledge nor the solitary knower as subject, but upon the site at which the act of knowing takes place, and the range and quality of relationships that constitute this site. Given the qualitative dimension of knowing, implicit in this question, "How?" is "How well?" That is, how productive is the knowing of the world in this way?

The *Zhuangzi* contains a passage in which this notion of "locus" or "place" is presented as being integral to what it means to know:

> Zhuangzi and Hui Shi were strolling across the bridge over the Hao river. Zhuangzi observed, "The minnows swim out and about as they please—this is the way they enjoy themselves."
>
> Huizi replied, "You are not a fish—how do you know what they enjoy?"
>
> Zhuangzi returned, "You are not me—how do you know that I don't know what is enjoyable for the fish?"

Huizi said, "I am not you, so I certainly don't know what you know; but it follows that, since you are certainly not the fish, you don't know what is enjoyment for the fish either."

Zhuangzi said, "Let's get back to your basic question. When you asked 'From where do you know what the fish enjoy?' you already knew that I know what the fish enjoy, or you wouldn't have asked me. I know it from here above the Hao river."[52]

Angus Graham, in interpreting this passage, observes that the expression *anzhi* 安知 can mean both "how do you know . . ." and "from where do you know . . ." But Zhuangzi is not just depending upon this linguistic ambiguity in order to win a sophistical argument. He has a more philosophic point to make: He wants to deny the "objectivity" of knowledge in the sense of the independence of the world known, from the knower. For Zhuangzi, knowledge is performative and a function of fruitful correlations. It is a "realizing" of a world in the sense of "making it real." And the knower and the known are inseparable aspects of this same event. Agency cannot be isolated from action. As the *Zhuangzi* says elsewhere, "There can only be genuine understanding when there is a genuine person."[53] One and one's posture or perspective is thus integral to what is known. Knowledge entails proximity. Zhuangzi's experience with the fishes makes his world continuous with the world of the fishes, and as such, his claim to knowledge is a claim to having been there.

Being continuous with the fishes and collaborating with them in the experience does not deny the fishes their difference. In fact, it is only through Zhuangzi's deference to their difference—allowing them to be what they are—that the experience can be optimally fruitful, and he can really come to know these particular fishes.

The expression "sire of the many (*zhongfu* 眾父)" balances the familiar metaphor for way-making "mother of everything that is (*wanwu zhi mu* 萬物之母)" and "the mother of the heavens and earth (*tianxia mu* 天下母)," underscoring the androgyny of the process. It should be noted that mother is the impregnated female, and father is the siring male. Each of them entails the other.

## CHAPTER 22

曲則全，枉則正，洼則盈，敝則新，少則得，多則惑。是以聖人執
一以爲天下牧。不自視，故章；不自見，故明；不自伐，故有功；
弗矜，故能長。夫唯不爭，故莫能與之爭。古之所謂曲全者，幾語
哉！誠全歸之。

Crimped then whole,
Warped then true,
Hollow then full,
Worn then new,
Modest then satisfied,
Demanding then bewildered.[54]

It is for this reason that the sages grasp oneness
To be shepherds to the world.[55]

Those who are not self-promoting are distinguished,
Those who do not show off shine,
Those who do not brag have lots to show,
Those who are not self-important are enduring.[56]

It is only because they do not contend
That none are able to contend with them.

Isn't what the ancients called "giving up the crimped for the sake of
    the whole"
Getting close to what these words mean!
This expression indeed says it all.


## *Commentary*

A major theme that runs through the *Daodejing* is the continuity
between the focus and its field. The ever-shifting focus is constituted by an intrinsic pattern of relationships that locates it within
its field of experience. These relationships are dynamic, and function in a way that can be discerned in the richness and complexity
of nature itself. That is, any predicate we use to parse a particular
focus will, in the course of the relentless, ineluctable process of
transformation, entail its opposite as well.

The moon that has waxed full will eventually wane; the stand of cypress that has grown old will gradually be renewed; the star that is burning brightly will in time give itself up to the dark night. That is, a thing can be isolated provisionally as an event punctuated in terms of its present phase, and can also be seen in terms of the process as a whole. This being the case, we understand and function within the field of experience most effectively if we can resist the discriminating and judgmental attitude toward things that comes with a partial view of them, and instead relate to them on the basis of the wholeness implicated within any phase of their process.

This insight into the "wholeness" of the process that we discern in nature where everything in due course gives rise to its opposite can be instructive in guiding the human experience. In our desires, for example, less produces more, and more, less. In our social relationships, modesty leads to distinction, and accommodation gives rise to deference.

## CHAPTER 23

希言自然。飄風不終朝，暴雨不終日。孰爲此？［天地。］天地而弗能久，又況於人乎？故從事而道者，同於道，德者，同於德；失者，同於失。同於德者，道亦德之；同於失者，道亦失之。

It is natural to speak only rarely.
Violent winds do not last a whole morning
And torrential rains do not last a whole day.
What is behind these occurrences?
[It is the heavens and the earth.]57
And if the heavens and the earth cannot sustain things for long,
How much less the human being.

Thus, those who are committed to way-making (*dao*) in what they do
Are on their way.
Those who are committed to character (*de*) in what they do
Achieve this character;

While those who lose it
Are themselves lost.[58]
Way-making is moreover enhanced[59] by those who express character,
Just as it is diminished by those who themselves have lost it.

## Commentary

Throughout the *Daodejing* there is a sustained suspicion of language. Chad Hansen has even characterized this text as being fundamentally "anti-language." In describing the evolution of Daoism, Hansen suggests that "Since language is an instrument of social control, we should avoid it—and everything that goes with it."[60] One point that Hansen is making here is well taken: "Trained discriminations are not a constantly reliable guide to behavior. Culturally motivated preferences based on those distinctions are, on the whole, unreliable. And they control us in insidious, unnatural ways."[61] But it might be a case of throwing out the baby with the befouled bathwater to extrapolate from the entirely reasonable claim about Laozi's Daoism that "as anarchy, it rebels not only against political authority, but *all social authority*" and then to infer that this means "the way to remove the authority of society totally from your life is to remove language."[62]

While we might find a palpable irony in one of the world's literary classics offering a critique of the language in which it is written, it is undeniably the case that a major theme of the *Daodejing* is that an uncritical use of language can lull us into a distorted understanding of the nature of the world in which we live. That said, language also has an important function for the Daoists who rely heavily upon oral transmission to pass on their ideas to subsequent generations. Broadly speaking, in the absence of the divorce between philosophy and rhetoric that occurred in classical Greece, there is an appreciation in the classical Chinese tradition of the performative and perlocutionary power of language that not only describes a world, but more important, commands a desired world into being. The *Daodejing* is not an exception to this sensibility.

What then is the Daoist reticence in the use of language? The *Daodejing* is not a discursive, expository Aristotelian treatise that, in a linear and sequential way, sets out to explain the way the world is. Rather, it is a deliberately collated and edited collage of largely rhymed wisdom literature that was drifting about in the early Chinese tradition. Michael LaFargue offers an alternative reading strategy for the *Daodejing* in suggesting that, rather than anticipating some literal, univocal interpretation for each passage, we ought to search the text empathetically for the point that it is trying to make relative to concrete life situations.[63] After all, even though empirically the claim that "a watched pot never boils" is demonstrably false, that does not diminish the saying's psychological insight for those people who are given to watching pots.

The philosophical problem that provokes the Daoist mistrust of language lies in the possibility that a misunderstanding of the nature of language has the potential to promote the worst misconceptions about the flux and flow of experience in which we live our lives. There is an obvious tension between the unrelenting processual nature of experience and the function of language to separate out, isolate, and arrest elements within it. To the extent that it is the nature of language to arrest the process of change and discipline it into a coherent, predictable order, there is the likelihood that an uncritical application of language might persuade us that our world is of a more stable and necessary character than it really is.

The assumption, for example, that there is a literal language behind the metaphorical can introduce notions of permanence, necessity, and objectivity into our worldview that can have deleterious consequences. Corollary to such notions are dualistic categories, such as reality and appearance, right and wrong, good and evil, true and false, reason and rhetoric, that encourage a finality and thus a kind of dogmatism in our judgments about the world. Such assumptions in parsing our experience lead to the exclusionary prejudices familiar in foundational ways of thinking.

Of course, the alternative to this "myth of the given" foundationalism is not its twin: a divisive and intolerant relativism that promises a different yet equally final judgment for each discrete person or community. In the Daoist processual worldview, there are not the gaps in experience that would permit either an exclusive foundationalism or an equally exclusive relativism. The ethos of the world is not a given, but an ecological achievement that is increased or diminished by human participation and behavior. Morality, then, is an ongoing negotiation in which some consensual and thus appropriate good can be produced by considering the needs and possible contributions of all things concerned.

## CHAPTER 24[64]

吹者不立；自視者不章；自見者不明；自伐者無功；自矜者不長。
其在道也，曰餘食贅行，物或惡之，故有欲者弗居。

> Blowhards have no standing,
> The self-promoting are not distinguished,
> Show-offs do not shine,
> Braggarts have nothing to show,
> The self-important are here and gone.
>
> As these attitudes pertain to way-making (*dao*),
> They are called indulgence and unseemliness.
> Such excess is so generally despised
> That even those who want things
> Cannot abide it.

## *Commentary*

Arrogance is disintegrating. It is both an unrealistic obsession with the importance of one's own role and a blindness to the contributions of those around one. Ironically, it has the opposite of the desired effect. Rather than persuading the community of one's own singular worth, it turns them away in irrepressible disgust. And of course, such disgust is rationalized by those who are smug and self-important as jealousy, quite ironically inspiring an even higher opinion of themselves. Such excess, despised by most, has precious little to offer to the quality of our experience.

## CHAPTER 25

有物混成，先天地生。寂呵寥呵，獨立而不改，[周行而不殆，]可以為天地母。吾未知其名，字之曰道，吾強為之名曰大。大曰逝，逝曰遠，遠曰反。道大，天大，地大，王亦大。國中有四大，而王居一焉。人法地，地法天，天法道，道法自然。

> There was some process that formed spontaneously[65]
> Emerging before the heavens and the earth.[66]
> Silent and empty,
> Standing alone as all that is, it does not suffer alteration.[67]
> [All pervading, it does not pause.][68]
> It can be thought of as the mother of the heavens and the earth.
> I do not yet know its name (*ming*).
> If I were to style it,[69]
> I would call it way-making (*dao*).
> And if forced to give it a name,
> I would call it grand.
> Being grand, it is called passing,
> Passing, it is called distancing.
> Distancing, it is called returning.
>
> Way-making is grand,
> The heavens (*tian*) are grand,
> The earth is grand,
> And the king is also grand.
> Within our territories
> There are four "grandees"
> And the king occupies one of them.
>
> Human beings emulate the earth,
> The earth emulates the heavens,
> The heavens emulate way-making,
> And way-making emulates what is spontaneously so (*ziran*).

## Commentary

Among other things, this chapter represents a valiant although self-consciously inadequate attempt to do what Wittgenstein says cannot be done. According to Wittgenstein, one cannot predicate the whole. That is, one cannot say that the totality of things is either large or small if there is nothing beyond it with which to compare.

The ongoing process of experience predates the configuration of our cosmology and our terms of understanding it. A familiar interpretation of this chapter is that it offers one of the earliest Chinese cosmogonies, referencing some primal origin behind the discriminations of our everyday world. This reading becomes problematic if we think in terms of some initial beginning that is independent of the process itself. For the Daoist, the flow of experience has no beginning and no end. However, as the world continues to transform, in due course and with a sufficient passage of time, an increasingly novel world emerges that outruns and makes obsolete any earlier explanatory vocabulary.

So beyond but certainly not excluding the appropriateness of reading this chapter as an account of the ongoing process of experience, this chapter is also a description of the way in which this process in the continuing present proliferates in producing the manifold of particulars that constitute it. Diachronically, each event within this grand and fluid process emerges, is consummated in achieving the uniqueness and complexity that makes it truly distinctive and thus "distant" from its context, and then subsequently returns. As such, the process in any moment is being reconstituted by the various stages of growth and creativity that each phenomenon moves through. The process produces the events; the events produce the process.

Synchronically, then, each event when regarded in terms of its distinctness has a certain distance from its context, and when viewed in terms of its continuity with its context, has returned.

In early Chinese natural cosmology, there is no appeal to some substratum or independent metaphysical origin, no "One" behind the many. Tang Junyi offers a proposition about the ontological parity among the myriad of things expressed as "the inseparability of the one and the many, continuity and multiplicity (*yiduo bufenguan* 一多不分觀)."[70] A process worldview is one of radical contextuality, where the particular and its context are at once continuous and distinct. In the *Yijing*, this sense of continuity and discreteness is captured in the image of the four seasons that are distinct from each other and yet continuous as well:

> In their flux (*bian* 變) and their continuity (*tong* 通) the processes of nature are a counterpart to the four seasons.[71]

Just as the myriad particulars are implicated within the notion of way-making, so the myriad people are implicated within the notion of "kingship." The human experience, far from being incidental to the unfolding of the cosmos, is an integral part of its majesty.

## CHAPTER 26

重爲輕根，靜爲躁君。是以君子終日行不離其輜重。唯有環觀，燕處則超。若若何萬乘之王，而以身輕於天下？輕則失本，躁則失君。

> The heavy is the root of the light;
> Equilibrium (*jing*) is the lord of agitation.
>
> It is for this reason that the ruler[72] in traveling the entire day
> Will not take leave[73] of his heavy wagons.
> It is only when he is ensconced in familiar chambers encircled by
> watchtowers
> That he rises above such concerns.
>
> How could someone be the king of a huge state
> And treat his own person as less important than the world?
>
> If he treats his person lightly, he loses the root;
> If he becomes agitated, he loses his throne.

## *Commentary*

All polarities are reconciled in the relationship between the particular focus and its field. To use singularity and plurality as a familiar polarity, a person is certainly a unique, nonsubstitutable individual, but as a radically contextualized matrix of relationships, this same person is also a manifold of selves all implicated within this individuality. Focus and field is thus another way of declaring the inseparability of the one and the many, of continuity and multiplicity, of uniqueness (aloneness) and commonality (sharedness).

The reconciliation of polarities means that in any particular event, there is a continuity between the inconsequential and the important, between equilibrium and agitation. This being the case, the *Daodejing* insists that if small matters are not attended to, they can have cascading consequences in which equilibrium gives way to turmoil.

In giving this apothegm a political application, the text evokes the image of a royal progress in which the ruler must be unrelentingly attentive to the basics—to the provisioning supply wagons upon which the well-being of not only the ruler, but all the travelers depends. Within the walls of the state itself, the ruler's person is no different from all the other matters of concern to the court, and as such, must be given appropriate care.

This chapter might well be read together with chapters 7 and 13. If rulers treat all things with equal seriousness and respect, their own persons will be taken care of as a matter of course. The way to be rid of such personal concerns is to be rid of the distinction between one's person and the world in which we live. One both values one's person and loses one's person in a thoroughgoing integration into one's field of experience. This is what the *Zhuangzi* calls "hiding the world in the world."[74] After all, "those who begrudge their persons as though they were the world can be put in charge of the world" (chapter 13).

## CHAPTER 27

善行者，無轍迹；善言者，無瑕謫；善數者，不用籌策；善閉者，無關籥而不可啓也；善結者，無繩約而不可解也。是以聖人恆善救人；而無棄人；物無棄財。是謂恦明。故善人，善人之師；不善人，善人之資也。不貴其師，不愛其資，雖知乎大迷。是謂妙要。

Able travelers leave no ruts or tracks along the way;
Able speakers make no gaffes that might occasion reproach;
Able reckoners have no use for tallies or counting sticks;
Able sealers make no use of bolts or latches yet what they close off
     cannot be opened.
Able cinchers make no use of ropes or cords yet their knots cannot
     be undone.

It is for this reason that the sages in being really good at turning
     others to account
Have no need to reject anyone,
And in dealing with property,
Have no need to reject anything.
This is what is called following their natural acuity (*ming*).

Thus able persons are teachers of the able
While the inept provide them with raw materials.

While perhaps wise enough,
Those who fail to honor their teachers and to be sparing with their
     raw materials
Have gotten themselves utterly lost.
This is what is called being subtle and getting to the essentials.

## Commentary

True efficacy means having the acuity to take things on their own
terms and in so doing, to turn them to optimum account. The
*Daodejing* itself makes frequent reference to "natural acuity (*ming*
明)," as in chapter 16: "Using common sense is acuity, while failing to use it is to lose control." The *Zhuangzi* offers further elaboration upon the relationship between acuity and efficacy:

> Where neither "this" nor "that" has an opposite is called the hinge
> of way-making. As soon as this hinge finds its way to the center of
> the circle, it can respond without end. What is right is on an endless
> continuum, and so is what is wrong. Thus it is said: There is nothing
> like having acuity (*ming*).[75]

In the Daoist worldview, "evil" is the opposite of efficacy. It is a
failure of imagination, the inability to make the most of things, a

missed opportunity. It is the failure to recognize and appreciate the worth of both people and things, and as a consequence, to misuse them. There is no need either to pick and choose, or to squander anything. For those who are truly proficient at what they do, there is no wastage—nothing left over, no loose ends. And there is nothing beyond their own proficiency that they are dependent upon to be successful in what they do.

When something or someone measures up to the mark, they can serve as a standard. And when they fall short of it—even far short of it—they become the best reason for having a standard in the first place.

## CHAPTER 28

知其雄，守其雌，為天下谿。為天下谿，恆德不離。恆德不離，復歸嬰兒。知其白守其辱，為天下谷。為天下谷，恆德乃足。恆德乃足，復歸於樸。知其白，守其黑，為天下式。為天下式，恆德不貣。恆德不貣，復歸於無極。樸散則為器，聖人用，則為官長。夫大制無割。

Know the male
Yet safeguard the female
And be a river gorge to the world.
As a river gorge to the world,
You will not lose your real potency (*de*),
And not losing your real potency,
You return to the state of the newborn babe.

Know the clean
Yet safeguard the soiled
And be a valley to the world.
As a valley to the world
Your real potency will be ample,
And with ample potency,
You return to the state of unworked wood.

Know the white
Yet safeguard the black

And be a model for the world.
As a model for the world,
Your real potency will not be wanting,
And with your potency not wanting,
You return to the state of the limitless.

When unworked wood is split,
It is made into utensils.
When the sages are employed,
They are made into head officials.

There is no cutting, however, in the very best tailoring.

## Commentary

The continuity between polarities, a persistent theme in the *Daodejing*, is here applied specifically to gender, suggesting that the Daoist image of the most consummate and fertile person is an androgyne who has access to the full range of gender traits. A similar profile of this person is found in chapter 10: "With nature's gates swinging open and closed are you able to remain the female?" It is the river gorge of the impregnated female that gives birth to the world.

This image of the dark, moist, and seemingly vacant concavity of the birthing female is pervasive in the *Daodejing*. In chapters 6, 32, 39, and 61, this river valley image is invoked to express the idea of inexhaustible cosmic fecundity.

Again, this gender distinction has two sides. First, it represents a whole range of other dichotomies that in their breadth demarcate the rich scope of possible behaviors available to the human being: being first and last, strong and weak, hard and soft, aggressive and recessive, agitated and still, and so on. Secondly, the androgyny of the consummate person resists any exclusivity among these traits. Under different circumstances, the authentic person might seem to be either aggressive or recessive, but in fact is both at the same time.[76] While splitting up the world and making distinctions within it might seem to have a functional value, it always entails a diminution. The most effective way of cultivating order in the world invariably relies upon the power of inclusivity.

## CHAPTER 29

將欲取天下而爲之，吾見其弗得已。夫天下神器也，非可爲者也。
爲者敗之，執者失之。物，或行或隨，或熱或吹，或强或磓，或培
或墮。是以聖人去甚，去泰，去奢。

> If someone wants to rule the world, and goes about trying to do
>     so,
> I foresee that they simply will not succeed.
> The world is a sacred vessel,
> And is not something that can be ruled.
> Those who would rule it ruin it;
> Those who would control it lose it.
>
> In the way of things:
>     Some move ahead while others follow behind;
>     Some breathe to warm themselves while others breathe to cool
>         themselves down;
>     Some are strong while others are disadvantaged;[77]
>     Some accumulate while others collapse.
> It is for this reason that the sages eschew the excessive, the superlative,
>     and the extravagant.

## Commentary

The world is constituted by a boundless sumptuousness of strange and wonderful things that often contradict each other in their life-patterns. This complex tension is not disciplined into order by some external controlling hand, imposing its considered design upon experience. And yet the oppositions that exist among things in nature resolve themselves into a self-adjusting balance and harmony. The spirituality we find pervasive in nature, far from being a gift bestowed by some external source, is rather the flowering of this thriving harmony. In fact, this harmony is not only autogenerative and self-sustaining, but persists only as long as it remains free from calculated manipulation, well-intended or otherwise.

When the patterns of nature are taken as counsel for political order in the empire, they teach us that the human world too will flourish if left to its own internal impulses. Coercive interventions from "above," while perhaps temporarily efficacious, are, in the long term and in the big picture, a source of destabilization and impoverishment. It is thus that sagacious rulers stay close to the center, and simply oversee a world that can be relied upon to order itself.

## CHAPTER 30

以道佐人主，不以兵強於天下，其事好還。師之所居，楚棘生之。
[大軍之後，必有凶年。]善者果而已矣，毋以取強焉。果而毋驕，
果而勿矜，果而勿伐，果而勿得已，居是謂果而不強。物壯而老，
是謂之不道，不道蚤已。

Those who use way-making (*dao*) to minister to the ruler
Do not seek to make him the strongest in the world by force of arms.
Such a business would likely come back to haunt them.[78]
Wherever armies bivouac
Brambles and thistles will grow.[79]
[In the wake of great armies
Lean years are sure to follow.][80]

Able commanders look only to achieve the right results
Without seeing victory as a source of empowerment.
They get their results without arrogance,
They get their results without becoming self-important,
They get their results without bragging about them,
They get these results and accommodate them only as a last resort.[81]
This is called getting the right results without forcing them,[82]
And creates a situation that is likely to endure.[83]

For something to be old while in its prime
Is called a departure from the way of things.
And whatever departs from the way of things will come to an untimely end.[84]

## Commentary

To achieve enduring results in all we do, we should be consistent with the way of things. To depart from this course of action and take any situation to an extreme will only backfire on us, producing untoward consequences. A good example of this precept is the use of arms to effect order.

The *Daodejing* offers a philosophy of warfare not unlike that of the *Sunzi*. It begins from the assumption that the prosecution of war is always a losing proposition, and should be undertaken only when all other avenues of reconciliation have been exhausted. While embracing this caution, the *Daodejing* like the *Sunzi* recognizes the fact that under some circumstances we are left with no choice but to resort to arms. Still, we must look to optimizing the possibilities of the situation, even when success is only minimizing our losses. This means that force can be justified only when a failure to respond aggressively would entail a great degree of coercion.

The most able commanders do only what is necessary to restore order without attempting to parlay the temporary military gain into long-term political capital. They are fully aware that with coercion, less is better, and do not regard their unfortunate role in having to restore order a personal recommendation. While military force might be a necessary evil in overcoming a particular obstacle, it is only an interim intervention, and is totally inappropriate as a policy for sustaining lasting social and political stability.

Martial order is an oxymoron, and being an offense against the way things ought to be, it is as vulnerable to natural correction as any other monstrosity.

## CHAPTER 31

夫兵者，不祥之器也。物或惡之，故有欲者弗居。君子居則貴左，用兵則貴右，故兵者非君子之器也。兵者，不祥之器也，不得已而用之，恬淡爲上。勿美也，若美之，是樂殺人也。夫樂殺人，不可以得志於天下矣。是以吉事上左，喪事上右。是以偏將軍居左，上將軍居右，言以喪禮居之也。殺人衆，以悲哀莅之，戰勝以喪禮處之。

Military weapons are inauspicious instruments,
And are so generally despised
That even those who want things
Cannot abide them.[85]

Rulers under normal circumstances take the left side as the seat of
    honor,
But when they go to war, they honor the right.
Thus, military weapons are not the instruments of true rulers.

Military weapons are inauspicious instruments,
And so when you have no choice but to use them,
It is best to do so coolly and without enthusiasm.
Do not glorify weapons,
For to do so is to delight in killing people,
And anyone who delights in killing people
Will come up short in the world.

It is for this reason that on auspicious occasions we honor the left
    side,
While at funerals we honor the right.
Analogously, the lieutenant commander stands to the left
And the supreme commander takes up his position on the right.
This means that they are positioned as they would be at a funeral.

When the casualties are high,
Inspect the battleground with grief and remorse;
When the war is won,
Treat it as you would a funeral.

## Commentary

Coercion is anathema to human flourishing, and perhaps nothing
is a more poignant symbol of coercion than the instruments of war.
Far from being celebrated as the trappings of the strong and mighty,
weapons should be regarded for what they really are: a most unfortunate if perhaps sometimes necessary evil.

This chapter sets out to demonstrate the tragic character of war. The full human life includes a broad spectrum of experiences, some of which are occasions for celebration and others for mourning. These two extremes are marked in Chinese custom by reversing the seat of honor. That is, in those ceremonies that punctuate the happy moments, the left is honored, and in those formalities that mark the moments of grief and heartache, the right is honored. The fact that whenever the military is involved, it is the right that is the seat of honor locates warfare and all of its horrors squarely and unmistakably on the side of life's misfortunes.

Warfare ought not to be glorified. It is always a losing proposition, and there are no victors. Although on occasion unavoidable, it is nothing better than methodical state-sanctioned killing. Even in the event of victory, triumph on the killing fields should never be confused with the proper seasons of celebration, but instead should be treated as what it is: a state funeral properly marked by grief and mourning.

## CHAPTER 32

道恆無名。樸雖小，而天下弗敢臣。侯王若能守之，萬物將自賓。
天地相合，以降甘露，民莫之令而自均焉。始制有名，名亦既有，
夫亦將知止。知止所以不殆。譬道之在天下也，猶小谷之與江海
也。

Way-making (*dao*) is really nameless (*wuming*).
Although in this unworked state it is of little consequence,[86]
No one in the world[87] would dare to condescend to it.
Were the nobles and kings able to respect this,
All things (*wanwu*) would defer of their own accord.
The heavens and the earth would come together
To send down their sweet honey,[88]
And without being so ordered,
The common people would see that it is distributed equitably.

When we start to regulate the world we introduce names.
But once names have been assigned,
We must also know when to stop.
Knowing when to stop is how to avoid danger.

As an analogy to describe way-making in the world:
The small creeks flow into the rivers and seas.

## Commentary

The ongoing shaping of experience entails working with the as yet inchoate and thus seemingly insignificant phases of the process. Each step requires a quantum of imagination and inspiration that does not reference the world as it is, but flies ahead of what has already been articulated to forge a new way forward. The value of this novelty and the respect due it lies in its potential to reshape our world.

Were those who have responsibility for order in the human world sufficiently deferential to this effort to maximize the available resources, the world would respond with natural plenty and the people would cooperate with fairness in the distribution of its bounty.

In order to function effectively in managing our environment, we need distinctions. These distinctions in themselves are functional and enabling, but once established, can take on a life of their own. We quickly fall into the trap of turning names into things, so that these names identify some more real "I-know-not-what" that stands independent of the now "superficial" way in which we actually experience any particular event. We misinterpret the persistence within process as some underlying foundation of our experience. Rational structures become institutionalized and, given enough time, petrified. The regimen of values they carry with them, empowering some against others, become entrenched and uncompromising. What began as a convenience takes over, constraining the very experience it was created to facilitate, and in so doing, robs life of its creative vigor.

Some commentators have balked at the analogy offered here, worried that way-making should in fact be the larger and more expansive rivers and seas, rather than their many tributaries. The point, however, is that *dao* as the ongoing process of experience is both *in* the world and *is* the world, is both the foci and their fields. In chapter 25 we invoked Tang Junyi's characterization of this natural cosmology as "the inseparability of the one and the many, of continuity and its multiplicity (*yiduo bufenguan* 一多不分觀)" to explain how the process is both one and many at the same time, depending on which is foregrounded. Way-making is not the One behind the many, but is rather the somewhat determinate many that constitute the somewhat indeterminate and ever continuous process.

## CHAPTER 33

知人者知也，自知者明也；勝人者有力也，自勝者強也。知足者富也。強行者有志也。不失其所者久也。死而不忘者壽也。

To know others is wisdom;
To know oneself is acuity (*ming*).[89]
To conquer others is power,
To conquer oneself is strength.
To know contentment is to have wealth.

To act resolutely is to have purpose.
To stay one's ground is to be enduring.
To die and yet not be forgotten is to be long-lived.[90]

## Commentary

The radical contextualization that is a pervasive feature of Daoist philosophy entails a priority of situation over agency. That is, agency is itself an abstraction from the complex web of constitutive relations that locates one within a specific, concrete situation. Thus, "to know" is to understand fully the reflexivity and mutually shaping relationship between self and context; "to conquer" is to be in full control of oneself within the shifting conditions of the life experience.

As chapter 46 states, to be content is simply "knowing when enough is enough." This satisfaction is neither a state of mind nor the acquisition of some absolute quantum of stuff, but rather the quality of reciprocal appreciation that gives character to a specific matrix of relationships. Appreciating one's relationships requires a knowledge of oneself as well as others, and the adjustments necessary to remain self-possessed in one's interactions.

The dominant assumption in classical Chinese natural cosmology is that the energy of transformation is not invested in some external efficient principle that stands independent of its creature, but rather that this energy for change resides within the world itself. The world is autogenerative and "spontaneously so" without initial beginning and without presumptive end.

Within such a world, this notion of the correlativity of life and death is anything but mystical or obscure. Quite simply, life and death have no separate status. The absence of cosmogonic thinking means that life and death are not distinguished as events distinct from the normal, more gradual processes of change.

Important for understanding the notion of "perishing *wang* 亡" is its cognate relationship with "forgetting *wang* 忘," a relationship that is made explicit here in the *Daodejing*. There is a strong sense that real dying occurs when one is forgotten. In a cultural tradition in which persons are understood to be irreducibly social, constituted by the pattern of roles and rituals of their lives' narratives, the answer to the question What is lost and what is left? is important. As long as a person is remembered, he or she has a place and a life. The emphasis on genealogical continuity, the ethic of filiality, the cultural requisite of returning the body to the ancestors intact, the elaborate structure of Chinese funerary rites, and the role of ancestor worship as the primary religious observance are all an expression of this social memory. On the other hand, "not being around," "being exiled," and "disappearing" are all ways of dying while still being otherwise alive. Hence, it is not surprising that the two characters, "to perish *wang*" and "to be forgotten *wang*," are found in alternative readings of this chapter 33.

The thread that seems to tie these lines of the text together is that it is purpose, place, and persistence that in sum give one an enduring role as a discernible current in the unfolding flow of experience.

## CHAPTER 34

道汎呵，其可左右也。成功遂事而弗名有也，萬物歸焉而弗爲主，
[則恆，無欲也]可名於小。萬物歸焉而弗爲主，可名於大。是以聖
人之能成大也，以其不爲大也，故能成大。

Way-making (*dao*) is an easy-flowing stream[91]
Which can run in any direction.[92]

With all things accomplished and the work complete,[93]
It does not assume any proprietary claim.

Since all things (*wanwu*) offer it allegiance
And yet it does not act as master,[94]
It can be counted among things of the most minor significance.

And since all things offer it allegiance
And yet it does not act as master,
It can also be counted among things of the greatest significance.

It is thus that the capacity of the sages to become great
Is simply because they do not try to do great things.
This is why they are indeed able to be great.[95]

## Commentary

While the ongoing stream of experience has a disposition and a propensity, it has no predetermined direction. Although within this stream all things find their completion, yet there is no isolatable, efficient agency within it that claims a controlling ownership over the process. The successful maturation of each thing within experience is achieved only through a collaboration with its environing others that entails both contribution and deference.

Persons find the greatest satisfaction within their families, for example, by contributing themselves utterly to the well-being of their contextualizing relations, and at the same time, by deferring to the appropriate needs of the other members. Their personal realization and the flourishing of their families are mutually entailing and coterminous.

Ecologically, it is the ongoing investment of each participant in the process that sustains the habitat, with often the failure of any one element being significant enough to threaten the symbiosis of the system. The habitat facilitates the process only by deferring to the importance of each element within it. From this perspective, the system is merely a function of the flourishing of each participant, with the importance residing in these constituents. In fact, with each participant being a holograph of the system, there is no superordinated system at all, but only the associated living of the participants.

On the other hand, the thriving of each participant is dependent upon a conducive (rather than a controlling) environment that allows for its uninterrupted growth. It is this positive absence of control that is vital in sustaining the system. Less is indeed more.

The effective "governing" of the sage is analogous to the flourishing of an ecological habitat. The community is self-defining, with its ethos emerging out of the collaboration of its constituents. Sages are simply virtuoso coordinators, getting the most out of their populations without the imposition of any personal agenda. Their "sagacity" at its most excellent is not only uncelebrated, but even goes unannounced. Such sagacity is the spontaneous emergence of the flourishing community as it comes to be implicated in their persons as some lofty emblem of continuity. Greatness lies not in the sages themselves, but in their catalytic capacity to maximize the creative possibilities of their people. Again, for the sages, less is more. That is, from the perspective of their people, "we are spontaneously like this."

## CHAPTER 35

執大象，天下往。往而不害，安平泰。樂與餌，過客止。故道之出
言也，曰淡呵其無味也，視之不足見也，聽之不足聞也，用之不可
既也。

Seize the great image[96]
And the world will flock to you.
Flocking to you they come to no harm,
And peace and security prevails.

Passing travelers will interrupt their journey
For music and fine fare.
But were way-making (*dao*) to be put into words:
It could be said to be so bland and insipid[97] that it has no taste.

Look for it and there is nothing to see,
Listen for it and there is nothing to hear,
And yet in availing oneself of it, it is inexhaustible.

### Commentary

Seizing the great image is having an aspiration, and having the
strength of character and imagination to forge a way that leads the
human community forward to live in their most productive manner.
Those who have the vision will win the people, and in pursuing this
vision, will secure their well-being.

The central metaphor that pervades the *Daodejing* (and the
*Analects of Confucius* as well) is making our way in the world.
Many travelers along the road of life are distracted by the alluring
pleasures of the senses. But way-making fairly described does not
resolve itself into this taste or that. Drinking one's cup of experience deeply is like partaking of artesian spring water that is at once
the blandest of things, and the most delicious. Again, like spring
water, effective way-making goes unnoticed, and yet it is not only
essential to sustaining life, but without argument it is the most precious commodity in the world.

CHAPTER 36

將欲翕之，必固張之；將欲弱之，必固強之；將欲去之，必固與之；將欲奪之，必固予之。是謂微明。柔弱勝剛強。魚不可脫於淵，邦之利器不可以示人。

Whatever is gathered in
Must first be stretched out;
Whatever is weakened
Must first be made strong;
Whatever is abandoned
Must first be joined;
Whatever is taken away
Must first be given.
This is what is called the subtle within what is evident.

The soft and weak vanquish the hard and strong.
Fishes should not relinquish the depths.
The sharpest instruments of state should not be revealed to others.

## Commentary

This chapter begins by describing the mutual implication of opposites, a phenomenon that is pervasive in our experience of the world. This is the same insight we find in chapter 40: "'Returning' is how way-making moves, and 'weakening' is how it functions." Any particular situation or condition that is most potent in its inchoate beginnings ultimately and inevitably gives way to its opposite.

Some commentators follow Han Feizi in interpreting this passage as a conscious political strategy for having one's way. In wanting to accomplish great things, you initiate policy surreptitiously. On this reading, generosity is a calculated strategy used to subvert other people: You give in order to get. But such self-serving manipulation is not consistent with Daoist sensibilities.

Another interpretation might be that the mutual entailment of opposites can serve us as a caution against becoming preoccupied with one side of a situation. Such a comprehensive awareness of the ineluctable transformation of events can serve as a general precept in anticipating the eventual outcome and consequences of any particular situation.

The concluding three lines might be popular sayings that can be explained by the mutuality of antinomies. Any condition on reaching its extreme will subsequently give way to its opposite. Since the natural milieu of fishes is the deep water, for them to surrender the depths is an extreme that will precipitate disaster. State security depends upon knowledge—both what we know of our neighbors and, importantly, what they know of us. To allow one's conditions to become transparent for one's enemy invites disaster.

## CHAPTER 37

道恆無名，侯王若能守之，萬物將自化。化而欲作，吾將鎮之以無
名之樸。鎮之以無名之樸，夫將不欲。不欲以靜，天地將自正。
道　二千四百廿六

Way-making (*dao*) is really nameless (*wuming*).[98]

Were the nobles and kings able to respect this,
All things (*wanwu*) would be able to develop along their own lines.[99]

Having developed along their own lines, were they to desire to de-
    part from this,
I would realign them
With a nameless scrap of unworked wood.

Realigned with this nameless scrap of unworked wood,
They would leave off desiring.
In not desiring, they would achieve equilibrium,[100]
And all the world would be properly ordered of its own accord.[101]

(Dao *section:* 2426 characters)[102]

## Commentary

In the classical Chinese worldview, as in many others, language has power. "To name (*ming* 名)" is "to command (*ming* 命)." If you have something's name, you not only know it, but can contain it and hold it subject to your will. To invoke a name brings power and mastery with it. The custom of respecting a taboo on the names of one's elders and superiors is a reflection of this belief. To have the vocabulary of a particular area of experience, then, is to assume charge over it and to control it.

But fixed principles, closed systems, the pretense of absolutes and initial origins are intellectually and practically suffocating. Dogma, artificiality, and finality close off the openness and fresh air of new directions in thought and action.

Indeed, the flow of experience is "nameless" and self-ordering. In making our way, it is the spontaneous aspect of experience and its irreversibility that enables us to overcome the pressure to conform to those existing structures that would obstruct the ineluctable process of self-transformation. In seeking to assist in removing such constraints and to help in reestablishing an equilibrium among things, perhaps the best tool in the toolbox is the uncalibrated set-square—a nondescript scrap of unworked wood that realigns things by disaligning them.

## CHAPTER 38

上德不德，是以有德，下德不失德，是以無德。上德無爲而無以爲
也；上仁爲之而無以爲也；上義爲之而有以爲也。上禮爲之而莫之
應也，則攘臂而扔之。故失道而后德，失德而后仁，失仁而后義，
失義而后禮。夫禮者，忠信之薄也，而亂之首也。前識者，道之華
也，而愚之首也。是以大丈夫居其厚，而不居其薄；居其實，而不
居其華。故去彼取此。

It is because the most excellent (*de*) do not strive to excel (*de*)
That they are of the highest efficacy (*de*).
And it is because the least excellent do not leave off striving to excel
That they have no efficacy.[103]
Persons of the highest efficacy neither do things coercively
Nor would they have any motivation for doing so.
Persons who are most authoritative (*ren*) do things coercively

And yet are not motivated in doing so.
Persons who are most appropriate (*yi*) do things coercively
And indeed do have a motive for doing so.
Persons who are exemplars of ritual propriety (*li*) do things coercively
And when no one pays them any heed,
They yank up their sleeves and drag others along with them.

Thus, only when we have lost sight of way-making (*dao*) is there excellence,
Only when we have lost sight of excellence is there authoritative conduct,
Only when we have lost sight of authoritative conduct is there appropriateness,
And only when we have lost sight of appropriateness is there ritual propriety.

As for ritual propriety, it is the thinnest veneer of doing one's best and making good on one's word,
And it is the first sign of trouble.
"Foreknowledge" is tinsel decorating the way,
And is the first sign of ignorance.

It is for this reason that persons of consequence:
Set store by the substance rather than the veneer
And by the fruit rather than the flower.
Hence, eschewing one they take the other.

## Commentary

For the Daoist, premeditated morality is a sham. Preassigned responses are forced and, because coercion only serves to diminish the creative possibilities of a situation, they are dehumanizing. Even in the cultivation of one's own character, efforts to excel according to stipulated behaviors only compromise one's natural moral proclivities, and will not do the job. There is a fundamental distinction to be made between actions that are inspired by and conduce to the formation of character, and those that are little more than an external show of proper conduct.

Technical morality, imposed from without, is no more than a record of steady moral deterioration. The more elaborate the terms of such norms, the clearer is the indication that morality has slipped from what we do spontaneously and unconsciously as the spirit moves us, to what we do for some self-conscious reason. Morality becomes increasingly instrumentalized, reduced to a means to some ulterior end in this spiraling decline. For the Daoist, the more that conduct is choreographed in the burlesque of Confucian ritualized living, the thinner and more diluted spontaneous moral sentiments become. This contrast is captured in the last section: the gulf between substance and veneer, between fruit and flower.

This chapter joins the anti-Confucian polemic of chapters 18 and 19 in which there is real concern that the Confucian celebration of increasingly artificial moral precepts will overwhelm the unmediated expression of natural feelings. It is for this reason that the full arsenal of Confucian moral values comes under assault.

To be fair to the early Confucian tradition, the *Analects*, the *Mencius*, and the recently recovered Confucian document, *Five Modes of Proper Conduct* (五行篇), all share this purportedly Daoist concern for moral authenticity as an uncontested value.[104]

## CHAPTER 39

昔之得一者：天得一以淸；地得一以寧；神得一以靈；谷得一以盈；侯王得一以爲天下正。其致之也。謂天毋已淸將恐裂；謂地毋已寧，將恐發；謂神毋已靈，將恐歇；謂谷毋已盈，將恐竭；謂侯王毋已貴以高，將恐蹶。故必貴而以賤爲本，必高矣而以下爲基。夫是以侯王自謂孤、寡、不穀。此其賤之本與非也？故至譽無譽。是故不欲祿祿若玉。硌硌若石。

Of old there were certain things that realized oneness:
    The heavens in realizing oneness became clear;
    The earth in realizing oneness became stable;
    The numinous in realizing oneness became animated;
    The river valleys in realizing oneness became full;

The lords and kings in realizing oneness brought proper order to the world.[105]

Following this line of thinking,
We could say that if the heavens had not become clear
They may well have fallen to pieces;
We could say that if the earth had not become stable
It may well have collapsed;
We could say that if the numinous had not become animated
It may well have faded away;
We could say that if the river valleys had not become full
They may well have dried up;
We could say that if the lords and kings had not brought proper
    order to the world
They may well have stumbled and fallen from power.[106]

Thus for something to be noble it must take the humble as its root;
For something to be high it must take the low as its foundation.

It is for this reason that the lords and kings use "friendless," "unworthy,"
    and "inept" as terms to refer to themselves.[107]
This is a clear case of taking the humble as the root, is it not?

The highest renown is to be without renown.
They do not want to be precious like jade,
But common like stone.

## Commentary

Tang Junyi's use of "the inseparability of one and many, of continuity and multiplicity (*yiduo bufenguan* 一多不分觀)" to describe
Chinese natural cosmology is a good place to begin in understanding the use of "one" in this chapter. In chapter 10, we have the
passage, "In carrying about your more spiritual and more physical
aspects and embracing their oneness (*bao yi* 抱一), are you able to
keep them from separating?" And again in chapter 22 there is an
efficacy associated with "grasping oneness (*zhiyi* 執一)":[108] "the
sages grasp oneness to be shepherds to the world."

While it is easier to see things as a manifold of separate events,
it is more difficult not only to understand the "oneness" and "con-

tinuity" of the process, but to further act upon this understanding in our transactions with the world. The support that we derive from each element in our experience—the sustaining forces of the heavens and the earth, the sacredness of the numinous dimension of life, the nourishment provided by circulation of the life forces, and the security enjoyed by virtue of an appropriate political order—is due to the persistence of these lifelines within the process. What we call common sense is simply coordinating our own behavior with all that is coherent and persistent within the life experience.

One insight that is available in understanding the "oneness" and "continuity" of things is the mutual implications of opposites. The lofty are lofty only by virtue of the lowly that sustain them, and if the lofty ever forget this interdependence, they stand the real danger of toppling from prominence.

A second insight provided by an awareness of the radical continuity of things is the efficacy of inclusivity. While fame and reputation make one singular, and might raise one high above the people, the greatest renown is to be an intimate friend to the least among one's countrymen. While rare items might be precious, the basic commodities that we depend upon, such as wind and water, stone and mortar, are even more so.

## CHAPTER 40

反也者道之動也；弱也者道之用也。天下之物生于有，有生于無。

> "Returning"[109] is how way-making (*dao*) moves,
> And "weakening" is how it functions.
> The events of the world arise from the determinate (*you*),
> And the determinate arises from the indeterminate (*wu*).[110]

## Commentary

The swinging doors of the gateway open and, embarking upon its initial phase of becoming increasingly determinate, the inchoate "thing" or "event" emerges within its already determinate context.

Culminating in its full maturation, the event then begins its gradual process of decline. As the journey continues, any persisting determinate aspects are ultimately weakened and overtaken by indeterminacy, concluding this sojourn into determinacy by its return to the indeterminate.

Just as being born is a certain death sentence, any phenomenon or event in its first steps on this journey toward consummation has set off on the road home. From the very start as it makes its way forward, its movement is one of "returning." And its optimum potency is not in its consummation, but in its initial generation. From that point onward, it is a downhill slide.

## CHAPTER 41[111]

上士聞道，僅能行之；中士聞道，若存若亡；下士聞道，大笑之。弗笑不足以爲道。是以建言有之曰：「明道如曹，進道如退，夷道如纇，上德如谷，大白如辱，廣德如不足，建德如偷；質眞如渝，大方無隅，大器晚成，大音希聲；大象無形。」道褒無名，夫唯道善始且善成。

When the very best students learn of way-making (*dao*)
They are just barely able to keep to its center.[112]
When mediocre students learn of way-making
They are sporadically on it and off it.
When the very worst students learn of way-making
They guffaw at the very idea.
Were they not to guffaw at it
It would be something less than way-making.

It is for this reason that in the *Established Sayings*[113] we find it said:

Radiant way-making seems obscured,
Advancing way-making seems to be receding,
Smooth way-making seems to have bumps,[114]
The highest character (*de*) seems like a deep gorge,
The most brilliant white seems sullied,
The most broadminded character seems deficient,

The most steadfast character seems dubious,
The most pristine and authentic seems defiled.
The greatest square has no corners,
The greatest vessel is last to be attended to,
The greatest sound is ever so faint,
The greatest image has no shape.

Way-making is so profuse as to be nameless (*wuming*).[115]
It is only way-making that is as efficacious in the beginnings of things
As it is in their completion.

## Commentary

Forging a way for the world is a demanding business, and is not something that everyone is able to do. Throughout the *Daodejing*, a distinction is pursued between those of superior character and those of lesser parts. Indeed, there is a cultural elitism in Daoism that is reminiscent of classical Confucianism. It is Confucius himself who says: "The common people can be made to travel along the way, but they cannot be made to realize it" (*Analects* 8.9). Importantly, both the Confucian and the Daoist are proactive, and what makes one "common" for both of them is a lack of concentrated effort within their somewhat different regimens of self-cultivation. Said another way, what makes one "uncommon" for both Confucian and Daoist is the attainment of a disposition that conduces to optimally productive relationships, where the nature, scope, and priority given to these constitutive relationships differ respectively.

The way is always under construction. It is being built and extended by the best of every generation. But the way is both made and followed, and even when the common lot do not participate in constructing it, they can find a place along it.

We need to distinguish *dao* from classical Greek metaphysics. For Aristotle, a principle (*arche*) is 1) that from which a thing can be known, 2) that from which a thing first comes to be, or 3) that at whose will that which is moved is moved, and that which changes, changes.[116] *Dao* or way-making is anarchic or unprincipled. It is without a beginning or origin. It is the indefinite in search of definition, the unlimited requiring limitation. It is lawless, obeying no strict causal rules. As such, it is open to infinite characterizations. It is the resource from which all things come, though it is in no sense separate from that for which it is the source.

In addition to the indeterminate qualities of experience, the determinate qualities are also integral to way-making. Although without character itself, way-making is nonetheless responsible for the character of every existing thing. As the locus of all characterizations, it cannot be predicated, and if predicated, it is both the predicate and its opposite as well. If bright, then dark also; if hard, then soft also.

There is another important feature of way-making that must be noticed. Way-making is the locus of creativity, where creativity is the self-construing activity of finite events in their processes of becoming. Co-creativity is present both in their beginnings and in their consummation. This function of way-making as the site and source of creativity is discovered only in and through things. Further, as the forum of creativity, way-making must remain provisional and incomplete. Otherwise true novelty—the spontaneous, uncaused, and unexplained emergence of the new and unique— would not be possible.

## CHAPTER 42

道生一，一生二，二生三，三生萬物。萬物負陰而抱陽，中氣以爲和。天下之所惡，唯孤、寡、不穀。而王公以自名也。物或損之而益，益之而損。故人之所教，亦議而教人：故强梁者不得死，我將以爲學父。

> Way-making (*dao*) gives rise to continuity,
> Continuity gives rise to difference,
> Difference gives rise to plurality,
> And plurality gives rise to the manifold of everything that is happening (*wanwu*).

Everything carries *yin* on its shoulders and *yang* in its arms
And blends these vital energies (*qi*) together to make them harmonious (*he*).

There is nothing in the world disliked more
Than the thought of being friendless, unworthy, and inept,
And yet kings and dukes use just such terms to refer to themselves.[117]
For things, sometimes less is more,
And sometimes, more is less.

Thus, as for what other people are teaching,
I will think about what they have to say, and then teach it to others.

For example: "Those who are coercive and violent do not meet their
natural end"—
I am going to take this statement as my precept.

## Commentary

In chapter 25 we evoked Tang Junyi's characterization of the Daoist
natural cosmology as "the inseparability of the one and the many,
of continuity and multiplicity (*yiduo bufenguan* 一多不分觀)."
Daoism construes oneness and manyness as interdependent ways
of looking at the process of experience. In this chapter, *dao* is said
to engender both "one" and "many," both "continuity" and
"difference." Viewed as the creative source of all things that, at the
same time, is only experiencable through them, *dao* is both continuity and proliferation. A bare-bones reading of the opening passage of this chapter might be:

Dao engenders one,
One two,
Two three,
And three, the myriad things.

This might also be read as we have done here:

*Dao* gives rise to continuity,
Continuity to difference,
Difference to plurality,
And plurality, to multiplicity.

Since the proliferation of things are constitutive of *dao* and continuous with each other, they can be viewed several different ways: In their flux and flow they are "passing (*shi* 逝)," in their proliferation into distinct and unique particulars they are "distancing (*yuan* 遠)," and in their radical contextuality and continuity with other things they are "returning (*fan* 反)" (chapter 25).

If we chose to view this process of proliferation and differentiation from the perspective of the particular in its production of continuity, we could as legitimately claim that:

> The myriad things engender three,
> Three two,
> Two one,
> And one, *dao*.

Or, said another way:

> Multiplicity gives rise to plurality,
> Plurality to difference,
> Difference to continuity,
> And continuity to *dao*.

That is, the multiplicity of things seen from another perspective is the continuity among things: Each unique focus is holographic, entailing its contextualizing field.

*Yin* and *yang* is a vocabulary of contrast, suggesting the possible width of experience and the degree of its diversity. Particular events in the world emerge as unique combinations of this diversity. In this creative process, it is a balancing and harmonizing of extremes that is most productive. Hence, sometimes less is indeed more.

## CHAPTER 43

天下之至柔，馳騁天下之至堅。無有入於無間。吾是以知無爲之有益也。不言之敎，無爲之益，天下希能及之矣。

The softest things in the world ride roughshod over the hardest things.[118]

Only the least substantial thing can penetrate the seamless.

This is how we know that doing things noncoercively (*wuwei*) is beneficial.

Rare are those in the world who reach an understanding of the benefits of teachings that go beyond what can be said, and of doing things noncoercively.

## Commentary

The way to optimize the creative possibilities of all the elements in any particular situation is to allow them to collaborate in doing what they do noncoercively (*wuwei*). These participating elements are constituted relationally, and their most productive relationships are those in which they are able to contribute themselves fully to the shared nexus without being diminished by the friction of contentiousness. It is thus that the "softest" are in fact the hardest, and the thing that offers the least resistance penetrates the deepest.

As rehearsed in the Introduction above, the teachings of the *Daodejing* seem largely to be a collating of and an elaboration upon traditional wisdom sayings. The text does not pretend to any singular originality or radical disjunction with the ways of the past. Chapter 42 allows quite plainly: "As for what other people are teaching, I will think about what they have to say, and then teach it to others."

The notion of "teachings that go beyond what can be said" also occurs in chapter 2 where, as here, it appears in tandem with "doing things noncoercively (*wuwei*)."

The "irrelevance charge" most often leveled against philosophy is a consequence of its being out of touch with the ordinary business of the day. Philosophy can be and often is a relatively systematic body of ideas accessed by its initiates through an elaborate technical vocabulary. Such professional philosophizing is "external" to life to the extent that it is esoteric, exclusive, and introduced to students through formal instruction.

The *Daodejing* in this respect is an object lesson in what it has to teach. By contrast with "professionalized" philosophy, the *Daodejing* appeals to a rich vein of shared wisdom sedimented into the everyday lives and language of the people. The "natural" disposition of the people that can be tapped for optimum harmony and equilibrium is an aggregate of unmediated feeling transmitted from generation to generation. By invoking sayings that are widely known, and by challenging its readers to make sense of associations that it draws among these sayings, the text simply orchestrates a popular transformation inspired by the internal impulse of the tradition itself.

## CHAPTER 44

名與身孰親？身與貨孰多？得與亡孰病？甚愛必大費，多藏必厚亡。故知足不辱，知止不殆，可以長久。

Your reputation or your person—which is dearer to you?
Your person or your property—which is worth more?
Gaining or losing—which is the greater scourge?

Miserliness is certain to come at a huge cost;
The hoarding of wealth is certain to lead to heavy losses.

Therefore, those who know contentment avoid disgrace,[119]
And those who know where to stop avoid danger.[120]
They will be long-enduring.

## Commentary

Wealth and reputation are familiar preoccupations, and are frequently sought at the expense of one's own personal well-being. This chapter goes about calculating the cost of dedicating oneself to fame and fortune, and weighs such an ambition against the familiar theme of finding contentment in what you have. Chapter 46 defines contentment as simply "knowing when enough is enough." The choice is between an endless cycle of wanting and getting on the one hand, or finding satisfaction with what you have. The cycle of getting is endless because getting begets wanting, and wanting only increases with getting. Satisfaction with what you have, on the other hand, is neither the attainment of some subjective state of mind nor the acquisition of some objective standard of property, but rather an ongoing attunement of the relationships that locate one within one's natural, social, and cultural environments. Just as "trusting" is more important than "truth," so "being satisfied" is more important than "satisfaction."

## CHAPTER 45

大成若缺，其用不敝。大盈若沖，其用不窮。大直如詘，大巧如拙，大贏如絀，大辯如訥。躁勝寒，靜勝炅，清靜可以為天下正。

> What is most consummate seems defective,
> Yet using it does not wear it out.
> What is fullest seems empty,
> Yet using it does not use it up.

> What is truest seems crooked;
> What is most skillful seems bungling;
> What is most prosperous seems wanting.
> What is most eloquent seems halting.[121]

> Staying active beats the cold,
> Keeping still beats the heat.
> Purity and stillness can bring proper order to the world.

## Commentary

The first line of chapter 45 is often translated as some variation on "what is most perfect" (Lau, Waley, Karlgren, Henricks). This rendering of *dacheng* 大成 raises an interesting philosophical issue that provides an opportunity to underscore some distinctions between a substance ontology and the Daoist process cosmology. It is sometimes claimed that "perfect" is an absolute term such as "prime" or "true" that precludes modification by qualifiers of degree such as "more," "quite," or "relatively." If we accept this claim, then "perfect" as an absolute term entails finality and closure, and as such, is inappropriate for describing the always provisional consummation that we find in a process cosmology.[122]

The world-in-process that shapes and is shaped by human creativity is always open, always provisional, always changeable, always in some degree a unique disclosure. We might appeal to Gilbert Ryle's distinction between "task or process" words on the one hand, and "achievement or success" words on the other, in locating an appropriate vocabulary to discuss the never-ending story of process cosmology. In the contrast between "to study" versus "to learn," "to listen" versus "to hear," "process" words are more appropriate for describing the human "task" of continuously going beyond one's present conditions. Process words are a language of continuing disclosure and aspiration. "Success" words on the other hand are less appropriate to describe this processional sense of order because they can be construed as a vocabulary of closure and finality: "perfection," "completion," "ideal," "absolute," "eternal," "immutable," "universal," and so on.[123]

In the absence of a language of closure, we must look to the notion of "consummation" as a sensibility that allows for the continuing process to be punctuated in terms of discriminated and distinct "events." Process does not override singularity and uniqueness; on the contrary, it celebrates it.

It is the process of experience itself that is sumptuous in all respects. Because this process is fluid and creative, it is always pregnant with the vital energies of imminent transformation and incipient potentiality. Something is always about to happen. The provisional nature of experience gives the quite appropriate impression that nothing is perfect or complete. That is, something is missing and has yet to come. The most consummate thus arises out of this absence, this deficiency, this lack. It is the inconclusiveness of experience together with the bottomlessness of its possible permutations that makes the anticipation of what has yet to come so poignant and delicious.

## CHAPTER 46

天下有道，卻走馬以糞。天下無道，戎馬生于郊。罪莫大於可欲，
禍莫大於不知足；咎莫憯於欲得。故知足之足，恆足矣。

When way-making (*dao*) prevails in the world,
The finest racing steeds are used to provide manure for the fields;
But when way-making does not prevail in the world,
Warhorses are bred just outside the city walls.

There is no crime more onerous than greed,
No misfortune more devastating than avarice.
And no calamity that brings with it more grief than insatiability.

Thus, knowing when enough is enough
Is really satisfying.[124]

## Commentary

One of the central themes of the *Daodejing* is how the human need
to own, to get, to possess, throws the natural rhythms of life into
convulsions. While the horror of war is perhaps the most dramatic
consequence of wanting what you do not have, words such as
"crime," "misfortune," and "calamity" are all common consequences of greed and avarice.

A distinction is necessary between simply "desiring," which, in
itself and exercised in an appropriate way, is a natural condition of
the human experience, and the insatiable need to own as an invidi-
ous habit of living that feeds on itself. As the Buddhist scholar Pe-
ter Hershock is wont to say: The more we get, the more we want.
The better we get at getting what we want, the better we get at
wanting. But the better we get at wanting, the less we want what
we get. The trouble is, in this endless spiral, with each iteration of
the cycle of wanting and getting what we want, the wanting gets
deeper. Not only are we unable to find satisfaction in what we
have gotten, but in direct proportion to our increase in getting, our
satisfaction becomes increasingly elusive. Hence, what is truly satisfying has little to do with what we have gotten, but is simply

knowing contentment. Perhaps what is most satisfying is getting the most out of what we already have.

## CHAPTER 47

不出於戶，以知天下；不窺於牖，以知天道。其出也彌遠者，其知彌尟。是以聖人不行而知，不見而名，弗爲而成。

> Venture not beyond your doors to know the world;
> Peer not outside your window to know the way-making (*dao*) of
>     *tian*.
> The farther one goes
> The less one knows.
>
> It is for this reason that sages know without going anywhere out of
>     the ordinary,
> Understand clearly[125] without seeing anything out of the ordinary,
> And get things done without doing anything out of the ordinary.[126]

## *Commentary*

"Knowing," "seeing," and "doing" in Daoism (and early Chinese natural cosmology broadly) are always local. "Knowing" entails not only "know-how" and "know-what," but also "know-whence." That is, the world is always known from one perspective or another, and never from nowhere. Knowledge is not the subjective representation of some objective reality, but a quality of the local experience itself. It is the "realizing" of a particular kind of experience in the sense of bringing it about and making it real.

"Knowing" thus construed is achieved through responsive and efficacious participation in one's environments, and through one's full contribution at home in the local and the focal relationships that, in sum, make one who one is. In other words, making one's way in the world is not "discovered" by traveling to distant lands and experiencing strange and wonderful things, but rather is "made" by participating fully in one's defining roles and relationships.

In fact, "leaving home" effectively puts at risk precisely those specific relationships that, having been cultivated, constitute oneself as a "knowing" and "doing" perspective on the world. It is perhaps this consideration that justifies D. C. Lau's instrumental reading of the opening lines: "By not setting foot outside the door . . ." and "By not looking out of the window. . . ." This reading makes good sense of the line that follows: "The farther one goes the less one knows." It would suggest that concentrating on one's life locally is not only a desideratum for knowing the world, but is a necessary condition for it.

## CHAPTER 48

爲學者日益，聞道者日損。損之又損，以至於無爲。無爲而無不爲也。將欲取天下也恆無事。及其有事也，又不足以取天下也。

> In studying, there is a daily increase,
> While in learning of way-making (*dao*), there is a daily decrease:
> One loses and again loses
> To the point that one does everything noncoercively (*wuwei*).
> One does things noncoercively
> And yet nothing goes undone.[127]

> In wanting to rule the world
> Be always non-interfering in going about its business (*wushi*);[128]
> For in being interfering
> You make yourself unworthy of ruling the world.

## *Commentary*

The most productive activities in the correlative world of classical Daoism are a function of optimally productive relations. And since coercion as either aggressor or victim diminishes the creative possibilities of a situation, optimally productive relations are the outcome of deferential dispositions in which all members of a social and natural nexus are able to express themselves fully in their relationships. It is under such conditions that a thriving community can accomplish the most, where "the most" is defined as the unique and productively diverse character of the community itself.

At issue here are two different ways of knowing a world. Most courses of study involve an ever-expanding range of knowledge and experience. To "master" a subject means to be able to predict and control a situation within a certain domain of the human experience. Not only is the Daoist suspicious of this kind of authority as a basis for interacting with our environments, but further the Daoist is persuaded that such "knowledge" promotes attitudes of mind that frustrate its own intentions. The development of a really deferential disposition requires largely a letting go of those barriers to associative and synergistic living that prevent full participation and contribution.

Perhaps one rather obvious example of these two approaches to functioning effectively in our world is our attempt over the last century to control water on the North American continent through the construction of dams and levies. Such construction feats certainly require a sophisticated level of engineering expertise, but to the extent that there is an insufficient respect for the way in which the processes of nature work, these projects have wreaked havoc on water supply, fish stocks, and natural reserves, and have precipitated human disaster where we have built our population centers on the floodplains.

Is the Daoist a Luddite, then? The problem is not the technology but the technological mind. The familiar passage from *Zhuangzi* about the farmer's response to the use of the well-sweep is a most appropriate gloss on this very question. On hearing about the well-sweep as a more efficient substitute for his pitcher for irrigating his fields, the old farmer is incensed, and draws a straight line between the use of such contrivances and a contriving heart-and-mind. For him, the cost is too great:

> If one has a contriving heart-and-mind lodged in his breast, he will be impure, and if he is impure, his spirit will be agitated, and the way (*dao*) will not carry someone whose spirit is agitated.[129]

CHAPTER 49

聖人恆無心，以百姓之心爲心。善者善之，不善者亦善之，德善
也。信者信之，不信者亦信之，德信也。聖人之在天下也，歙歙
焉，爲天下渾心，百姓皆屬其耳目焉，聖人皆咳之。

Sages really think and feel immediately.[130]
They take the thoughts and feelings of the common people as their own.

To not only treat the able as able
But to treat the inept as able too
Is a quantum gain in ability.
To not only treat the credible as credible
But to treat those you do not trust as credible too
Is a quantum gain in credibility.

As for the presence of sages in the world, in their efforts to draw
    things together:
They make of the world one muddled mind.
The common people all fix their eyes and ears on the sages,[131]
And the sages treat them as so many children.

## Commentary

We can treat the expression *wuxin* 無心, "thinking and feeling
immediately," as a *wu*-form. Just as *wuwei* in meaning "to do things
noncoercively" is both a disposition and a quality of action, "thinking and feeling immediately" too is a sedimented habit of
engagement.

What makes the sages "sages"? Using the focus-field language,
sages are persons who through the quality of their transactions are
able to establish patterns of deference that implicate the entire population within their fields of activity. The basis of the flourishing
community is not ready-made individuals who distinguish themselves through their uncommon contributions, but rather a "functional" inchoate heart-mind emergent from productive relations. It
is through communication and associated living that the shared
knowledge, beliefs, and aspirations of individuals are formed.

Human realization is achieved, then, not through the whole-hearted participation in communal life forms, but by life in community that forms one whole-heartedly. We do not speak because we have minds, but become like-minded by speaking to one another in a communicating community. The "thoughts and feelings" of the common people describe the emergence of a heart-mind out of social transactions and effective communication. This is an optimizing process of self- and world-enlargement that is focused and consummated in the conduct of the sage. In creating community, to get the best out of the conventionally best is relatively easy; to find the best in those who have been weighed, measured, and dismissed as the least, is to get the most out of your ingredients. And it is getting the most out of your ingredients that is the very definition of sagacity.

The "immediacy" of sagacious thinking and feeling has several implications. First, the locus of sagacious thinking lies in inspiring and transforming the ordinary and routine business of the common people rather than in some "I-know-not-what" altered state of consciousness. Secondly, sagacious living in drawing together and focusing the aspirations of the community is not a process of homogenization that sacrifices uniqueness and particularity to the gods of a clarifying rationalization. It might not be "clear" why the community thinks and feels the way it does, but in its richness and complexity, it certainly feels good. And thirdly, the people are able to remain childlike and to be treated as such because there is no master narrative in place that would discipline their experience, and in so doing, make it "grown up." The unmediated potency of the child is a frequent image in the *Daodejing* (for example, chapters 10, 20, 28, and 55).

## CHAPTER 50

出生入死。生之徒，十有三；死之徒，十有三；而民生生動皆之死
地，亦十有三。夫何故也？以其生生也。蓋聞善執生者，陵行不辟
兕虎，入軍不被甲兵。兕無所揣其角，虎無所措其蚤，兵無所容其
刃。夫何故也？以其無死地焉。

In the cycle of life and death,
One third are the companions of life,
One third are the companions of death,[132]
And one third again are people who, because of their preoccupation
    with staying alive,
Move toward the execution ground with each and every step.
Now why do they do this?
Simply because of their preoccupation with staying alive.

I have heard it said that those who are good at holding on to life
Do not steer clear of rhinos and tigers when traveling in the hills,
And do not hide behind armor[133] and shields when entering the fray.
For the rhino finds nowhere to gore,
The tiger nothing to sink its claws into,
And the soldier nothing into which he can lodge his blade.
How can this be so?
Because there is not a whiff of the execution ground about them.

## Commentary

This is an important chapter in establishing a contrast between the presuppositions about life expectancy in the contemporary world, and those assumptions that attended life in classical China. Taken in their own context, the statistics offered here are probably quite accurate. Today there is an expectation that a full complement of life is some 75 or 80 years. If we turn the clock back a few generations, even in the relatively medically advanced environments of Western Europe and North America, childbirth was perilous for both infant and mother alike, not to mention the horror of plagues and pestilence that would occur at regular intervals.

It is hard to say how this precariousness of life would affect human relationships. On the one hand, such high mortality rates must have been at least a caution in the natural affection that parents would be willing to invest in their newly born children. In traditional China, there was the custom of calling infants pejorative names as a way of warding off those forces that would claim them and take them away.

On the other hand, such relentless temporality might well have made the fleeting relationship with a little life that much more precious. And when the perils of youth were successfully negotiated, a journey that reached longevity was certain to be much honored and celebrated.

The *Zhuangzi* can serve as a gloss here:

> Those who understand way-making (*dao*) certainly have a penetrating familiarity with the overall pattern of things; those who understand this pattern certainly know how to deal with contingencies. And those who know how to deal with contingencies will not find themselves harmed by other things. For those of the very best character, fire cannot burn them, water cannot drown them, heat and cold cannot harm them, birds and beasts cannot hurt them. This is not to say they don't pay any attention to such things, but rather that because they are alert to danger, secure amid changing fortunes, and careful in their undertakings, nothing is able to do them harm.[134]

## CHAPTER 51

道生之，而德畜之，物形之，而器成之。是以萬物尊道而貴德。道之尊也，德之貴也，夫莫之爵也，而恆自然也。道生之，畜之。長之，遂之，亭之毒之，養之覆之，生而弗有也，爲而弗恃也，長而弗宰也，此之謂玄德。

Way-making (*dao*) gives things their life,
And their particular efficacy (*de*) is what nurtures them.
Events shape them,
And having a function consummates them.
It is for this reason that all things (*wanwu*) honor way-making
And esteem efficacy.
As for the honor directed at way-making
And the esteem directed at efficacy,
It is really something that just happens spontaneously (*ziran*)
Without anyone having ennobled them.

Way-making gives them life and nurtures them,
Rears and develops them.

It brings them to fruition and maturation,
Nourishes and guards over them.

Way-making gives things life
Yet does not manage them.
It assists them
Yet makes no claim upon them.
It rears them
Yet does not lord it over them.
It is this that is called profound efficacy.

## Commentary

The world emerges as a collaboration between foci and their fields,
between particular events and their contexts, between one's effective character and one's way in the world, between *de* and *dao*. It is
only within the complexity of a contextualizing situation that particular events take shape and assume their productive functions.
Thus, within this process, respect is extended to both the energy of
insistent particularity and the environments that conduce to its
consummation.

While one's general field of experience is the locus within which
one finds the sustenance and shelter essential to achieve one's own
maturation, this environment in spite of its generosity does not make
proprietary or regulatory claims on the particular events that constitute it. Given that the disposition of the general field emerges out
of the expressed character of its constituents and is always construed from one perspective or another, the field itself is neither
objective nor generic, having its own profound particularity.

## CHAPTER 52

天下有始，以爲天下母。既得其母，以知其子。既知其子，復守其
母，沒身不殆。塞其兌，閉其門，終身不勤。啓其兌，濟其事，終
身不救。見小曰明，守柔曰强。用其光，復歸其明，毋遺身殃，是
謂襲常。

The world has its fetal beginning
That can be considered the mother of the world.
You have to have gotten to this mother,
Before you can understand her progeny.
And once you have understood her progeny,
If you go back and safeguard the mother,
You will live to the end of your days without danger.

Block up the openings
And shut the gateways,
And to the end of your days your energies will not be used up.[135]

But if you vent the openings
And multiply your responsibilities,
To the end of your days you will be incurable.

Making out the small is real acuity (*ming*),
Safeguarding the weak is real strength.
Taking into account the way things reveal themselves,
If you go back again and rely upon your acuity,
You will stay clear of calamities.

This is what is called according with common sense.

## Commentary

Life-experience as we know it has its fetal beginning with the mother of the world, and the offspring of this matriarch are the pageant of novel events that emerge in the unfolding of each moment. Importantly, the fetal beginning of the world is a claim about the continuing present and generational divides in an ongoing genealogy rather than about some ultimate origin or initial beginning. That is, creativity is always expressed in situ, entailing both determinate and indeterminate aspects in a never-beginning and never-ending process. It is, indeed, turtles all the way down.

If we understand the nature of experience—both its determinate aspects (the existing context) and its indeterminate source (the mother)—then we have insight into the stream of novel events as they present themselves. And an insightful appreciation of what is happening in the ongoing transformation of things is the best way to secure ourselves within this world.

The need to conserve one's vital energies and to avoid the depletion that is caused by externally induced agitation is a familiar theme in the text. This leaking away of vitality reflects a lack of insight into the nature of experience, and the consequent inability to manage relationships efficaciously.

The concluding passage really repeats the distinction necessary for insight into the character of phenomena that is made in the opening section. We must grasp the determinate world in light of its indeterminate source. The mirroring activity that we associate with the Daoist *wu*-forms is a kind of active and nurturing understanding that allows things to shine forth as themselves, both in their transitoriness and in their particularity, without mediation. One's brightness of understanding, one's acuity (*ming* 明), is a conjunction between the determinate light given off by the things and events themselves, and the indeterminate (and thus non-distorting) light that the mirroring activity itself generates as it casts the world in its best light. Again, it is this quality of appreciation that precludes any destabilizing friction in the relationships that locate one in the world.

## CHAPTER 53

使我介有知也，行於大道，唯施是畏。大道甚夷，民甚好嶰。朝甚除，田甚蕪，倉甚虛，服文采，帶利劍，厭食而資，財有餘，是謂盜夸，盜夸，非道也哉！

> With the least modicum of wit,
> The only things we have to fear in traveling the grand thoroughfare
> (*dao*)
> Are the turn-offs.
> The grand thoroughfare is perfectly level and straight
> Yet people have a great fondness for mountain trails.

Their court is impeccably clean
Yet the fields are overgrown with weeds
And the granaries stand empty.
Their clothing is embroidered and colorful
And sharp swords hang at their sides;
They are stuffed with food
And have wealth and property to throw away.
This is called highway robbery (*dao*),
Which ought not to be confused with way-making (*dao*).

## Commentary

There is a strong propensity in favor of staying on course as we make our way in the world, with lapses being largely a matter of choosing unfortunate diversions. While the high road is always the good road, people exhibit an inexplicable penchant for wandering astray on paths that are as treacherous as they are draining.

One explanation for people getting lost along the way is thus of their own making: They are tempted from the straight and narrow by beckoning byways and shortcuts. Another familiar story is captured in a pun between two different kinds of rulers: There are those "robbers (*dao* 盜)" who live an opulent life-style on the backs of the common people. They are not to be confused with proper rulers who take the lead as "way-makers (*dao* 道)."

## CHAPTER 54

善建者不拔，善抱者不脫，子孫以祭祀不絕。脩之身，其德乃眞；脩之家，其德有餘；脩之鄉，其德乃長；脩之邦，其德乃豐；脩之天下，其德乃博。以身觀身，以家觀家，以鄉觀鄉，以邦觀邦，以天下觀天下。吾何以知天下之然哉？以此。

What has been well-planted cannot be uprooted;
What is embraced tightly will not escape one's grasp;
And with one's children and grandchildren performing the custom-
    ary rites
The autumnal sacrifice will never be interrupted.

Cultivate it in your person,
And the character you develop will be genuine;
Cultivate it in your family,
And its character will be abundant;
Cultivate it in your village,
And its character will be enduring;
Cultivate it in the state,
And its character will flourish;
Cultivate it in the world,
And its character will be all-pervading.

Thus you can use your person to survey other persons,
Your family to survey other families,
Your village to survey other villages,
Your state to survey other states,
And your world to survey worlds past and yet to come.

How do I know that the world is really so?
From this.

## Commentary

Many commentators point out the resonances between this chapter and the *Great Learning* (*daxue* 大學), one of the Confucian foundational texts included in the *Four Books*. A comparison with the most relevant portion of this Confucian classic is instructive:

The ancients who sought to highlight illustrious character for the world first brought proper order to their states; seeking to bring proper order to their states, they first established parity for their families; seeking to establish parity for their families, they first cultivated their persons; seeking to cultivate their persons, they first established what was proper in their own hearts-and-minds; seeking to establish what was proper in their own hearts-and-minds, they first achieved integrity in their thoughts; seeking to achieve integrity in their thoughts, they first broadened their own understanding of things. And broadening understanding lies in getting to the bottom of things and events.

When one gets to the bottom of things and events, understanding will be as broad as it can be, and once understanding is thus broadened, one's thoughts will have integrity, and once one's thoughts have integrity, the heart-and-mind will do what is proper, and once the heart-and-mind does what is proper, the person will be cultivated, and once the person is cultivated, families will have parity, and once families have parity, the state will be properly ordered, and once the state is properly ordered, there will be peace in the world.

From the emperor down to the common folk, everything is rooted in the cultivation of one's person. There is no such thing as healthy branches when the root is rotten, and it has never happened that what is invested with importance is treated lightly, or what is treated lightly is invested with importance.

The *Daodejing* seems to be using "well-planted" and "embraced tightly" in the opening passage as a metaphor for the effective cultivation of one's personal disposition. Such personal cultivation encourages growth in every quarter of the cosmic order, and has enduring consequences for the proliferation of generation after generation of one's continuing lineage.

The *Daodejing* like the *Daxue* rehearses the concentric and mutually entailing circles through which the rippling effect of cosmic cultivation takes place, beginning here with one's own personal character and extending through the familiar social and political institutions to include the farthest reaches of the cosmos. Such overlapping and synergistic cultivation of a cosmic ethos establishes a touchstone—a standard of quality—that can be appealed to in continuing and sustaining the process.

## CHAPTER 55

含德之厚者，比於赤子。蜂蠆虺蛇弗螫，攫鳥猛獸弗搏。骨弱筋柔而握固。未知牝牡之會而朘怒，精之至也。終日號而不嗄，和之至也。知和曰常，知常曰明，益生曰祥，心使氣曰強。物壯即老，謂之不道，不道蚤已。

One who is vital in character (*de*)
Can be compared with a newborn baby.

Wasps and scorpions will not sting a baby,
Snakes and vipers will not bite him,
And birds of prey and ferocious beasts will not snatch him up.
Though his bones are soft and his sinews supple
His grip is firm.

As yet oblivious to the copulation of male and female
His member still stands erect:
Such is the height of potency.

He screams through the entire day
And yet his voice does not get hoarse:
Such is the height of harmony (*he*).

Understanding harmony is common sense,
And using common sense is acuity (*ming*).[136]
On the other hand, trying to increase one's quantum of life is certainly a bad omen,[137]
While allowing the heart-mind to use up the *qi* one has, is to overdo things.

For something to be old while in its prime
Is called a departure from the way of things (*dao*).
And whatever departs from the way of things will come to an untimely end.[138]

## Commentary

Vitality is managing one's energy effectively across the seasons of one's lifetime. The newly born child is an image of the fullness of potency: a robustness that makes it immune from environing evils. This image is instructive. What gives the baby its vigor is its capacity to respond from the center, being supple yet firm, flexible yet potent. The baby, unconsciously and without motivation, is the embodiment of harmony and equilibrium. Vitality, then, is sustaining this kind of balance in the rhythms of the day. Common sense—insight into the ordinary and everyday—is the relatively uncommon ability to optimize one's quantum of life-energy by using it up in a measured way, remaining ever responsive to the cadence of one's experience.

To try either to add to or to overspend this vitality is to introduce an element of coercion into the life process that produces the opposite effect. Persons still young can quickly become old and dry when they exhaust their resources by straining against the world.

## CHAPTER 56

知之者弗言，言之者弗知。塞其兌，閉其門，和其光，同其塵，挫其銳，解其紛，是謂玄同。故不可得而親，亦不可得而疏；不可得而利，亦不可得而害；不可得而貴，亦不可得而賤。故爲天下貴。

> Those who really understand it do not talk about it,
> And those who really talk about it do not understand it.[139]

> Block up the openings,
> Shut the gateways,[140]
> Soften the glare,
> Bring things together on the same track,
> Blunt the sharp edges,
> Untangle the knots.[141]
> This is what is called the profoundest consonance.

> Thus, there is no getting too intimate
> Or staying aloof from it;
> There is no benefiting
> Or causing it harm;
> There is no ennobling
> Or debasing it.
> It is thus the most precious thing in the world.

## Commentary

We can only assume that the subject of this chapter is way-making. In chapters 2 and 43, way-making is similarly characterized with the expression "teachings that go beyond what can be said (不言之

教)" that suggests the limitations of language in communicating adequate insight into how best to make our way in the world. This is of course a familiar refrain that begins with the very first lines of the text: "Way-making that can be put into words is not really way-making, and naming that can assign fixed reference to things is not really naming."

This chapter describes the process of effecting the most productive relationships within one's field of experience. While maintaining one's particular integrity, one comes together with other things in relationships that have no sharp edges or tangles. In this equilibrium between integrity and integration, between insistent particularity and the coordination of the shared creative opportunities that emerge, the optimization of the process of experience, like the most elegant dance or the most remarkable bronze, precludes the possibility of adding to or taking away from it. It is simply right.

## CHAPTER 57

以正治邦，以奇用兵，以無事取天下。吾何以知其然也哉？以此：
夫天下多忌諱，而民彌貧；民多利器，而邦家滋昏；人多知慧，而
奇物滋起；法物滋章，而盜賊多有。是以聖人之言曰：「我無爲，
而民自化；我好靜，而民自正；我無事，而民自富；我無欲，而民
自樸。」

Bring proper order to the state by being straightforward
And deploy the military with strategies that take the enemy by
    surprise,[142]

But in ruling the world be non-interfering in going about its business (*wushi*).[143]
How do I know that this is really so?
From the following.[144]

The more prohibitions and taboos there are in the world,
The poorer the people will be.[145]
The more sharp instruments in the hands of the common people,

The darker the days for the state.
The more wisdom hawked among the people,[146]
The more that perverse things will proliferate.
The more prominently the laws and statutes[147] are displayed,
The more widespread will be the brigands and thieves.

Hence in the words of the sages:
    We do things noncoercively (*wuwei*)
    And the common people develop along their own lines;
    We cherish equilibrium (*jing*)
    And the common people order themselves;
    We are non-interfering in our governance (*wushi*)
    And the common people prosper themselves;
    We are objectless in our desires (*wuyu*)[148]
    And the common people are of themselves like unworked wood.[149]

## Commentary

The key expression that sets the theme for this chapter is the *wu*-form, *wushi* 無事: "being non-interfering in going about the business of governing." The contrast that is established in applying the *wu*-forms to political administration is between a top-down and impositional attitude toward governing, and a bottom-up and emergent approach in which the people themselves define the terms of order. Heavy-handed rule is counterproductive, generating problems in direct proportion to the degree of interference in the authentic lives of the people. To the extent that those with political responsibility are able to leave the people to their own devices, the people will govern themselves.

Is Daoism a political anarchism? Definitely, with the proviso that there is an unquestioned assumption that rulership is a natural feature of human organization. Of course, such a presupposition about the nature of political organization is not unique to Daoism, being itself a precondition in many forms of anarchist theory.

What then is the function of sagely political leadership? Ironically from a Daoist perspective, the first occurrence in the classical corpus of the expression *wuwei*, "doing things noncoercively," belongs to the *Analects of Confucius* 15.5:

The Master said, "If anyone could be said to have effected proper order while remaining noncoercive, surely it was the sage-king Shun. What did he do? He simply assumed an air of deference and faced due south."

In the processual and relational cosmology of early China, implicated within the persons of the sage-rulers are the evolving patterns of associated living. These rulers are icons of the worlds over which they preside. Focused in their persons, they embody and lend their names to a particular generation of coherent behavior. Their very presence is an axis around which the complexity of change and multiplicity yields to persistence and coherence. As such, they have quite literally an integral role in the "inseparability of one and many, of continuity and multiplicity" that is a hallmark of this cosmology.

## CHAPTER 58

其政閔閔，其民屯屯；其政察察，其邦夬夬。禍福之所倚，福禍之所伏。孰知其極？其無正也。正復爲奇，善復爲妖。民之迷，其日固久矣！是以方而不割，廉而不刺，直而不肆，光而不耀。

When the government is at sixes and sevens,
The common people sail right along,
But when the government is everywhere vigilant
These same people are always at fault.[150]

It is upon misfortune that good fortune leans,
It is within good fortune itself that misfortune crouches in ambush,
And where does it all end?

There is no straightforward maneuver
Because the straightforward reverts to surprise
And what is going well again becomes dark and ominous.
It has been a long time now that we human beings have lost the way.

Hence be square but do not cut anyone;
Be pointed but do not pierce anyone;
Be true but do not act willfully and without restraint;
Shine forth but do not be dazzling.[151]

## Commentary

Opposites always entail each other, and can only be separated abstractly and at the risk of upsetting the rhythm of life by treating them as really separable. Enforcing order produces disorder. Attempts at overt control on behalf of one half of a dyad at the expense of the other half, whether such manipulation be political or otherwise, simply makes things worse. The more we enact and implement laws, the more lawbreakers there are on the streets and in the jails. Coercion arises in a pointless attempt to promote one antinomy over the other, pushing any situation to an extreme.

How do we respond to this never-ending spiral of reversion? If we have an understanding of the process as a whole, we can, while staying balanced at the center, anticipate the movement between opposites. While we can certainly live a robust and healthy life, we can also, in the fullness of time, enjoy a consummatory and healthy death.

Death is real and, wherever there is life, it is not far away. However, to separate death out from the life experience and inveigh against it as something to be avoided at all costs prevents us from appreciating the fragility and preciousness of life that is made possible by this same delicious temporality. Life is made meaningful by death. Death as natural closure punctuates a most particular event in the ongoing transformation of things. Properly understood, a healthy death can be lived well and can enhance the lives of all involved; misunderstood, a resentful death can sour life and become a focus of dread and loathing that robs everyone, especially those left to carry on, of their life energy.

The *Zhuangzi* as a sustained reflection on the relationship between life and death provides many insightful anecdotes that take us beyond grief and suffering. For example:

> Not long thereafter, Ziyu fell ill, and Zisi went to ask after him. "Extraordinary!" said Ziyu. "The transformer of things continues to make me all gnarly and bent. He hunches me up so badly that my vital organs are above my head while my chin is buried in my bellybutton. My shoulders are higher than my crown, and my hunch-

back points to the heavens. Something has really gone haywire with the *yin* and *yang* vapors!" . . .

"Do you resent this?" asked Zisi.

"Indeed no," replied Ziyu. "What's to resent? If in the course of things it transforms my left arm into a cock, I'll use it to tell the time of day. If it goes on to transform my right arm into a crossbow bolt, I'll use it to shoot me an owl for roasting. If it then transforms my buttocks into wheels and my spirit into a horse, I will ride about on them without need of further transportation. . . . What's to resent?"[152]

Zhuangzi's conception of life and death is commonsensical. Empirically we know nothing of permanence and annihilation. In fact, all we know of experience is persistence within change. It is on this basis that the *Zhuangzi* concludes:

"Once we take the heavens and earth to be a giant forge and transformation to be the great ironsmith, wherever I go is just fine. Relaxed I nod off and happily I awake."[153]

## CHAPTER 59

治人、事天，莫若嗇。夫唯嗇，是以蚤服，蚤服是謂重積德。重積
德則無不克。無不克則莫知其極。莫知其極，可以有國。有國之
母，可以長久。是謂深根固柢，長生久視之道也。

For bringing proper order to the people and in serving *tian*,
Nothing is as good as husbandry.
It is only through husbandry that you come early to accept the way,
And coming early to accept the way is what is called redoubling
    your accumulation of character (*de*).
If you redouble your accumulation of character, all obstacles can be
    overcome,
And if all obstacles can be overcome, none can discern your limit.
Where none can discern your limit,
You can preside over the realm.[154]
In presiding over the mother of the realm[155]
You can be long-enduring.

This is what is called the way (*dao*) of setting deep roots and a se-
    cure base,
And of gaining long life and an enduring vision.

## Commentary

The translation of *se* 嗇 as "husbandry" is felicitous because this
character means both husbandry in the agricultural sense of growing and harvesting, and also in the economical sense of being sparing.
Both ideas are at play in this chapter. Cultivation and frugality are
major themes.

Robert Henricks (2000):84–5 analyzes the meter and rhyme
structure of the chapter, suggesting that it is quite striking in its
prominence and complexity. Perhaps one way of appreciating this
text is to take this internal rhythm as an object lesson for its message.
The last two lines summarize the positive consequence of accumulating and expending the vital energies of our lives in a properly
measured way.

Repeatedly the *Daodejing* enjoins its readers to conserve and
nourish their quantum of vital energy in both their human and
natural environments. We should never force life either in attempting to add to it or in allowing it to be unnecessarily squandered.
Building effective character and spending it as we go, we are able
to survey the lay of the land and participate fully in constructing
the way for our place and time. We secure our role and make the
most of our creative energies by expending them judiciously, always staying in step in the dance of life.

This chapter works on two levels. On one plane, it focuses on a
regimen of self-cultivation and the nourishing of one's life-force.
There is much in the text that might well be construed as formal
meditative practices. On the other hand, the text uses a political
vocabulary to suggest that on a second plane, such a personal regimen prepares one to take a leading role in establishing a vision for
the human community, and in bringing this vision to fruition.

CHAPTER 60

治大國若烹小鮮。以道莅天下，其鬼不神。非其鬼不神也，其神不傷人也。非其神不傷人也，聖人亦弗傷也。夫兩不相傷，故德交歸焉。

> Bringing proper order to a great state is like cooking a small fish.
> When way-making (*dao*) is used in overseeing the world,
> The ghosts of the departed will not have spiritual potency.
> In fact, it is not that the ghosts will not have spiritual potency,
> But rather that they will not use this potency to harm people.
> Not only will the ghosts not use their potency to harm people,
> But the sages will not harm people either.[156]
> It is because the ghosts and sages do no harm
> That their powers (*de*) combine to promote order in the world.

## *Commentary*

Bringing proper order to a great nation requires patience and a lightness of touch on the part of those who would assume this responsibility. There is a subtle and deliberate choice of language in this chapter that reflects the project it describes. The term "overseeing," for example, suggests a need for a gentle hand in concentrating and shaping the available energies to their most positive effect.

The world around us is enchanted, with its spiritual forces residing high and low in different corners of the human experience. Such power, potentially both pernicious and benign, can be a source of either benefit or tremendous harm, depending upon how it is directed. This reservoir of spiritual potency is available to promote the flourishing community, which is to say that it can be channeled to maximum advantage by using it to forge a way forward for the community. Such way-making brings with it an awareness that these raw concentrations of power are both potent and fragile, and that interacting productively with them can only proceed with alertness and enormous care.

## CHAPTER 61

大邦者下流也，天下之牝也，天下之交也。牝恆以靜勝牡，爲其靜
也，故宜爲下也。故大邦以下小邦，則取小邦；小邦以下大邦，則
取於大邦。故或下以取，或下而取。故大邦者不過欲兼畜人，小邦
者不過欲入事人。夫皆得其欲，則大者宜爲下。

A great state is like the lower reaches of water's downward flow.
It is the female of the world.

In the intercourse of the world,
The female is always able to use her equilibrium (*jing*) to best the
    male.
It is this equilibrium that places her properly underneath.

Hence if the great state is able to get underneath the small state,
It can rule the small state;
If the small state is able to get underneath the large state,
It can get to be ruled by the large state.[157]
Hence some get underneath in order to rule
And some get underneath in order to be ruled.

Now, the great state wants no more than to win over the other state
    and tend to it,
While the small state wants no more than to offer the other state its
    services.
If they are both getting what they want in the relationship,
Then it is fitting for the great state to take the lower position.

### Commentary

The theme of this chapter is not to set a contrast between an
essentialized male and female, but is rather a reflection upon how
modesty is the best way to maintain a fruitful relationship between
the sexes. The great state is compared to the lower reaches of a
river that is a confluence of all of the streams that flow into it at its
higher levels. What it brings to the relationship is its greatness: that
is, an abundance of vital energy.

Importantly, the female does not bring a stillness or passivity to her relationship with the powerful male, but an achieved equilibrium, an "underneath." As we see in chapter 6 and elsewhere, she is the river valley. Her deference is a function of her capacity to accommodate and stabilize the relationship by drawing the energy into her emptiness. She "bests" the male by being able to absorb and reinvest any excess energy in her reproductive role.

Both the great and the small state understand that "ruling" and "being ruled" (literally, "taking" and "being taken") is a fiduciary relationship justified by the quality of care and service that is invested in it. While it is vitally important that equilibrium is maintained in the small state being ruled by the great state, it is perhaps more difficult and yet essential that coercion does not surface in the great state channeling its resources to rule over the small. Hence, all things being equal, it is best for the great state to have the responsibility of reclining and assuming the receptive posture.

## CHAPTER 62

道者，萬物之注也。善人之葆也，不善人之所保也。美言可以市尊，行可以加人。人之不善也，何棄之有？故立天子，置三卿，雖有拱之璧以先四馬，不若坐而進此。古之所以貴此者何也？不謂求以得，有罪以免與？故爲天下貴。

Way-making (*dao*) is the flowing together of all things (*wanwu*).

It is prized by those who are able
While safeguarding those who are inept.

Certainly fine words can be used in negotiations
And noble behavior can enable one to surpass others.
But why would we want to get rid of those who are inept?

At the coronation of the Son of *tian*
And at the inauguration of the three high ministers,
Better to respectfully present them with the tribute of this way-
    making
Than to offer up discs of jade followed by teams of horses.

Why was it that this way-making was so revered in antiquity?
Is it not said that way-making enables those who seek to get what
    they want,
And those who have done wrong to avoid retribution?
Thus it is the most valuable thing in the world.

## Commentary

Way-making as the flowing together of all things is properly prized
as the enabling context that makes everything possible. It is the
locus within which all things come to fruition. Indeed, way-making
properly pursued gets the most out of all of its tributaries, including the very thinnest stream. Within the human experience, facility
in language and conduct that is properly used might be entirely
worthy, but there is a place for those who are less proficient as
well.

Way-making in its capacity to accommodate all things is an
appropriate model of rulership, and would be much more valuable
to those taking on political responsibility than the usual expensive
yet largely worthless symbols of office. After all, it is from way-
making that the rulers can learn the tolerance and compassion necessary to find a place in community for all of their people, however
humble and inept the lowest might be. And there is fair recognition
that comforting the least among us and surviving through the most
trying of times are occasions for those who are better off to grow in
greatness. Those who are suffering provide those more fortunate
the precious opportunity to be generous and share what they have.

From time immemorial, way-making has been an object of continuing reverence. It is a term of art that attempts to capture the
endless natural processes that yield up the bounty of the earth, the
wondrous human cycle that reproduces the beauty of its own kind,
and the accumulating cultural artifacts and institutions that enchant the world. At the same time, way-making as a healer and as
hope for those who have strayed, is forgiving. After all, in the flow
of experience, most if not almost all transgressions go unpunished.

## CHAPTER 63

為無為，事無事，味無味。大小多少，報怨以德。圖難乎其易也；
為大乎其細也。天下之難作於易；天下之大作於細。是以聖人終不
為大，故能成其大。夫輕諾必寡信，多易必多難。是以聖人猶難
之，故終於無難。

Do things noncoercively (*wuwei*),
Be non-interfering in going about your business (*wushi*),[158]
And savor the flavor of the unadulterated in what you eat.[159]

Treat the small as great
And the few as many.

Requite enmity with character (*de*).[160]

Take account of the difficult while it is still easy,
And deal with the large while it is still tiny.
The most difficult things in the world originate with the easy,
And the largest issues originate with the tiny.

Thus, it is because the sages never try to do great things
That they are indeed able to be great.[161]

One who makes promises lightly is sure to have little credibility;
One who finds everything easy is certain to have lots of difficulties.

Thus, it is because even the sages pay careful attention to such things
That they are always free of difficulties.

## Commentary

This chapter opens with several of the *wu*-forms, the implications
of which have been discussed at some length in the Introduction.
What the *wu*-forms have in common is that they describe an active
disposition that is conducive to getting the most out of the relationships that locate one within any particular situation.

By way of gloss on the less common *wu*-form, "savoring the
flavor of the unadulterated (*wuwei* 無味)," we might appeal to chapter 35, which says of way-making itself that were it "put into words,
it could be said to be so bland and insipid that it has no taste." In

culinary terms, those who have the most comprehensive and inclusive taste make no final discriminations. They just try with imagination to find a productive use for things, and to enjoy all things big and small as they come.

In chapter 12 too it says that "the five flavors destroy the palate." The relevant distinction here is between a preoccupation with instrumentalized and thus distracting sensual pleasures, and sustaining a focused way of life.

But is the Daoist a gourmet or a gourmand? Probably the best answer is Chinese cooking itself. There are distinctive characteristics of good Chinese cooking. A primary feature reflected in the never-ending menu is the stubborn attempt to optimize a finite number yet surprisingly imaginative range of ingredients. This is done by inventing any number of ways of preserving and extending them, and then combining them in different sequence, color, texture, flavor, fragrance, and so on. Use a little bit of the more pricey ingredients to flavor a lot of the more common ones. Take advantage of seasonableness. Prepare the food to provide maximum surface area and cook it so as to sear in the nutrients while minimizing the expenditure of fuel.

Importantly, getting the most out of your ingredients means keeping the garbage can empty. This effort at maximization is pursued with minimum wastage.

If "savoring the flavor of the unadulterated (*wuwei* 無味)" has an analog in Cook Ding's "doing things noncoercively (*wuwei* 無爲),"[162] it would be cooking and eating in such a way as to tease one's unique ingredients into productive relationships that allow the natural flavors to speak for themselves.

There is also the porous line between food and medicine in the Chinese world, where one gathers and consumes from one's external landscape those elements that promise a balanced and healthy body. The seemingly most innocuous resources in nature have their unique properties.

Part of getting the most out of your ingredients in the life-experience has to do with deference to detail. Understanding things in their relationship to the process as a whole enables one to anticipate a developing situation while it is still embryonic. By responding to circumstances while they are inchoate, one is able to coordinate them both positively and negatively to best effect. Said another way, Daoists would probably agree with both negative concerns about the need for full awareness such as "the devil is in the details" and "nip it in the bud," as well as more positive expressions such as "you are what you eat" and "seize the moment."

There is a passage in *Sunzi: The Art of Warfare* that shares with this chapter an insight into being doubly prepared:

> He whom the ancients called an expert in battle gained victory where victory was easily gained. Thus the battle of the expert is never an exceptional victory, nor does it win him reputation for wisdom or credit for courage. His victories in battle are unerring. Unerring means that he acts where victory is certain, and conquers an enemy that has already lost.[163]

## CHAPTER 64

其安也易持也；其未兆也易謀也；其脆也易判也；其微也易散也。爲之乎其未有，治之乎其未亂也。合抱之木，作於毫末；九成之台，作於纍土；百仞之高，始於足下。爲之者敗之；執者失之。是以，聖人無爲也，故無敗也；無執也，故無失也。民之從事也，恆於其成而敗之。故曰慎終若始，則無敗事矣。是以聖人欲不欲，而不貴難得之貨，學不學，而復衆人之所過。能輔萬物之自然而弗敢爲。

It is easy to keep one's grip when things are stable,
It is easy to plan for a situation that has yet to happen,
It is easy to snap something that is brittle,
It is easy to break something up that is just beginning.

Deal with a situation before it happens;
Bring it under control before it gets out of hand.

A tree with the girth of a person's embrace
Grows from the tiniest shoot.

A pavilion nine stories high
Rises from one basketful of earth.
A thousand foot wall
Begins from the soil under one's feet.[164]

Those who would do things ruin them;
Those who would control things lose them.[165]
Hence because the sages do things noncoercively (*wuwei*)
They do not ruin them,
And because they do not try to control things
They do not lose them.

The common people always ruin the things they do
Just on the very brink of success.
Thus it is said:
    If you are as careful at the end as you are at the start,
    You will be free of failure.[166]

It is for this reason the sages in leaving off desiring[167]
Do not prize property that is hard to come by,
And in studying not to study[168]
Return to what most people have passed over.
Although they are quite capable of helping all things (*wanwu*) fol-
    low their own course (*ziran*),
They would not think of doing so.

## Commentary

In the inseparability of continuity and multiplicity, the *Daodejing*
encourages two mutually reinforcing levels of awareness: focal and
field. The field awareness allows one to locate a particular event
within the process of reversion: the mutual entailment of opposites.
It foregrounds the relational character of the web of events, and
the symbiotic continuities that obtain among them. This kind of
insight—the capacity to see where a situation has come from and
to anticipate where it is going—precludes the habit of resolving the
fluid process of experience into isolated "things" and discourages
the one-sided and exclusive judgments that come with it.

On the other hand, focal awareness is the full appreciation of the particular foci that are constitutive of the field, and are the medium through which field awareness is entertained. A detailed understanding of the minutia within situations enables one to encourage or discourage processual fluctuations in their inchoate phase before they evolve into the overwhelming force of circumstances.

This chapter stresses the importance of focal awareness. For example, it is salutary to understand that each major event has a modest beginning, that minor changes can have cascading consequences, and that the devil and the angels, too, are in the details.

## CHAPTER 65

古之爲道者，非以明民，將以愚之也。夫民之難治也，以其知也。故以知知邦，邦之賊也；以不知知邦，邦之德也。恆知此兩者亦稽式也。恆知稽式，是謂玄德。玄德深矣，遠矣，與物反矣，乃至大順。

> Those of ancient times who engaged in way-making (*dao*)
> Did not use it to edify the common people,
> But rather to keep them foolish.
> What makes it difficult to bring proper order to the people
> Is that they already know too much.
>
> Thus to use knowledge in governing the state[169]
> Is to be a bane to that state;
> To use a lack of knowledge in governing the state
> Is to be its benefactor.[170]
>
> Those who really know the distinction between using knowledge or
>     a lack of it in governing the state will moreover become its model.
> And those who really know this model are said to be profoundly
>     efficacious (*de*).[171]
>
> Profound efficacy runs so deep and distant
> Only to turn back along with other things to reach the great flow.

## Commentary

This chapter is an example of applying Daoist natural cosmology normatively to the pursuit of an anarchistic political order. It is also a good example of how Daoism entails an epistemology of immediate feeling.

There is much here that resonates with chapters 25, 32, and 40. Cosmologically, there is this focus and its field. The insistent particularity of the focus, facilitated but not controlled by its environing others, is expressed in a process of growth and consummation in which it achieves its own distinctiveness. In this self-creating process, it "distances" itself from the flow of experience and realizes its own individuality. But this attainment is not for the particular alone. At the same time, it is a source of enrichment for its field of experience. It is in this sense that it is reflexive, always returning into the great flow of experience. Making this life significant makes the cosmos significant too.

To translate rather abstract language into a more concrete example, in a classroom experience, this student can be conceptually isolated as a particular focus within the group. As a focus, she is looking from one perspective among many at the project of the group—to try to understand Daoism better. The group, always being entertained from one perspective or another, when seen from her perspective, constitutes her particular field of experience. Whatever anyone else might contribute, she will interpret it from where she stands. Said another way, there is no "objective" group or "objective" interpretation that stands independent of the many perspectives that constitute it.

The optimum learning experience for this student is when she is provided the space to grow and realize her distinctiveness within the class environment without being overwhelmed by assumptions and precedents that are not her own. The creative potential of this student lies in the extent to which she is able to engage and realize the project at a level of concrete, unmediated feeling. While other available interpretations might stimulate her to see Daoism in one way or another, they do her and the class a distinct disservice when they close off her capacity to think independently of them. The bane of the learned commentaries is that, in their persuasiveness, they conceal novel ways to think about the text.

The self-creative process at its best is one free of coercion and constraint. To the extent that this student has distinguished herself as a particular person with her own unique interpretation, she has distanced herself from the group. But then the quality of interpretation she has achieved that foregrounds her as a particular person provides a resource for other particulars in her field of experience, thereby enhancing the creative possibilities of the group.

## CHAPTER 66

江海之所以能爲百谷王者，以其善下之也，是以能爲百谷王。是以聖人之欲上民也，必以其言下之；其欲先民也，必以其身後之。故居前而民弗害也。居上而民弗重也。天下皆樂推而弗厭也。非以其無爭與，故天下莫能與之爭。

What enables the rivers and seas to be king over all the valleys
Is that they are good at staying lower than them.
It is this that enables them to be the king of all the valleys.

This is the reason that the sages in wanting to[172] stand above the
  common people
Must put themselves below them in what they have to say;
In wanting to stand before the common people
They must put themselves behind them in their personal concerns.
Hence, they dwell above them yet the people do not find them a
  heavy burden,
They dwell in front of them yet the people do not find that they
  block the way.[173]
The entire world delights in promoting them, and never tires of do-
  ing so.

Is it not because they strive without contentiousness (*wuzheng*) that
no one in the world is able to contend with them?[174]

## Commentary

The waters from all the valleys flow down into the rivers and seas. Although the rivers and seas have noble status as the confluence of the waters of the world, they have it because they occupy the low ground. Important in this analogy is the interdependence between the many and the one, between continuity and multiplicity, between the highly and lowly stationed. Also there is the mutual entailment of opposites: The rivers and seas are noble because they occupy the low ground.

A familiar theme in the *Daodejing* is captured in the last line: "Is it not because they strive without contentiousness that no one in the world is able to contend with them?" The *wu*-form used in this rhetorical question assumes that the sages have not only an active, participatory role in bringing order to the world, but an effective one as well. The sages like the rivers and seas perform a synchronizing function that, perceived from a particular perspective, has a nobility to it. Both sages and seas do what they do naturally and well.

Far from being merely passive players buffeted about in the emerging order, both sages and seas actively coordinate the massive quantum of energy that flows into them from their constituents, and maximize its circulation to the advantage of all. Because such coordination benefits all equally, the streams and the common people defer happily to their coordinators.

What distinguishes the contribution of both the waterways and the sages is that they are able to be as effective as they are because they use accommodation rather than coercion as the basis for organizing their worlds.

## CHAPTER 67

天下皆謂我大，大而不肖。夫唯不肖，故能大若肖久矣，其細也夫！我恆有三葆，持而葆之：一曰慈，二曰儉，三曰不敢爲天下先。夫慈，故能勇；儉，故能廣；不敢爲天下先，故能爲成器長。

今舍其慈且勇，舍其儉且廣，舍其後且先，則死矣。夫慈，以戰則勝，以守則固。天將建之，如以慈垣之。

The entire world knows me[175] as "great."
I am great, and yet bear a resemblance[176] to nothing at all.
Indeed, it is only because I resemble nothing at all that I am able to
   be great.[177]
If I did bear a resemblance to something else,
For a long time now I would have been of little consequence.

I really have three prized possessions that I cling to and treasure:
   The first of these is compassion,
   The second, frugality,
   And the third is my reluctance to try to become preeminent
      in the world.

It is because of my compassion that I can be courageous;
It is because of my frugality that I can be generous;
It is because of my reluctance to try to become preeminent in the
   world that I am able to become chief among all things.

To be courageous without compassion,
To be generous without being frugal,
And to take the lead without holding back—
This is courting death.

Compassion will give you victory in waging war,
And security in defending your ground.

When nature sets anything up
It is as if it fortifies it with a wall of compassion.[178]

## Commentary

The *Daodejing* uses the modifier "great or grand (*da* 大)" to refer
both to the process of way-making itself (chapters 18, 25, 35, 41,
and 53) and to the human embodiment of way-making, the king
and the sage (chapters 25, 34, and 63). In this chapter, the first
person pronoun "I" is used as the person who embodies way-
making. It is my uniqueness that is the source of my greatness.
What then are the conditions of this uniqueness?

The text describes these conditions as "three treasures," but in fact they are three dimensions of the same temperament. A sense of frugality reflects an abiding respect for the integrity of things and an unwillingness to compromise them. It is this respect for other things that allows one to be magnanimous and accommodating in dealing with them.

And an unwillingness to contend for domination over other things is again a reluctance to sacrifice the creative possibilities of either oneself or one's environing others through recourse to coercion. It is precisely because I am noncoercive that other things defer to me in leading the way.

Finally, and most fundamentally, I must be compassionate. In the Daoist epistemology of unmediated feeling, what makes frugality and noncontentiousness appropriate for dispositional interactions is that both entail taking other things on their own terms. Compassion funds the concrete network of affective relationships that constitutes one in a particular nexus. Feeling each other is how we really know each other. All effective transactions are affective transactions, and require recourse to these invested relations.

The Daoist is not naïve. Struggle for survival is sometimes a part of the natural condition. Under such circumstances, "courage" expressed without reference to these concrete relationships is merely raw aggression, and raw aggression usually elicits a like response. Real courage is dependent upon the fellow-feeling of the army being dispatched into battle, and success in war is unlikely without it. In nature's own story, each thing emerges within a cocoon of familial feelings as a first line of defense that buffers it against a sometime hostile world.

## CHAPTER 68

善為士者，不武。善戰者，不怒。善勝敵者，弗與。善用人者，為之下。是謂不爭之德，是謂用人之力，是謂天，古之極也。

Those who are good as students are not militant;[179]
Those who are good at waging war are not belligerent;

Those who are good at vanquishing their enemies do not join issue;
Those who are good at employing others place themselves beneath
    them.[180]

This is what is called having noncontentious efficacy (*de*).
It is what is called making use of others.[181]
It is what is called an axis that is as old as the heavens.[182]

## Commentary

What is the *Daodejing*'s attitude toward war? Commentators often
cite chapters 30 and 31 as evidence that the text is anti-war, and
such an interpretation certainly has merit. But even in these overtly
pacific chapters, the guiding assumption seems to be that while
warfare is indeed deplorable, it is on occasion unavoidable. For
example, chapter 31 says that "military weapons are inauspicious
instruments, and so when you have no choice but to use them, it is
best to do so coolly and without enthusiasm." And again, in chapter 30 it allows that "able commanders . . . get these results and
accommodate them only as a last resort." The operative term here,
as in the *Sunzi* tradition,[183] is that warfare is always a losing
proposition, but sometimes you are left no other choice (*budeyi* 不
得已).

This being the case, the *Daodejing* like the military classics also
has a lot to say about the appropriate disposition to assume when
one has run out of options and must go to war. The point is that
even under war conditions, the insight that "the soft and weak
vanquish the hard and strong" (chapter 36) still applies. Hence,
"compassion will give you victory in waging war, and security in
defending your ground" (chapter 67).

The message of this chapter and the one that follows resonates
closely with the *Sunzi* tradition. For example, line two is similar to
the *Sunzi*'s caution:

主不可以怒而興軍，將不可以慍而戰。

A ruler cannot mobilize his armies in a rage; a commander cannot
    incite a battle in the heat of the moment.[184]

And line three is similar to the *Sunzi*'s advice:

是故百戰百勝非善之善者，不戰而屈人之兵善之善者。

So to win a hundred victories in a hundred battles is not the highest
    excellence; the highest excellence is to subdue the enemy's army
    without fighting at all.[185]


## CHAPTER 69

用兵有言：曰「吾不敢爲主，而爲客；吾不進寸，而退尺。」是謂
行無行，攘無臂，執無兵，扔無敵。禍莫大於無敵，無敵近亡吾葆
矣。故稱兵相若，則哀者勝矣。

There is a saying about using the military:
    I would not think of taking the offensive
    But only of defending my ground;
    I would not think of taking an inch
    But only of giving up a foot.

This is what is called
Deploying forward without bringing the troops,
Throwing a punch without raising a hand,
Grasping tightly without having a weapon in hand,
Launching an assault without confronting an enemy.

There is no calamity greater than underestimating the enemy,
For underestimating the enemy is tantamount to losing your treasures.[186]
Hence, when two armies, evenly matched, cross swords in combat,
It is the side that laments the need to do so that wins the day.


## *Commentary*

This chapter might be read as an application of nominal rather
than verbal *wu*-forms to military philosophy. Here the equipment
of war is referenced, where in each case the element that would
occasion coercion is absent. Hence you have "a troopless forward
deployment" and "a handless punch."

Being successful militarily requires awareness. A lack of aggression reflects a field awareness and the recognition that in the over-

all process there will be a reversion of opposites. Just as control produces disorder, aggression leads to enervation, and arrogance to humiliation.

But such field awareness must be coupled with a focal awareness. For example, underestimating the enemy is a failure to pursue a detailed, concrete understanding of a relationship. The cost of treating the enemy lightly is the loss of the "three prized possessions" that are described in chapter 67 as compassion, frugality, and humility. As suggested in the commentary to chapter 67, it is the disposition constituted by these three attitudes that enables one to develop and sustain robust relationships at the level of unmediated feeling. This is what is meant in chapter 26 when it is said that to treat something lightly is to lose what is most fundamental.

Thus, the army that enters the battle with remorse is the one that has the deeper understanding of the relationship between itself and its enemy, and although it would not be deploying on the battlefield unless all other options had been exhausted, it still treats the relationship with this enemy with abiding respect.

## CHAPTER 70

吾言甚易知也，甚易行也。而人莫之能知也，而莫之能行也。夫言
有君，事有宗。夫唯無知也，是以不我知。知我者希，則我貴矣。
是以聖人被褐而懷玉。

What I have to say is very easy to understand
And is very easy to carry out,
Yet there is no one in the world who is able to understand it[187]
And no one who is able to put it into practice.

Now what is said has its lineage
And what is done has its lord.
It is only because it requires unprincipled knowing (*wuzhi*)
That they do not understand me.

But if those who understand me are rare,
I am to be highly prized.

Thus the sages dress in burlap
Yet conceal jade in their bosom.

## Commentary

One important point being made here is that, however one understands the teachings of the *Daodejing* intellectually, such an appreciation needs to be authenticated in practice in order to be really understood. Saying and doing are inseparable, and knowing is "realizing" in the sense of "making real."

There is a contrast that this text wants to pursue between what it has to say, and the substance of other philosophical doctrines. Most teachings require an archaeology of ideas and values, tracing the evolution of their governing theories and concepts from generation to generation, from master to student. These doctrines are systematic by appeal to governing principles, and require a formal initiation for their transmission.

The *Daodejing* has something different to offer. In fact, it eschews precisely what doctrinaire philosophies promote. It proffers a philosophy of immediate experience captured in its *wu*-forms. The function of the *wu*-forms is to dissolve philosophical concepts and theories, and return these constrained energies as concrete feelings and the immediate experience they animate. For it is affective feeling itself rather than simply cognitive "knowledge" that is the site of knowing. Even though these teachings about how best to make our way in the world could not be more straightforward, "when the very best students learn of way-making they are just barely able to keep to its center" (chapter 41).

The *Daodejing* recommends cultivating those habits of awareness that allow us to appreciate the magic of the ordinary and everyday. Like common sense, the rareness with which such habits are invoked as a test for what we ought to do makes them a treasured commodity hidden within the bosom of only the wisest among us.

## CHAPTER 71

知不知，尚矣，不知知，病矣。是以聖人之不病，以其病病也，是
以不病。

> Knowing that one does not know is knowing at its best,
> But not knowing that one knows is suffering from a disease.[188]
> Thus, the reason the sages are free of disease
> Is because they recognize the disease as a disease.
> This is why they are not afflicted.

## *Commentary*

The attainment of "unprincipled knowing (*wuzhi* 無知)" alluded
to in the previous chapter and elsewhere in the text is the habit of
embracing experience immediately and on its own terms without
allowing preconceptions to arrest one's exploration and appreciation short of a probing depth of awareness. Unprincipled knowing
is the stubborn attempt to know particularity exhaustively. A precondition for pursuing understanding at the level of concrete, affective feeling is knowing that one does not yet know it in a such a
way. On the other hand, the greatest obstacle in the quest for this
penetrating understanding is a failure to both acknowledge and
suspend those preconceptions that pass as knowing. This is mis-
taking the fish trap for the fish. As the *Zhuangzi* observes:

> The fish trap is how you catch the fish. Having caught the fish,
> forget the trap. The snare is how you catch the rabbit. Having caught
> the rabbit, forget the snare. Words are how you capture meaning.
> Having caught the meaning, forget the words. Where am I going to
> find someone who has forgotten the words so that I can have a
> word with him?[189]

In Chinese medicine, disease (*bing* 病) usually entails a blockage of
some kind in the healthy circulation of *qi*. In this case, epistemic
disease is the blockage of access to immediate experience. The English translation, "disease," is also felicitous in suggesting a condition that interrupts free and easy intercourse.

We invariably have a set of presuppositions that we bring to experience. To think otherwise is naïve. But a self-conscious awareness of such prejudices can go a long way toward immunizing us against the hardening of the categories and epistemic sclerosis.

This chapter can be contrasted rather clearly with passage 2.17 in the *Analects of Confucius*:

> The Master said: "Zilu, shall I instruct you in what it means to know something? To know what you know and know what you do not know—this then is what it means to know."[190]

For Confucius, an awareness of the limits of what you know is a necessary condition for the unrelenting pursuit of proper education. It is this self-cultivation that is the signature of the Confucian project of self-consummation. Confucius gives a positive value to both acquired knowledge and a knowledge of limits, while for the *Daodejing*, it is acquired knowledge itself that sets limits on unmediated knowing.

This *Daodejing* chapter can also be contrasted instructively with the well-known passage in the *Apology* in which the oracle's pronouncement that Socrates is the wisest person in Athens is explained when the ever-modest Socrates is able to conclude that what the god means is "The wisest of you men is he who has realized, like Socrates, that in respect of wisdom he is really worthless."[191]

For Socrates like Confucius, a positive value is attached to both knowledge and a knowledge of limits. The important difference between Socrates and Confucius which does not really concern us here is that the content of knowledge for Socrates is the wisdom of God as opposed to human wisdom, while for Confucius, it is human wisdom itself as a continuing source of spirituality.

## CHAPTER 72

民之不畏威，則大畏將至矣。毋狹其所居，毋厭其所生。夫唯弗厭，是以不厭。是以聖人自知而不自見也，自愛而不自貴也。故去彼取此。

If the common people do not hold your authority in awe,
Then some greater authority is on its way.[192]

Do not reduce the size of their places of residence
And do not lower their standard of living.
It is only because you do not lower their standard of living
That they do not become disaffected.

It is for this reason that sages know themselves
But do not show off;
They love themselves
But are not precious.
Hence, eschewing one they take the other.

## Commentary

It is only by being people-centered that those entrusted with governing can exercise the authority appropriate to bringing proper order to the world. If the people feel mistreated and become estranged from those holding political responsibility, the days of the present regime are numbered, and political change is imminent.

Sagely rule is not a choice between self-abnegation and alienation. Proper governance is always inclusive, where the self-worth of the ruling authority is certainly in evidence, but not to the extent that it overwhelms its responsibility for the well-being of the people. For the rulers, knowing themselves is understanding and being responsive in the relationships that are implicated in their own persons; loving themselves is embracing fully the relationships that locate them within their social and political institutions. Importantly, the intrinsic relatedness of ruler and people means that self-regarding is also other-regarding.

## CHAPTER 73

勇於敢者，則殺，勇於不敢者，則活。此兩者，或利或害。天之所
惡，孰知其故？天之道，不戰而善勝，不言而善應，不召而自來，
繟而善謀。天網恢恢，疏而不失。

Those who are courageous in feats of daring will die because of
   it;
While those whose courage is tempered by prudence will preserve
   their lives.
In these two cases, courage can either put one in harm's way, or be
   beneficial.
Who can understand why *tian* despises the things that it does?[193]

*Tian*'s way (*dao*) is winning the war without going to battle,
Is answering effectively without saying a word,[194]
Is coming of its own accord without being summoned,
And is laying plans skillfully while remaining free and easy.

*Tian*'s net is cast wide,
And although coarse in its mesh, nothing slips through it.

## Commentary

The way of *tian* is the force of natural, social, and cultural conditions that give us context. That is, the patterns of nature and the
propensity of circumstance that provide the stage for the drama of
life are an appropriate guide for human conduct. These contextualizing operations are rich and complex, and yet unfold efficiently
and without any defect that does not ultimately find correction. A
distinctive feature of nature's efficacy is its *yinyang* width and
comprehensiveness. However we choose to predicate its activities,
the opposite correlation is true as well. The events of the world
around us are both light and dark, gross and fine, fast and slow.
*Tian* wins yet does not fight; it communicates yet does not speak; it
comes yet is not on call; it is designing yet is impromptu and casual;
its net is coarse yet fine enough that nothing escapes.

   On *tian*'s model, real strength entails flexibility, real wisdom
entails uncertainty, and real endurance entails patience. So, too,
real courage is most effective only when it is tempered by prudence.

## CHAPTER 74

若民恆且不畏死，奈何以殺懼之也？若民恆且畏死，而為畸者，吾
將得而殺之，夫孰敢矣？若民恆且必畏死，則恆有司殺者。夫代司
殺者殺，是代大匠斲也。夫代大匠斲者，則希不傷其手矣。

> If the common people are really not afraid of dying
> How can one frighten them by threatening to kill them?
>
> But if the people are really afraid of dying
> And know that we will arrest and kill those who do perverse things,
> Who among them would dare to do them?
>
> If the people are really afraid of dying[195]
> Then there will always be an executioner.
>
> To stand in for the executioner in killing people
> Is to stand in for the master carpenter in cutting his lumber.
> Of those who would thus stand in for the master carpenter,
> Few get away without injuring their own hands.

## Commentary

One might speculate that the kinds of differences between the two MWD documents and the WB version suggest that editors in the process of transmission were trying to bring some clarity to an otherwise ambiguous text. For example, by leaving out the phrase "if the people are really afraid of dying" and simply stating "there will always be an executioner," the WB text takes the step of resolving the ambiguity between government-sanctioned executioner and the natural executioner in favor of the latter.

But the MWD version does seem to be unproblematic as it stands. It makes basically three points. First, if the conditions of the common people become so extreme that their very survival is in question, the political authority of the state, reinforced as it is by the sanctioned violence of penal laws and punishments, will cease to have any deterrent effect on the conduct of the people. As far as they are concerned, death has become a foregone conclusion whatever course of action they take.

Secondly, political authority depends upon the people being able to exercise the choice of life over death. The better the lives of the people, the more they will fear death. It is this choice that, in the image of the executioner, introduces the very possibility of sanctioned violence, and is an encouragement for the people to refrain from untoward conduct. Political authority might set the conditions, but particular people make the choice. As the popular saying cited in chapter 42 has it, "those who are coercive and violent do not meet their natural end."

However—and this is the third point—foreclosing on the lives of people is properly the province of our natural circumstances, and any real reliance upon this corporal strategy for enforcing order will usually backfire to one's own detriment. Importantly, the *Daodejing* as a text is neither pollyannic nor categorical. Although it would embrace the precept that coercion is always a losing proposition, it leaves open the possibility that under certain and decidedly rare circumstances, sanctioned violence in the shape of capital punishment and even military intervention might be the lesser of two evils.

## CHAPTER 75

人之飢也，以其取食稅之多也，是以飢。百姓之不治也，以其上有以爲也，是以不治。民之輕死也，以其求生之厚也，是以輕死。夫唯無以生爲者，是賢貴生。

> The people's hunger is because those above[196] are eating too much
>     in taxes—
> This is why they are hungry.
> The people's lack of order is because those above manipulate them—
> This is why they are not properly ordered.
> And the people's scoffing at death is because those above are exact-
>     ing so much from life[197]—
> This is why they scoff at death.
>
> It is precisely those who do not kill themselves in living
> Who are more enlightened than those who treasure life.

## Commentary

Much of the *Daodejing* is a treatise directed at exhorting those in political office on the people's behalf. The general premise is that much if not most of the suffering of the common people is an immediate result of bad government. Excessive taxation and heavy-handed interference in the lives of the people closes the distance between the joy of life and the pain of death to a matter of little consequence.

This chapter continues the idea that forcing life and trying to get too much out of it is as bad as squandering it. As stated in chapter 55: "Trying to increase one's quantum of life is certainly a bad omen, while allowing the heart-mind to use up the *qi* one has, is to overdo things."

## CHAPTER 76

人之生也柔弱，其死也蕕仞堅強。萬物草木之生也柔脆，其死也枯槁。故曰堅強者死之徒也，柔弱者生之徒也。是以兵強則不勝，木強則梔，故強大居下，柔弱居上。

> While living, people are supple and soft,
> But once dead, they become hard and rigid cadavers.[198]
> While living, the things of this world and its grasses and trees are pliant and fragile,
> But once dead, they become withered and dry.
>
> Thus it is said: Things that are hard and rigid are the companions of death;
> Things that are supple and soft are the companions of life.
>
> For this reason,
> If a weapon is rigid it will not prevail;
> If a tree is rigid it will snap.[199]
>
> Thus, the rigid and great dwell below,
> While the supple and soft abide above.

## Commentary

The *Daodejing* is constantly challenging our uncritical assumptions with its theory of the correlative relationship among antinomies. What is living is soft and supple, and thus flexible; what is dead is hard and rigid, and thus easily broken. It is the weak that is really strong, and it is the strong that is really weak. Thus, contrary to our conventional inclinations, we should honor and defer to the weak and look down upon the strong.

## CHAPTER 77

天之道，猶張弓者也？高者抑之，下者舉之，有餘者損之，不足者補之。故天之道，損有餘而益不足。人之道則不然：損不足而奉有餘。夫孰能有餘而有以取奉於天者乎？唯有道者乎。是以聖人爲而弗有，成功而弗居也，若此其不欲見賢也。

The way of *tian* is like archers drawing their bows.
To hit something high in the air, they pull the string downward;
To hit something lower, they pull the string upward.
When they have drawn the string too far back, they let some go,
And when they have not drawn it far enough, they pull harder.[200]

The way of *tian* is also to let some go where there is excess
And to augment where there is not enough.

The way of human beings on the other hand is not like this at all.
It is instead to take away from those who do not have enough
In order to give more to those who already have too much.

Who then in having too much is able to draw on this excess to make
an offering to the world?[201]
Perhaps only those who are way-making (*dao*).

It is thus that sages act on behalf of things but do make any claim on
them,
They see things through to fruition but do not take credit for them.
It is in such a way that they refrain from making a display of their
worth.

## Commentary

The way of the world in which we live is one of sustained equilibrium. Excess and insufficiency in our various ecological environments certainly occur, but in the course of time they are righted through a process of redistribution, and balance is restored. As chapter 23 observes, "Violent winds do not last a whole morning and torrential rains do not last a whole day."

While we human beings would do well to imitate this pattern, we instead create a vicious circle in which the rich get richer, and the poor get poorer. Chapter 75 states what is a familiar refrain in the *Daodejing*: "The people's hunger is because those above are eating too much in taxes." It is only the enlightened among us who are able to coordinate fully their participation in their natural, social, and cultural environments, and who in so doing, extend the way forward for all concerned. The bonus, of course, is that while sagacious conduct conduces substantially to a thriving world, the persons responsible make no claims upon the dividends that such efficacious living produces.

## CHAPTER 78

天下莫柔弱於水，而攻堅強者莫之能先也，以其無以易之也。柔之
勝剛也，弱之勝強也，天下莫弗知也，而莫之能行也。是故聖人之
言云：「受邦之詬，是謂社稷之主；受邦之不祥，是謂天下之
王。」正言若反。

Nothing in the world is as soft and weak as water
And yet in attacking what is hard and strong,
There is nothing that can surpass it.
This is because there is nothing that can be used in its stead.

There is no one in the world that does not know
That the soft prevails over the hard
And the weak prevails over the strong,
And yet none are able to act accordingly.

This is the reason that the words of the sages say:
> Only the person who accepts invective against the state
> Is to be called its legitimate ruler;
> Only the person who accepts the misfortunes of the state
> Is to be called its true king.

Appropriate language seems contradictory.

## Commentary

The unfolding of experience is described in chapter 40 as "returning" and "weakening." Hot is "hot-becoming-cold"; hard is "hard-becoming-soft." All conditions of experience are alloyed with their opposites, and in the fullness of time, will ultimately manifest them. The young grow old, the powerful become effete, the high are laid low. In the processual cosmology of classical Daoism and in the passage of experience between the correlative *yin* and *yang* phases, words that properly capture this dynamic process certainly mean what they mean, but also mean their opposite.

An hour spent with the Oxford English Dictionary might persuade us that, in spite of our common sense assumptions about the literalness and specificity of language, this linguistic phenomenon of the inseparability of opposites—"appropriate language seems contradictory"—is not unfamiliar within the evolution of the English language itself, perhaps recalling an earlier processual sensibility. "Terrific," for example, is both "bad" and "good"; "prodigious" is both "marvelous" and "ominous"; "enormity" is both "immense" and "horrendous"; "awful" is both "unpleasant" and "inspiring."

The classic Daoist example of the inseparability of opposites is water that is at once soft and hard, weak and strong, noble and base. Although this insight into the working of things is obvious enough, it seems that only a few people are able to apply it to the way they live their lives. When this characteristic of experience is applied to the political order, for example, privilege invariably entails responsibility, and the attainment of high office is anything but an unmixed blessing.

## CHAPTER 79

和大怨，必有餘怨，焉可以爲善？是以聖人執左契而不以責於人。
故有德司契，無德司徹。夫天道無親，恆與善人。德 　三千四一

> In bringing harmony (*he*) to a situation of intense enmity,
> There is sure to be some animosity remaining.
> How can such reconciliation be considered a success?
>
> The sages, holding on to the left half of the tally,
> Do not demand payment from others.
>
> Persons of character (*de*) take charge of the tally
> While persons who are lacking in character look to calling it due.
>
> The way of *tian* shows no partiality;
> It is really on the side of people who are good in their relationships.

(De *section*: 3041 characters)[202]

## Commentary

By the time relationships have disintegrated into a situation of intense enmity, it is almost impossible to restore them. Much better to have managed these relationships through deference and accommodation in the first place. We can invoke two insights from chapter 63 that inform such a recommendation. First, "requite enmity with character," and secondly, "take account of the difficult while it is still easy, and deal with the large while it is still tiny."

The fifth chapter of the *Zhuangzi*, the title of which is "Character (*de*) Satisfies the Tally," can serve as a gloss on these lines of the *Daodejing*. This chapter in the *Zhuangzi* contains a series of anecdotes about a menagerie of mutilated cripples who, under normal circumstances and under the sway of conventional values, would be ostracized from their communities. Their disfigured physical forms, often the result of amputary punishments, would be certain grounds for societal rejection. However, having overcome discreteness and extended the influence of their character to contribute to the community, they "satisfy the tally," and not only integrate harmoniously into their societies, but further come to exercise considerable sway in establishing the importances of their respective worlds. The weight and quality of their character is such that they are important factors in the ongoing process of defining values and establishing an aesthetic and moral order.

To contextualize this rather obscure chapter of the *Daodejing*, we remember that the Daoist tradition is generally critical of the Confucian willingness to limit its concerns to the human world alone. At the same time, as in this chapter, the *Daodejing* does not preclude such a focus. It does not reject the "extension" of oneself in the development of one's humanity, but seeks to go further in extending oneself to all things by "acting authentically and without coercion (*wuwei*)." The Daoist texts, like their Confucian counterparts, see resistance to the emergence of a discrete and discriminating self as a precondition for integrative action and the extension of character (*de*) that follows from mutual accommodation. In one of the *Zhuangzi* parodies on Confucius, it describes this process:

> Yan Hui said, "I have made progress."
> "How so?" inquired Confucius.
> "I have sat and forgotten."
> Confucius, noticeably flustered, inquired:
> "What do you mean by 'sitting and forgetting'?"
> "I have demolished my appendages and body, gotten rid of my keenness of sight and hearing, abandoned my physical form, and cast off knowledge, and in so doing, have joined with the Great Extender," said Yan Hui. "This is what I call 'sitting and forgetting.'"
> . . . Confucius replied, "Please let me become your follower."[203]

Perhaps the most helpful metaphor available in the Daoist texts to elucidate this notion of "extension" is that of the tally. Relationships are like tallies shared between persons, and those with character are able to make the most of them.

In the Daoist tradition, the extension of one's character is described in more pervasive terms than in the Confucian literature. As in the Confucian tradition, at times such a person becomes the embodiment and protector of the human order, a styler of new culture, and a source of new meaning. But the Daoists take it beyond this into the natural world. The *zhenren,* the Daoist version of the consummating person, embraces the character (*de*) of the natural as well as the human environment. By becoming coextensive with the *de* of the ox, for example, Cook Ding in butchering its carcass is able to penetrate and interpret its natural lineaments and interstices without distraction, and hence is able to become an efficacious butcher; by becoming coextensive with the *de* of the wood, Carpenter Qing is responsive to the quality and potential of his materials without distraction, and hence is able to become an efficacious craftsman.[204]

The absence of a "*dis*-integrating" discrete self makes these exemplars open to the ethos of their natural environments, so that the environment contributes to them, making them potent and productive, and they contribute to their environments, interpreting and maximizing the possibilities of those things that constitute their worlds.

## CHAPTER 80

小邦寡民。使有十百人之器而勿用；使民重死而遠徙。有舟車，無所乘之；有甲兵，無所陳之。使民復結繩而用之。甘其食，美其服，樂其俗，安其居。鄰邦相望，雞狗之聲相聞，民至老死，不相往來。

You want a small state with a minimal population.

Have ready to hand weaponry for a sufficient number of military units
Yet have no recourse to use them.

Make sure that the common people take dying seriously
So that they have no taste for venturing far from home.

Though you have ships and chariots enough
Have no reason to man them;
Though you have armor and weapons enough
Have no reason to parade them.

Bring the common people back to keeping their records with knot-
ted string,
To relishing their food,
To finding beauty in their garments,
To enjoying their customs,
And to finding security in their homes.

Although your neighboring states are within eyesight
And the sounds of their dogs and cocks are within earshot,
Your people will grow old and die without having anything to do
with them.

## Commentary

Commentators are inclined to read this chapter as a primitivist
document, rejecting the distractions of living within a larger world,
and recommending a return to the simplicity of a village life un-
tainted by the trappings of "civilization." While this interpretation
might have some merit, it does not exhaust what seems to be a
more profound sensibility. After all, this small state has all of the
resources on hand, military and otherwise, to protect itself against
those undeserved yet perhaps inevitable forces that would threaten
it. The message might be pacific, but it is not naïvely pacifistic.

The Heshanggong commentary observes:

Even though the sages govern a large state, it is as though it were
small. Being frugal they do not demand too much. Even though the
people are numerous, it is as though they are few. The sages would
not think of wearing them out.

Wu Yi (2001):454 puts this commentary together with chapter 60:
"Bringing proper order to a great state is like cooking a small fish."
The point is not the absolute size of the state, but the way in which
it is governed.

There is much in this chapter that can be given a military
interpretation, locating the text squarely within the pressing concerns of the Warring States Period in which it was compiled. The
ruler must make a choice between raising and deploying an army
in conquest of foreign lands, or leaving the people to tend their

crops at home. In order to go to war, a culture must be created that glorifies combat and the spoils of victory above the risks entailed on the battlefield, thereby making light of death and injury. Of course, the recommendation offered here would seem to be that it is better to remain on the land, while at the same time prudently encouraging that preparations be made in case someone else is less deliberate and decides to bring the battle to you.

We might also read this chapter as a celebration of local living, resonating as it does with chapter 47: "Venture not beyond your doors to know the world; . . . The farther one goes the less one knows."

A life is lived most fully in the immediacy and concreteness of ordinary experience. We can only thrive by further articulating and extending ourselves within those constitutive relationships that locate us in a specific time and place. We must grow from here to there. Whatever the temptations to wealth and grandeur that lure us away from these relationships, such distractions from what we really are serve only to diminish our opportunities for consummate experience. On the other hand, a fully responsive appreciation of the local redirects us back to unmediated feeling as the real site of efficacious knowing and living.

## CHAPTER 81

信言不美，美言不信。知者不博，博者不知。善者不多，多者不善。聖人無積，既以爲人己愈有，既以予人矣己愈多。故天之道，利而不害；聖人之道，爲而不爭。

> Credible words are not eloquent;
> Eloquent words are not credible.
>
> The wise are not erudite;
> The erudite are not wise.
>
> The adept are not all-around;
> The all-around are not adept.[205]

The sages do not accumulate things.
Yet the more they have done for others,
The more they have gained themselves;
The more they have given to others,
The more they have gotten themselves.

Thus, the way of *tian* is to benefit without harming;
The way of the sages is to do without contending.[206]

## Commentary

This chapter recalls chapter 67, in which frugality, modesty, and compassion are celebrated as the mutually entailing conditions of effective living. Given the inseparability of opposites, frugality suggests a focused respect for the integrity of other things, and allows one to be magnanimous and accommodating in dealing with them. Likewise, modesty in one's language, learning, and abilities does not in any way diminish one's character, and yet opens up a space that facilitates harmonious and mutually productive relationships.

Given the inseparability of opposites, acting on behalf of others is gaining oneself, and giving to others is getting oneself. In the Daoist epistemology of unmediated feeling, frugality and the non-contentiousness that it entails is a disposition that allows one to take other things on their own terms. Indeed, it is only in feeling each other deeply that we are really able to know each other in the co-creative sense of realizing each other. All effective transactions are affective transactions, and require recourse to these invested relations.

## NOTES TO THE *TRANSLATION AND COMMENTARY*

1. Or more simply, perhaps, "Speakable way-making—this is not really way-making, nameable naming—this is not really naming." See *Yijing Dazhuan* A4 神無方易無體 "spirituality is without squareness and change is without body." Willard Peterson (1982):103 offers an interpretation of this commentary: "To have no 'squareness' is to be not susceptible of being differentiated into parts and to be not adequately delimited

by any conceptual bounds." Also see *Zhuangzi* 6: "Now understanding is dependent upon something before it can be on the mark, and yet that which it depends upon is never fixed. 夫知有所待而後當，其所待者特未定也 ."

To interpret this passage a bit closer to home, Ralph Waldo Emerson in celebrating the sacredness of one's uniqueness and one's spontaneity, decries doctrine and conformity. Indeed, "this conformity makes them not false in a few particulars, authors of a few lies, but false in all particulars. Their every truth is not quite true." Emerson (1883):56.

2. An alternative punctuation of these lines would produce a text that would read:

> The indeterminate (*wu*) is the beginning of everything that is happening;
> While the determinate (*you*) is the mother of everything that is happening.

Chapter 32, which resonates with this chapter, is consistent with the reading we have offered here.

3. Phenomena are never either atomistically discrete or complete. See *Zhuangzi* 5.2.40 and commentary on it in 63.23.58; compare Graham (1981):54 and 104, and Watson (1968):41 and 257.

4. D. C. Lau amends the MWD text here, adding the two characters 之玄 on the basis of the WB.

5. Lau (1982) reconstitutes this line as it occurs in the WB text as "as soon as everyone knows the able as the able, there is ineptness." He extrapolates on the basis of the opening line. But there is no lacuna in the MWD versions that would allow for this, and the GD text is also abbreviated in this same way.

6. The GD text has the final past particle *yi* 已 at the end of these first two phrases, giving the sense of "already." But the MWD texts both have the present progressive particle *yi* 矣 at the end of the second phrase denoting a continuing state of affairs.

7. The GD text does not have this line.

8. We are "restoring" this phrase on the basis of the WB version: The particle *ze* 則 seems to require the subordinate phrase *weiwuwei* 爲無爲.

9. Reading "to surge up (*chong* 沖)" as "empty (*zhong* 盅)."

10. Reading "the determinate (*you* 有)" as its cognate, the grammatical particle "*you* 又."

11. *Zhuangzi* 75.27.1. See Graham (1981):106 and Watson (1968):303.

12. Some commentators give *buren* 不仁 a negative value, interpret-

ing it as "not humane" (Henricks) or "ruthless" (Waley, Lau). *Ren* 仁 appears elsewhere in the *Daodejing* (chapters 8 [in the WB version], 18, and 19) as a suspect Confucian value that emerges only when genuine moral feeling has been overwritten by conventionalized rules for living.

13. The expression "straw dogs (*chugou* 芻狗)" appears in the *Zhuangzi* 37.14.31. These sacrificial objects are artifacts that are treated with great reverence during the sacrifice itself, and then after the ceremony, discarded to be trodden underfoot.

14. Some commentators suggest the "what you have within (*zhong* 中)" should be read as "your inner emptiness (*zhong* 盅)," thereby making a connection with the notion of the boundless productive capacity of emptiness found both in chapter 4 and in the bellows image in this same chapter.

15. Some commentators read the expression "*buzisheng* 不自生" as "does not give itself life," but this contradicts the "self-so-ing (*ziran* 自然)" character of nature. The rest of the chapter takes the conduct of the sages as an analogy, making the point that it is their unselfishness that enables them to realize themselves.

16. The WB text has "In giving it is how authoritatively 與善仁."

17. See *Xunzi* 28. Compare Knoblock (1994):244.

18. Compare chapters 22 and especially 39 that also discuss "grasping" and "embracing oneness."

19. The WB text has the expression "original character 元德" rather than "profoundest character 玄德" here and in chapters 51 and 65.

20. The MWD texts do not have "to make a dwelling 而為室." D. C. Lau reconstructs this line on the basis of the preceding sentence.

21. Although the five colors are specifically white, black, red, green, and yellow, the text is referring to the vast range of possibilities that the combination of these colors produces. The same is true with the five flavors and five notes.

22. This phrase also occurs in chapters 3 and 64.

23. The order of these phrases is considerably different in the WB text: 1, 5, 4, 2, and 3.

24. The WB text does not have the phrase "in the proper governing 之治也."

25. This contrast between the propriety of guaranteeing basic needs and the dangers inherent in indulging intellectual diversions resonates with a similar passage in chapter 3:

It is for this reason that in the proper governing by the sages:

They empty the hearts-and-minds of the people and fill their stomachs,

They weaken their aspirations and strengthen their bones.

26. The GD text has 何謂寵辱 "What does it mean in saying 'Favor *and* disgrace'?"

27. *Zhuangzi* 26.11.13. Compare Graham (1981):212 and Watson (1968):116.

28. James (2000):112.

29. The GD text has *shan wei shi* 善爲士 ("good as students") instead of *shan wei dao* 善爲道 ("good at forging their way in the world").

30. The GD text begins this line with *bi* 必 ("were certainly").

31. The GD text does not have this line.

32. The GD text has *shiyi wei zhi song* 是以爲之訟 ("For this reason were I to sing their praises").

33. The GD text does not have this line.

34. The GD text differs from the MWD A and B, but like the Wang Bi, begins these two lines with *shu neng* 孰能 ("who is able"), so this would read "Who is able while muddy, through stillness, to gradually become clear; who is able while settled, through agitation, to gradually come to life."

35. The GD text has *shang* 尙 ("surpass") in this sentence, meaning "surpassing fullness."

36. The GD text does not have these last two lines.

37. The GD text has *zhong* 中 ("focus," "balance") instead of *jing* 靜 ("equilibrium").

38. The GD text has *ju* 居 ("to dwell") instead of the graphically similar *wu* 吾 ("we"), and *xu* 須 ("to wait for") instead of *guan* 觀 ("to observe"), with the alternative reading "And we tarry to await their return."

39. The GD text has "the way of *tian* (天道)" rather than "things (*fu wu* 夫物)," which might be translated as:

In the way of the world in all of its profusion,

Each thing again reverts and returns to its root.

40. James (2000):76.

41. This phrase also occurs in chapter 34, but there it refers to the facility provided by the workings of *dao* rather than "the most excellent rulers."

42. This chapter in the MWD A and B and in the GD all begin with *gu* 故, usually translated "thus" or "therefore," suggesting that these lines

are a continuation from the previous chapter. On this basis, Henricks (1989:220–5 and 2000:112) suggests that 17 and 18 should be read as one unit. But *gu* is not always inferential, and in fact sometimes serves as a grammatical particle which simply separates passages.

43. The GD text does not have these two lines.

44. The six relationships referred to here are father and son, elder and younger brother, and husband and wife.

45. The GD text has *zhengchen* 正臣 ("proper ministers"), while MWD A and B have *zhenchen* 貞臣 ("upright minister"). Robert Henricks (2000: 11–15) observes that there is much discussion on the issue of anti-Confucian polemic in the contemporary academic literature. On the basis of variants in GD chapter 19, Henricks adds his own argument that while the GD text is certainly anti-Confucian in general terms, at some later date this critique was made more explicitly anti-Mencian when a vocabulary prominent in the *Mencius* ("sage [*sheng*]," and the paired terms "authoritative conduct [*ren*]" and "appropriateness [*yi*]") was introduced by some later editor. Thus, the earlier GD chapter 19 lines that read "cut off wisdom (*zhi*) and get rid of discrimination (*bian*)" and "cut off transformation and get rid of deliberation" became by 168 BCE "cut off sagacity (*sheng*) and get rid of wisdom (*zhi*)" and "cut off authoritative conduct (*ren*) and get rid of appropriateness (*yi*)."

On the other hand, to sustain Henricks's argument that the text took an anti-Mencian turn, some account would have to be given for why the signature paired *ren* and *yi* also appear here in the GD chapter 18.

46. In the GD text, this line reads 絕知棄辨 "Cut off wisdom and get rid of discrimination."

47. In the GD text, this line occurs as 絕偽棄詐 "Cut off hypocrisy and get rid of deceit," and is located as the third saying instead of as the second as in MWD texts.

48. MWD A and GD have *he* 訶 and MWD B has *he* 呵. Both characters mean "to shout at, to scold." WB has *ah* 阿 that is taken to be an informal assent, a casual "yeah."

49. The MWD and GD texts all have "what is deemed beautiful and ugly 美與惡," while the WB text has "what is deemed efficacious and defective 善與惡."

50. At the Tailao banquet, all three animals (cow, sheep, and pig) would be killed, cooked, and eaten.

51. The MWD texts have "my needs alone 吾欲獨," while the WB text

has "I alone 吾獨."

52. *Zhuangzi* 45.17.87–91; compare Graham (1981):123 and Watson (1968):188–89.

53. *Zhuangzi* 15.6.4; compare Graham (1981):84 and Watson (1968):77.

54. Compare chapter 12, which advocates modesty in one's needs. Chapter 46, too, is concerned about insatiability:

> There is no crime more onerous than greed,
> No misfortune more devastating than avarice.
>
> And no calamity that brings with it more grief than insatiability,
>
> Thus, knowing when enough is enough
> Is really satisfying.

55. The WB text has "It is for this reason that the sages embraced oneness to be model to the world 是以聖人抱一爲天下式." Compare chapters 10 and 39, which also discuss "grasping" and "embracing oneness."

56. This passage is the same as chapter 24, only stated in negative terms.

57. MWD A and B are both missing this line. On examining a copy of the original text, one observes that although there is a lacuna here, it is not large enough to include this line. Lau (1982):159 speculates plausibly that the "ditto" mark might have been left out.

58. This passage is less than clear, and has given rise to a range of interpretations. But the symbiotic relationship between way-making (*dao*) and character (*de*) is not in doubt.

59. Grammatically, *de* 德 ("character") is parallel to *shi* 失 ("to lose"), suggesting a pun with *de* 得 ("to get") to mean "gain and loss."

60. Hansen (1992):211.

61. Hansen (1992):224.

62. Hansen (1992):229.

63. LaFargue (1994):133–174.

64. The MWD texts have this chapter following chapter 21. In WB, the last two lines read 故有道者弗居 "that those engaged in way-making cannot abide it." But the MWD version appears again at the beginning of chapter 31. See note 85 below.

65. *Hun* 混 is sometimes translated as "chaos," but this puts a negative twist on an idea that is basically positive in classical Chinese. "Spontaneity" might be a more appropriate rendering. See the *Zhuangzi* story of Lord Hundun discussed in Hall and Ames (1998):65–67.

66. All of the terms for "world," such as *tiandi* 天地 and *qiankun* 乾

坤, are bipolar and correlative, entailing "copulation" in the sense of joining together. Even *yuzhou* 宇宙 as the rounded eaves and the phallic ridgepole is a sexual image. The emergence of *dao* is prior to these familiar images of conception and birthing.

67. In the WB *Daodejing* 25, the text reads:

獨立不改，周行而不殆，可以爲天下母。

In describing *dao* 道, the first phrase has been almost uniformly translated into English as some variation on "it stands solitary and does not change" (Legge, Karlgren, Lau, LaFargue, Henricks, Ames and Young, and most others). Yet we must ask what could it mean to assert that *dao* "does not change" in the "eventful" world of classical Daoism? To the contrary, *Daodejing* 40 claims explicitly 反道之動: "Returning is the movement of *dao*." We must allow that "change" is so real in fact that it is expressed in many different ways, *gai* 改 being only one of them. If the assumption is that *dao* changes, then in order to avoid what is a rather obvious equivocation, a translation of this line might need to distinguish among several different senses of "change," some of which are: 1) *bian* 變 to change gradually across time, 2) *yi* 易 to change one thing for an other, 3) *hua* 化 to transform utterly where A becomes B, 4) *qian* 遷 to change from one place to another, and 5) *gai* 改 to alter or correct or reform or improve upon x on the basis of some external and independent standard or model, Y.

In the received text, of course, it is 5) *gai* that delimits the meaning of "change." The virtue of translating *gai* 改 as "alteration" is that it introduces the notion of "alterity" to dismiss the possibility that there is something other than *dao*. A failure to make this "altering" sense of *gai* clear has led to some classic misunderstandings in translating important texts (see Ames and Rosemont [1998]:279–82), one of the most obvious perhaps being this particular passage. While "does not change" might fall within the semantic tolerance of *gai*, this translation is hard to square generally and not insignificantly with everything else that is said about *dao* in the literature. For example, it is contradicted by the line which immediately follows in the WB text: 周行而不殆: "Pervading everything and everywhere it does not pause."

The meaning here is not that *dao* "does not change," but being the *sui generis* and autopoietic totality of everything that is, *dao* is not open to alteration by appeal to something other than itself. The Wang Bi commentary observes that *dao* has no counterpart—that is, there is nothing beyond it. As we read further on in this same chapter, one thing might emulate another thing—that is, "humans emulate the earth, and the earth emulates the heavens." But because *dao* is everything, and everything is *dao*, what can it emulate? "*Dao* emulates what is spontaneously so 道法 自然."

Fukunaga Mitsuji (1968):143–5 has avoided the equivocation so prevalent in the English translations when, on the basis of the received text, he offers the *kanbun* reading: *aratamezu* "is not reformed, revised." His interpretive translation in modern Japanese is the passive-causative *kaerarezu*: "is not made to change."

The variant in the GD *Daodejing* is of some value in suggesting the intended meaning of this passage. It has 獨立不亥, reinforcing MWD B, which has 亥 with the 玉 classifier. Don Harper has suggested that 亥 is a loan for the same character with the 日 classifier which the *Shuowen* takes as equivalent to *jian* 兼 ("to be paired with"). Such a reading, "solitary it has no counterpart," is close to Wang Bi.

Alternatively, making quite a different point, 亥 with the 日 classifier can also mean "complete, all-in-all, entire," again consistent with 兼 or 備 as "the total." When we claim that *dao* is everything and everything is *dao*, we have to qualify this statement with the observation that *dao* is processual and hence underdetermined. Thus, it is described as the fecund mother of the world. Perhaps the point here is that *dao* as 自然 *ziran* ("self-so-ing") entails the emergence of spontaneous novelty, and while always "grand 大 " it is never complete. There is no finality or closure.

Or perhaps the text is making both of these points—*dao* has no counterpart and is never complete—at the same time.

68. This line, found in the received text, does not occur in either the GD or the two MWD versions. Lau restores it to the MWD text.

69. A "style" is the proper title or term of address in speaking to someone. In China it was a common practice among the literati on reaching majority at 20 years to take on and be referred to by such a name as a reflection of one's sense of oneself and one's aspirations.

70. Tang Junyi (1988):16.

71. *Yijing dazhuan* A6.

72. The WB text has "the sage 聖人."

73. The MWD B text has "does not get far away from 不遠."

74. See *Zhuangzi* 16.6.26; compare Graham (1981):86 and Watson (1968):81.

75. See *Zhuangzi* 4.2.30–1; compare Graham (1981):53 and Watson (1968):40.

76. See our discussion of androgyny in Hall and Ames (1998):79–100.

77. MWD B is missing this line, but MWD A has a lacuna that would accommodate the missing characters. Lau reconstructs it on the basis of the WB text.

78. "Backfire" captures the meaning here, but would be anachronistic. MWD A and B are missing this line, although MWD B does have the first character *qi* 其, and according to Lau (1982) and Henricks (1989), there is a lacuna that would accommodate the remaining three characters. Lau (1982) restores the line. The GD text does not have this line or the four that follow it.

79. The MWD A text has the character *chu* 楚 in this line, translated as "brambles." This character, as the name of the father of Qin Shihuang, the first emperor of the Qin, was taboo. Its presence here suggests with some certainty that it was either a copy that predates the Qin dynasty or a fair copy of a text that did. See Lau (1982):161–2.

80. These two lines occur in the WB text. Their absence in the MWD and GD texts supports the common assumption that they are interpolated commentary.

81. The language of "the able commander 善者" and "as a last resort 不得以" is reminiscent of the *Sunzi* and *Sun Bin*. See Ames (1993): 91–3, 191, and especially Lau and Ames (1996):34–5, 153. The GD text does not have this line. The WB text has "He gets these results only as a last resort 果而不得已," while the MWD texts both have "He gets these results and accommodates them only as a last resort 果而毋得已居."

82. The GD text like the MWD versions has the phrase "this is called 是謂," while the WB text does not.

83. Adding this line from the GD text: 其事好長, although it is likely a relocated version of the second line that the GD text is missing: 其事好還. Neither the WB nor the MWD versions have it.

84. These final three lines also occur in chapter 55. See Henricks (2000):15–16 for his discussion of the "bare bones" GD version of this chapter.

85. The WB text has "Fine weapons are inauspicious instruments, and are so generally despised that those who are engaged in way-making cannot abide them." Only MWD A has "who want things 有欲者" rather

than "who are engaged in way-making 有道者." The MWD B has a lacuna. The problem with overriding the MWD A version is that the same phrase occurs in chapter 24, where both MWD texts have "who want things."

86. The Guodian text has 妻, which means "legitimate wife, peer," rather than 小, which means "small, unimportant, lowly." Alternatively, Li Ling (Henricks 2000:208 n. 36) reads this as 細, meaning "delicate, subtle, of little consequence."

87. The Guodian text has "world 天地" rather than "empire 天下."

88. Arthur Waley (1934) points out that this term, literally "sweet dew 甘露," is a substance like barley sugar or honey that supposedly falls only when a kingdom is at complete peace.

89. The *Sunzi* has a passage: "He who knows the enemy and himself will never in a hundred battles be at risk." Ames (1993):96. This allusion might suggest that these are not exclusive propositions being offered here: One does best to know others *and* to have self-understanding.

90. The WB text has "To die and yet not perish is to be long-lived 死而不亡者壽." See Ames (1998) for an argument that in this tradition of ancestor reverence, to be forgotten is to perish.

91. MWD B has *feng* 渢 for *fan* 汎. Note that these are cognate terms, and that *fan* can also be pronounced *feng*.

92. In the WB version, this phrase is followed by "All things depend upon it for their lives, and yet it does not control them." A similar phrase is found in chapter 2, and the idea of "benefiting but not managing" as a characterization of *dao* pervades the text. This phrase does not occur in the MWD texts.

93. This phrase also occurs in chapter 17, although in that context, it refers to the facility provided by "the most excellent rulers."

94. Both MWD texts are interrupted at this point with the phrase "Then it is constantly without desires 則恆無欲也." The WB text has it as a subordinate clause, "and is constantly free of desires 常無欲." This phrase compromises the parallel structure, so that on the unlikely chance it belongs here, there should be a similar phrase in the subsequent parallel refrain. We have chosen to remove it.

95. A similar although expanded version of these lines appears in chapter 63 with a context that offers clarification for this characterization. The subject in the WB version of this chapter is way-making rather than the sages.

96. The *Book of Changes* comes to mind with the use of "image

(*xiang* 象)," where a proactive sense of "vision" complements the more passive sense of "revelation."

97. The expression "bland and insipid (*dan* 淡)" is instructive, given the water metaphor that pervades the text. Of course, for those who frequent the drinking fountain at the Honolulu Academy of Arts, artesian spring water is at once the blandest of things and the most delicious.

98. The WB text opens with the two phrases "Way-making really does things noncoercively, yet everything gets done. 道常無爲而無不爲." The GD and MWD texts have only the first phrase, with the MWD as we have translated it here, and the GD as "Way-making really does things noncoercively 道恆無爲也."

99. These three opening lines are almost identical to lines 1, 3, and 4 of chapter 32.

100. These few lines have many variations in the different texts, suggesting a general dissatisfaction with the wording. The WB text has "As a nameless scrap of unworked wood, they would be objectless in their desires 無名之樸夫亦將無欲." The GD text does not have line 7, following line 6 with "They would then be satisfied, and being satisfied, they would achieve equilibrium 夫亦將知足，知〔足〕以靜萬物將自定."

101. The WB and GD texts have "stable (*ding* 定)" rather than "proper (*zheng* 正)."

102. The MWD B text has the title and a character count for this section.

103. The mutuality of formation (structure) and function, agent and action, allows us to translate *de* 德 as both action ("to excel") and agency ("excellence, efficacy, character").

104. This chapter is reminiscent of *Mencius* 4B19:

孟子曰：人之所以異於禽獸者幾希，庶民去之，君子存之。舜明於庶物，察於人倫，由仁義行，非行仁義也。

Mencius said: "What distinguishes the human being from the brutes is ever so slight, and where the common run of people are apt to lose it, the exemplary person preserves it. Shun was wise to the way of all things and had insight into human relationships. He acted upon authoritativeness and appropriateness rather than simply doing what was authoritative and appropriate."

The *Mencius* 2B2 has the expression "acting on character (*dexing* 德行)" and 2B3 has the passage "those who act authoritatively by virtue of their character are true kings 以德行仁者王."

It is likely that Mencius was influenced in his ideas about the formation of character by the treatise *Five Ways of Proper Conduct* 五行篇, copies of which have been recently recovered in both the MWD and GD finds. In spite of its Confucian vocabulary, there is a real resonance between *Five Ways of Proper Conduct* and this chapter of the *Daodejing*. Note the same sequence in listing the kinds of proper conduct. This document opens with:

> Authoritativeness (*ren* 仁) taking shape within is called the formation of character (*de* 德); where it does not take shape within it is simply called proper conduct. Appropriateness (*yi* 義) taking shape within is called the formation of character; where it does not take shape within it is simply called proper conduct. Observing ritual propriety (*li* 禮) taking shape within is called the formation of character; where it does not take shape within it is simply called proper conduct. Wisdom (*zhi* 智) taking shape within is called the formation of character; where it does not take shape within it is simply called proper conduct. Sagacity (*sheng* 聖) taking shape within is called the formation of character; where it does not take shape within it is simply called proper conduct. There are five ways of the formation of character, where harmony among them is called character.

105. The WB version has an additional example just before this line: "The myriad things in realizing oneness came to life 萬物得一以生."

106. The WB version has another line before this one: "If the myriad things had not come to life, they may well have become extinct 萬物無以生將恐滅."

107. Compare chapter 42. In ancient times it was customary as a mark of humility for rulers to refer to themselves in first person singular as "the friendless," "the unworthy," and "the inept."

108. The WB version of chapter 22 has the same expression as chapter 10: "embracing oneness (*bao yi* 抱一)."

109. The GD and MWD texts topicalize the first character of the first two lines for emphasis, and GD has *fan* 返 rather than *fan* 反 in the first line, reinforcing the choice of "returning" over "reversing" in describing the movement of *dao*. Compare chapter 25:

> Being grand, it is called passing,
> Passing, it is called distancing.
> Distancing, it is called returning.

110. The *you* 有 and *wu* 無 here might be translated as "something" and "nothing" respectively. They refer to the more determinate and inde-

terminate aspects of the ongoing process of experience. Importantly, rather than ontological terms, these are explanatory categories necessary to make sense of the process of experience (see Hall [1978]).

111.   In the MWD texts, this chapter precedes chapter 40.

112.   The WB version has *qin* 勤 ("with real effort"). The MWD and WB versions of the text just have "walk it 行之." But the GD text has "keep to its center 行其中," which extends the "path" metaphor.

113.   Some of the commentaries treat the expression *jianyan* 建言 as "wisdom sayings" generally, while others treat it as a specific title of a work that is no longer extant.

114.   This line comes before the one above it in the GD text.

115.   The MWD and GD versions all have *bao* 襃 that D. C. Lau translates as "ample." The WB text is also viable: "Way-making is hidden in the nameless 道隱無名."

116.   *Metaphysics* 1012b34–1013a20.

117.   Compare chapter 39. See note 107 above.

118.   For the *Daodejing*, water and *qi* 氣 are symbols of the softest things, while rock and metal are the most unyielding.

119.   The two MWD and the GD text all have "therefore (*gu* 故)" at the beginning of this line, while the WB text has "therefore (*shigu* 是故)" before "miserliness" in line 4.

120.   This same line occurs in chapter 32.

121.   This sentence occurs in the WB edition, but not in the MWD or GD texts. However, we follow Lau in restoring it here on the basis of what seems to be a sufficiently long lacuna in the MWD B text.

122.   Of course, the claim that "perfect" is an absolute term, or at least functions as one, is dubious. Quantification of "perfect" is both frequent and familiar in common English usage: witness "in order to form a more perfect Union," or "a no more perfect spot could be found," or "she was absolutely perfect."

123.   Ryle (1949):149–153.

124.   These three lines are ordered differently in different texts. The MWD texts have 1, 2, and 3. The WB has only two lines: 2 and 3. The GD text does not have the first four lines that open this chapter, and has a 1, 3, 2 sequence. In wording, the GD text has "more onerous than (*hou* 厚)" in place of "greater than (*da* 大)," and "greed (*shenyu* 甚欲 )" in place of "being desirous (*keyu* 可欲)." The GD text has "understanding when enough is enough (*zhi zu zhi wei zu* 知足之爲足)" in place of "Therefore,

the satisfaction of being content (*gu zhi zu zhi zu* 故知足之足)." The order of the GD would seem superior because its sequence is a natural transition into the last two lines. Also the GD wording seems more varied and considered. We follow it in both respects here.

125. The MWD B and the WB text have "name, identify (*ming* 名)," but given the interchangeability between this character and "to understand clearly (*ming* 明)" and the parallel with "knowing (*zhi* 知)" and "getting things done (*cheng* 成)," we have translated this passage as *ming* 明. In fact, given the assumed relationship between "naming" and "knowing" in this tradition, this alteration does not make much difference.

126. This chapter presents a good example of how the MWD text with its more precise grammar clarifies the meaning. For the last line, the WB text has "And gets things done without doing 不爲而成." This reading with an intransitive "doing" would suggest simply that the sage does not do anything. But the point being made in the opening lines seems to be that the job gets done, only locally. Both MWD texts have "And gets things done without doing 'x' 弗爲而成," where "x" is the object of acting, that is, what is done. The MWD texts are missing the two lines preceding this one, but parallel structure allows us to extrapolate and assume that they too would have the *fu* 弗 negative, which requires an object.

127. D. C. Lau (1982):176–81 in his translation of MWD follows Gao Ming, who appeals to the fact that the expression "and all is done (*wu bu wei* 無不爲)" does not occur anywhere in the MWD texts to argue that "and has no motivation for doing so (*wu yi wei* 無以爲)" might be an earlier formulation of this idea. It certainly occurs in chapter 38 as a criterion second to "acting noncoercively (*wuwei* 無爲)" for superior conduct. The fact that the GD text does have *wu bu wei* makes Gao Ming's arguments less persuasive, although most versions of chapter 38 do have *wu yi wei* as an alternative formulation.

128. The *wushi* 無事 in this passage is another *wu*-form. What the *wu*-forms seem to have in common is efficacy through the absence of coercion and constraint.

129. *Zhuangzi* 31.12.52; compare Graham (1981):186 and Watson (1968):134. For a detailed discussion of this anecdote see Hall and Ames (1998):178–80.

130. The WB text has "Sages do not have real thoughts and feelings 聖人無長心."

131. The WB text does not have this phrase, but most of the other

received editions do. Further, Wang Bi's commentary on the text clearly suggests that this phrase is present in the edition that he was working from. Again, the WB "text" seems to be a version of the *Daodejing* that is markedly different from the one on which he wrote his commentary.

132. Compare chapter 76, which also uses the expressions "companions of life" and "companions of death."

133. The MWD B text has "armor (*bingge* 兵革)" rather than just "weapon (*bing* 兵)," found in the other versions.

134. *Zhuangzi* 44.17.48–50; compare Graham (1981):149 and Watson (1968):182.

135. The two MWD texts have *jin* 堇, a familiar abbreviation for *qin* 勤 that can mean either "to toil" or "to be used up." While the GD variant *wu* 務 "to work at" would encourage the former reading, "to toil," we follow chapter 6, which uses the same character to mean "to be used up." D. C. Lau does the same in translating it as "will not run dry." The subject of this passage seems to be one's quantum of vital energies (*qi*), and again it might be an allusion to some kind of meditative regimen.

136. A version of these two lines also occurs in chapter 16.

137. The term *xiang* 祥 in modern Chinese has come to mean "auspicious," but in the classical texts it could mean simply "omen," or as in this passage, even a "bad omen."

138. This final passage also occurs in chapter 30. The last line is not found in the GD text.

139. We follow the GD text, which has "those who really understand it 智之者" and "those who really talk about it 言之者." The first of these phrases is reminiscent of the wording in *Analects of Confucius* 6.20: "To truly cherish it is better than to just understand it, and to enjoy it is better than to simply cherish it."

140. These two lines also occur in chapter 52.

141. These four lines that also appear in chapter 4 occur here in both the MWD and GD texts in this sequence, but have a different order in the MWD versions of chapter 4. The order that we find in MWD versions of chapter 4 is in fact the same order that we find in the WB version of this chapter.

142. The terms "straightforward (*zheng* 正)" and "take by surprise (*qi* 奇)" are a technical military vocabulary. See Ames (1993):119 and Lau and Ames (1996):79–82 and 252–56.

143. A version of this line also occurs in chapter 48.

144. Neither of the MWD texts has this line 以此. But we follow Lau (1982):160 in restoring it on the basis of parallels in chapters 21 and 54.

145. The GD text has "the more rebellious the people will be 民彌叛."

146. The GD and MWD A versions just have "wisdom 知," while the MWD B text has the fuller expression "wisdom 智慧." The WB version is more interpretive, with "skill and expertise 技巧."

147. The WB text has "laws and edicts 法令."

148. The MWD B and GD texts have "we desire not to desire 我欲不欲," but the WB text has "we are objectless in our desires 我無欲." We follow the WB text here in order to maintain the parallel structure.

149. This correlation between being objectless in one's desires and being like unworked wood also occurs as a WB variant in chapter 37.

150. A collation of the MWD versions provides us with an opening passage that we can only speculate about. That such speculation is not always rewarded with the resolution we hope for is demonstrated by the fact that Lau and Henricks provide translations of the same characters that are not far short of contradictory. The WB version would appear to be someone's attempt to deal with this textual ambiguity. Within the context of the chapter as a whole, we can be relatively sure that a contrast is intended between a Daoistic government that does not intervene in the lives of the people, letting them get on with things, and a non-Daoistic government that is heavy-handed and judgmental, generating rules of conduct that are self-justifying in their application.

151. The WB text ascribes this conduct specifically to the sages.

152. *Zhuangzi* 17.6.47; compare Graham (1981):88 and Watson (1968):84.

153. *Zhuangzi* 17.6.53; compare Graham (1981):88 and Watson (1968):85.

154. Following Henricks (2000):84–5, where the GD text has the graphically similar character "realm (*yu* 域)" for "country (*guo* 國)." Note, however, that "*guo*" begins the following chapter.

155. This expression is familiar in the text, where "mother" is the image of the creative source of our experience. Compare chapters 1, 20, 25, and 52.

156. While this phrase is ambiguous in the MWD texts as "the sages will not harm them either 聖人亦弗傷也," where "them" could refer to either ghosts or people, the WB text resolves the ambiguity explicitly in favor of the people: "the sages will not harm the people either 聖人亦不傷人."

157. The WB text has the small state "... can rule the great state 則取
大國." Given that the lines that follow continue an assumed distinction
between the great state "ruling" and the small state "being ruled," it would
seem that the WB version is less clear than the MWD texts in its failure to
establish this subtle distinction at the outset.

158. In both chapters 48 and 57 this *wu*-form, "being non-interfering
in going about your business *wushi* 無事," is recommended as the most
appropriate disposition in governing the world.

159. Compare chapter 35.

160. Chapter 79 provides an extended discussion of this precept.

161. A similar couplet appears at the end of chapter 34. The phrasing
of these lines here is similar to the WB version of chapter 34, although the
subject in the WB text is way-making rather than the sages.

162. See *Zhuangzi* 7.3.2–12; compare Graham (1981):63–4 and
Watson (1968):50–1.

163. See Ames (1993):116.

164. A variation on this line that has become a popular saying in vernacular Chinese is "a journey of hundreds of miles begins with the soil
under one's feet 千里之行始於足下." But according to Henricks (2000):
63, this version that appears in the WB text (but not the Wang Bi
commentary) is a later revision that seems to have originated with the
Heshanggong recension. At least the GD and both MWD texts have the
version translated here.

165. These two lines occur in chapter 29 in a specifically political
context.

166. Instead of these three lines, one version of the GD text (for the
two different versions of the second half of this chapter, see Henricks
[2000]:44 and 122) has "As a guideline in overseeing affairs, if you are as
careful at the end as you are at the start, you will be free of failure 臨事之
紀慎終如始則無敗事矣."

167. Compare chapter 37. The interpretation of the expression "desiring not to desire 欲不欲" as "being objectless in one's desires 無欲" is
encouraged by this same variant in the WB version.

168. One of the two GD versions of this text has "And in teaching not
to teach 教不教."

169. The WB text has "to use knowledge in bringing proper order to
the state 以智治國."

170. The WB text has "is to confer good fortune upon the state 國之富."

171. Because of a taboo character, the WB text has "original efficacy 元德" rather than "profound efficacy 玄德" here and in chapters 10 and 51.

172. The GD text does not have "in wanting to 欲," which gives it a somewhat different meaning.

173. MWD A has these two phrases in reverse order, but GD and WB are the same order as MWD B.

174. The MWD versions have *wuzheng* 無爭 as a *wu*-form in this sentence: "they strive without contentiousness." The GD and WB texts have *buzheng* 不爭: "they do not contend." Only the MWD texts have this concluding line as a rhetorical question rather than a descriptive statement.

175. The WB text has "my way-making 我道."

176. Henricks (1989):160 points out that the character translated "to resemble (*xiao* 肖)" also carries the meaning of its homophone, "to be small (*xiao* 小)." Thus, this passage could also be read, "Being great, I am not small. Indeed, it is only because I am not small that I am able to be great. If I were small, for a long time now I would have been of little consequence."

177. As Lau (1982):157 points out, in MWD A this conditional is reversed to read "it is only because I am great that I resemble nothing." Lau argues for the superiority of the MWD B reading that we have here.

178. The WB text has "When nature is about to rescue something, it surrounds it with compassion 天將救之以慈衞之."

179. Many if not most of the traditional commentaries and contemporary translations interpret "students (*shi* 士)" in a military sense as "officers" or "warriors." While entirely plausible, such an understanding assumes that this same term is being used here differently from the two other chapters in which it occurs (15 and 41). Also, it surrenders a possible contrast between the best students of way-making, who are "subtle and mysterious, dark and penetrating" and whose "profundity was beyond comprehension" (chapter 15), and persons who are militant and aggressive.

180. Compare chapters 61 and 66.

181. The WB text has "it is called making use *of the strength* of others 是爲用人之力," adding two characters to the text. Lau follows the WB and restores this expression, although there is no lacuna in the MWD versions.

182. This is a rather obscure phrase, and commentators have often abandoned it as corrupt. The WB text includes a verb that makes it paral-

lel grammatically to the other two phrases preceding it at the expense of making it asymmetrical in the number of characters: "it is what is called matching up with an axis that is as old as the heavens 是謂配天古之極."

183. In this tradition we include the reconstructed *Sunzi* and the *Sun Bin*. See Ames (1993) and Lau and Ames (1996).

184. See Ames (1993):164–66.

185. See Ames (1993):110–11.

186. Compare the "three prized possessions" in chapter 67.

187. The MWD A text has "among people 人," while MWD B and the WB versions have "in the world 天下."

188. On the basis of what seems to be a "ditto" mark in the MWD A text, Henricks (1989):168 suggests that the text should read "not to know that you don't know is a flaw 不知不知病矣." Although he is responding to the rather forced attempts to make sense of this line in some of the other translations, there is no collaboration for this reading in any of the other texts. Grammatical differences between the MWD versions and the WB text suggest that scholars in the transmission of this chapter are puzzling over its meaning. In fact, we would argue that this line not only makes good sense as it stands, but further is a key to the chapter as a whole.

The WB text has an additional, somewhat redundant line following this one: "It is only if you recognize the disease as a disease that you will be free of disease 夫唯病病是以不病."

189. *Zhuangzi* 75.26.48–9; compare Graham (1981):190 and Watson (1968):302.

190. We follow the received text here. See Ames and Rosemont (1998) for an alternative reading found in the Dingzhou text, which would read:

> The Master said: "Zilu, shall I instruct you in what it means to be wise? To know what you know and know what you do not know— this then is wisdom."

191. Tredennick and Tarrant (1993):44.

192. The MWD versions, with the inclusion of a number of grammatical particles, are more precise than the WB version. Also, in this chapter, the meaning of the character *wei* 畏 is parsed to mean both "awe" and "authority," and the character *yan* 厭 to mean both "lower" and "disaffected."

193. And what *tian* despises are "those who are courageous in feats of daring." The WB text has a line following this one: "It is for this reason

that even the sages pay careful attention to such things 是以聖人猶難之." This line also occurs in chapter 63.

194. Compare chapter 23: "It is natural to speak only rarely."

195. This line does not occur in the WB text.

196. Although implicit in the MWD texts, identifying the oppression with "those above 其上" is made explicit in the WB text.

197. In the MWD texts the second part of this passage is unclear, and could be rendered "because they (the people) are trying to get too much from life 以其求生之厚也." Although this would connect comfortably with the closing lines, it violates what seems to be a parallel structure in condemning the excesses of those in power.

198. The WB text just has "hard and rigid," but the MWD versions have an additional two rather uncommon characters, which when combined mean something like (laid out six feet long =) "cadaver."

199. Although there is considerable variation in the different versions of these lines, the meaning is clear enough.

200. See Wu Yi (2001):444–45 for an alternative reading.

201. The MWD texts have "make an offering to *tian* 奉於天者," while the WB version has "to the world." The WB alternative makes a stronger connection with the unselfish and enlightened conduct that is subsequently described, so we have followed it.

202. The MWD B text has the title and a character count for this section. It has been placed at the end of chapter 79 because in the MWD versions, this is the last chapter. What other texts parse as chapters 80 and 81 occur between chapters 66 and 67.

203. *Zhuangzi* 19.6.89; compare Graham (1981):92.

204. For Cook Ding, see *Zhuangzi* 7.3.2–12; compare Graham (1981): 63–4 and Watson (1968):50–1. For Carpenter Qing, see *Zhuangzi* 19.50. 54–9; compare Graham (1981):135 and Watson (1968):205–6.

205. The WB version has "the adept do not dispute; disputers are not adept 善者不辯，辯者不善."

206. The MWD B text just has "the way of the human being 人之道," but the WB version has "the way of the sages 聖人之道," which seems more consistent with what has gone before.

# *Appendix*
## The Great One Gives Birth to the Waters

### INTRODUCTION

In the 1993 Guodian archaeological find, 71 strips of *Daodejing* text were found in three distinct bundles that have been called *Laozi* A, B, and C. The document that has been titled *The Great One Gives Birth to the Waters* from its opening phrase comprises 14 of these strips. Physically, in the length of the bamboo strips, in the cord markings, in general appearance, and in calligraphic style, it is indistinguishable from the other strips in the *Laozi* C bundle. Although it has been treated as a separate document by the editors initially responsible for the reconstruction of the Guodian texts, this has been done solely on the basis of content, using the extant *Daodejing* as a principle of exclusion. These same scholars allow that, as it stands, it is an integral part of *Laozi* C.

We can ask, then, what is the relationship between *The Great One Gives Birth to the Waters* and *Laozi* C? It is particularly interesting that this document in the present sequencing of the seven units that constitute *Laozi* C follows immediately on a version of the second half of chapter 64 that contains the phrase:

是以聖人…能輔萬物之自然而弗敢爲。

Although the sages . . . are quite capable of helping all things follow
   their own course,
They would not think of doing so.

This phrase allows that in Daoist cosmology, even though the wisest and most accomplished of people are able to assist in the way in which the myriad of events unfold, they would not think of interfering with the spontaneous issue of things.

First, as D. C. Lau has pointed out, a familiar element in textual coherence in the classical corpus is the repetition of characters. In fact, we can link up all of the seven units of *Laozi* C by appealing to this method of character association. In particular, the character *fu* 輔 ("to help"), which appears in the chapter 64 phrase cited above, occurs eight times in the opening paragraph of *The Great One Gives Birth to the Waters*.

Further, this second half of chapter 64 is the only piece of text that appears twice in the recovered text, once in bundle A and again in bundle C. The two versions of this portion of chapter 64 are markedly different. In fact, one point of difference is that the phrase describing the reticence of the sages to override cosmic spontaneity cited above appears in the *Laozi* A as:

是以聖人能輔萬物之自然而弗能爲。

Although the sages are quite capable of helping all things follow
    their own course,
They are not able to do so.

This version of the text is internally contradictory, and appears corrupt.

We can speculate that if *The Great One Gives Birth to the Waters* is not an integral part of the *Daodejing* at this point in its evolution, it is at the very least an explanatory commentary on a revised and improved version of chapter 64.

Textual issues aside, in the bigger picture, the importance of *The Great One Gives Birth to the Waters* lies in the considerable clarity it lends to the issue of how we are to understand Daoist cosmogony. This document is quite simply the earliest record of Chinese cosmogony that we have. It not only sheds important light on other brief and suggestive cosmogonic allusions that we find in the *Daodejing* (especially chapters 25, 39, 42, 51, and 52), but it also resonates rather explicitly with the language of these same chapters.

The Great One is identified as the first among the defining terms in the Daoist cosmology, followed by the heavens and the earth, the spiritual and the numinous, the *yin* and the *yang qi*, the four seasons, the hot and the cold, the wet and the dry, and finally the annual cycle. Still, in the continuing emergence of the world, all of these correlated elements constituting the cosmos collaborate to produce each other and the totality. Said another way, the Great One is not a transcendent, ordering principle—a single source— that stands independent of the world it produces. Rather, it is coterminous with this world, hidden within it, and circulating everywhere. While the Great One gives birth to the waters, it also lies hidden in them, and these same waters collaterally assist it in giving birth to the heavens and the earth. In this process, time is inseparable from the emerging world. Indeed, time is the very propensity of the world to transform.

Daoist cosmogony does not entail the kind of radical initial beginning we associate with those metaphysical cosmogonies that describe the triumph of Order over Chaos. In fact, the *Zhuangzi's* well-known account of the death of Lord Hundun 渾沌 —often translated negatively as Lord Chaos, but perhaps better rendered positively as Lord Spontaneity—provides a rather strong Daoist objection to such a "One-behind-the-many" reading:

> The ruler of the North Sea was "Swift," the ruler of the South Sea was "Sudden," and the ruler of the Center was "Hundun, or Spontaneity." Swift and Sudden had on several occasions encountered each other in the territory of Spontaneity, and Spontaneity had treated them with great hospitality. Swift and Sudden, devising a way to repay Spontaneity's generosity, said: "Everyone has seven orifices through which they can see, hear, eat, and breathe. Spontaneity alone is without them." They then attempted to bore holes in Spontaneity, each day boring one hole. On the seventh day, Spontaneity died.[1]

But why according to the *Zhuangzi* shouldn't one wish to bring order out of *hundun*?[2] A reasonable question, indeed, if *hundun* is the confusion and disarray—the formless surds—that other cosmogonies describe as primordial Chaos. But if *hundun* is the spontaneous emergence of novelty that honeycombs all construals of order in the continuing Daoist present, then the imposition of order upon it means the death of novelty. After all, it is spontaneity that makes the life experience deliciously indeterminate and, in some degree, unpredictable. To enforce a given design is simply to select one of a myriad candidates for order and to privilege that one over the rest. Swift and Sudden have transformed the unsummed and causally noncoherent *dao* into a single-ordered world.

Instead of invoking the language of initial beginnings and some independent efficient cause, this document and the *Daodejing* broadly, with their pervasive mothering and birthing metaphors, describe fetal beginnings in an ongoing cycle of autogenerative reproduction.[3] Where it perhaps looks most like classical cosmogony is when we allow that over time, the spontaneous emergence of novelty eventually makes obsolete any rational structures that we have available for describing or explaining experience. Process requires a continual reformulation of our terms of understanding. This is the meaning of the opening line of the *Daodejing* that is glossed by *The Great One Gives Birth to the Waters* when it explains that the reason for using *dao* is that we are trying to think beyond our present categories.

This cycle of reproduction is defined in terms of the mutuality of opposites: rising and then falling, advancing and then returning, waxing full and then waning empty. In this cycle, the workings of the world favor new life as the process brings existing growth to culmination and closure.

And finally, according to *The Great One Gives Birth to the Waters*, we could just as well call these ongoing processes "the world," or use another of the familiar names we have for describing the life experience that goes on around us. Why do we appeal to a notion like *dao*? Why do we use the "style" name rather than something more common and recognizable?

Those who have been successful in the past have invoked this term *dao* in framing their efforts, and have associated their persons and their accomplishments with it. Terms such as "the world" and its counterparts, on the other hand, are too well-established, and do not seem appropriate for doing the work of venturing beyond our known world. *Dao* brings with it the assumption that we are using our imagination to think past our present boundaries into a realm that we have yet to place theoretical and conceptual limits upon. Thus, it is the very vagueness and indeterminacy of *dao* that recommends it as a term of art.

## Text and Translation

太一生水，水反輔太一，是以成天。天反輔太一，是以成地。天地〔复相輔〕也，是以成神明。神明复相輔也，是以成陰陽。陰陽复相輔也，是以成四時。四時复相輔也，是以成滄熱。滄熱复相輔也，是以成濕燥。濕燥复相輔也，成歲而止。

故歲者，濕燥之所生也。濕燥者，滄熱之所生也。滄熱者，四時之所生也。四時者，陰陽之所生〔也〕。陰陽者，神明之所生也。神明者，天地之所生也。天地者，太一之所生也。

是故太一藏於水，行於時。周而或〔始，以己爲〕萬物母；一缺一盈，以己爲萬物經。此天之所不能殺，地之所不能厘，陰陽之所不能成。君子知此之謂…

天道貴弱，削成者以益生者。伐於强，責於〔剛；助於弱，益於柔〕。下，土也，而謂之地；上，氣也，而謂之天。道亦其字也。請問其名。以道從事者，必托其名，故事成則身長；聖人之從事也，亦托其名，故功成而身不傷。天地名字幷立，姑過其方，不思相〔當。天不足〕於西北，其下高以强；地不足於東南，其上〔高以强〕。〔不足於上〕者，有餘於下；不足於下者，有餘於上。

In the Great One[4] giving birth to the waters, the waters collaterally assist the Great One, thereby producing the heavens. The heavens collaterally assist the Great One, thereby producing the earth. The heavens and earth again assist each other, thereby producing the spiritual and numinous. The spiritual and numinous again assist each other, thereby producing *yin* and *yang qi*. *Yin* and *yang qi* again assist each other, thereby producing the four seasons. The four seasons again assist each other, thereby producing the hot and the cold. The hot and the cold again assist each other, thereby producing the moist and the dry. And the moist and the dry again assist each other, culminating in producing the yearly cycle.

Thus, it is the moist and the dry that give birth to the yearly cycle; it is the hot and the cold that give birth to the moist and the dry; it is the four seasons that give birth to the hot and the cold; it is the *yin* and the *yang qi* that give birth to the four seasons; it is the spiritual and the numinous that give birth to the *yin* and the *yang qi;* it is the heavens and the earth that give birth to the spiritual and the numinous; it is the Great One that gives birth to the heavens and the earth.

Thus it is that the Great One is hidden away in the waters, and travels with the seasons. It completes a cycle only to begin again, making itself the mother of everything that happens. It is alternatively deficient then full, making itself the guiding pattern of everything that happens. This is not something the heavens can diminish, nor something that the earth can alter, nor something the *yin* and the *yang qi* can bring to closure. Exemplary persons know this as what is called . . .

The way of *tian* is to prize softness. It pares away at what has culminated in order to benefit new growth. It attacks the strong, and punishes the hard; it aids the soft and benefits the weak.

The dirt beneath our feet we call the earth, and the *qi* above our heads we call the heavens. As for *dao*, it is just another style name for the same things. But what, may I ask, is its proper name? Those who would accord with *dao* in their undertakings must do so in the name of *dao*. It is thus that they are successful at what they do and are personally long-lived. Even the sages who accord with *dao* in their undertakings do so in its name. It is thus that they are successful in their accomplishments and personally go unharmed. The different names for the heavens and the earth—both their original name and their style name—are also well-established. It is just that in trying to venture beyond these categories, we do not think that such names are fitting.

The heavens are wanting in the northwest, but the earth beneath compensates for this deficiency by its height. The earth is wanting in the southeast, but the heavens above compensate for this deficiency by their height. Any deficiency above is made up for in what is below, and any deficiency below is made up for in what is above.

## NOTES TO THE *APPENDIX*

1. *Zhuangzi* 21.7.33; compare Graham (1981):98–99 and Watson (1963):97.

2. In fact, in the commentary that the translator James Legge ([1891]: 267) appends to his early English translation of the *Zhuangzi*, he opines: "But surely it was better that Chaos should give place to another state. 'Heedless' and 'Sudden' did not do a bad work."

3. Li Ling, Sarah Allan, Isabelle Robinet, and others in the discussion of *The Great One Gives Birth to the Waters* at the 1998 Dartmouth Conference made much of the cyclical nature of the creative process. See Allan and Williams (2000):162–71.

4. The editors of the *Guodian Chumu zhujian* (1998):125 n. 1 identify the *taiyi* 太一 with *dao* on the basis of a passage in the *Lushi chunqiu*:

道也者精也不可爲名强爲之名謂之太一。

As for *dao*, it is vitality. It cannot be given either form or name. If forced to name it, I would call it the Great One.

Li Ling (1995–6) has written extensively on the Tai Yi cult that appears in the state of Chu during the Warring States Period and on its later development.

# Thematic Index

We have identified those chapters of the text that we believe most immediately inform the stated themes. In so doing, we have relied upon meaning broadly rather than simply the explicit terms.

# Bibliography of Works Cited

Allan, Sarah, and Crispin Williams (2000). *The Guodian Laozi: Proceedings of the International Conference, Dartmouth College, May 1998*. Berkeley: The Society for the Study of Early China.

Alexander, G. G. (1895). *Lao-tsze: The Great Thinker with a Translation of His Thoughts on the Nature and Manifestation of God*. London: K. Paul, Trench, and Trubner & Co.

Ames, Roger T. (forthcoming). "Human Exceptionalism versus Cultural Elitism: Three in the Morning, Four at Night." In *A Communion of Subjects: Animals in Religion, Science, and Ethics*, edited by Paul Waldau and Kimberley Patton. Oxford University Press.

——— (1998). "Death as Transformation in Classical Daoism." In *Death and Philosophy*, edited by Jeff Malpas and Robert C. Solomon. London and New York: Routledge.

——— (trans.) (1993). *Sun-tzu: The Art of Warfare*. New York: Ballantine.

Ames, Roger T., and David L. Hall (2001). *Focusing the Familiar: A Translation and Philosophical Interpretation of the* Zhongyong. Honolulu: University of Hawaii Press.

Ames, Roger T., and Henry Rosemont Jr. (1998). *The Analects of Confucius: A Philosophical Translation*. New York: Ballantine.

Baxter, William (1998). "Situating the Language of the *Lao-tzu*: The Probable Date of the *Tao-te-ching*." In *Lao-tzu and the Tao-te-ching*, edited by Livia Kohn and Michael LaFargue. Albany: State University of New York Press.

Carus, Paul, and D. T. Suzuki (1913). *The Canon of Reason and Virtue: Lao Tzu's Tao Teh King*. Chicago: Open Court.

Ch'en Ku-ying 陳鼓應 (1977). *Lao-tzu: Text, Notes, and Comments*. Translated by Rhett Y. W. Young and Roger T. Ames. San Francisco: Chinese Materials Center.

Dewey, John (1976–83). *Middle Works, 1899–1924*. 15 vols. Edited by Jo Ann Boydston. Carbondale, Ill.: Southern Illinois University Press.

Emerson, Ralph Waldo (1883). *Essays by Ralph Waldo Emerson*. Boston and New York: Houghton, Mifflin, and Company.

Fukunaga Mitsuji 福永光司 (trans.) (1968). *Roshi* 老子. Tokyo: Asahi Shinbunsha.

Giles, Herbert A. (1886). *The Remains of Lao Tzu*. London: John Murray.

Giradot, Norman J. (1983). *Myth and Meaning in Early Taoism: The Theme of Chaos (Hun-tun)*. Berkeley: University of California Press.

Guo Yi 郭沂 (2001). *Guodian zhujian yu xian Qin xueshu sixiang* 郭店竹簡 與先秦學術思想 (The Guodian bamboo strips and pre-Qin thought). Shanghai: Shanghai jiaoyu chubanshe.

Graham, A. C. (1990). "The Origins of the Legend of Lao Tan." In *Studies in Chinese Philosophy and Philosophical Literature*. Albany: State University of New York Press.

——— (1989). *Disputers of the Tao*. Chicago: Open Court.

——— (trans.) (1981). *Chuang-tzu: The Inner Chapters*. London: George Allen & Unwin.

Granet, Marcel (1934). *La pensée chinoise*. Paris: Editions Albin Michel.

Grange, Joseph (1997). *Nature: An Environmental Cosmology*. Albany: State University of New York Press.

Hall, David L. (1994). "Buddhism, Taoism and the Question of Ontological Difference." In *Essays in Honor of Nolan Pliny Jacobson*, edited by S. Pulgandla and David Miller. Indianapolis: Indiana University Press.

——— (1987). "Logos, Mythos, Chaos: Metaphysics as the Quest for Diversity." In *New Essays in Metaphysics*, edited by R. Neville. Albany: State University of New York Press.

——— (1978). "Process and Anarchy: A Taoist Vision of Creativity." *Philosophy East and West* 28 no. 3 (July 1978):271–285.

Hall, David L., and Roger T. Ames (1998). *Thinking from the Han: Self, Truth, and Transcendence in Chinese and Western Culture*. Albany: State University of New York Press.